CITY OF SUPPLIANTS

T0349897

*Ashley and Peter Larkin Series in Greek and Roman Culture*

# CITY *of* SUPPLIANTS
## TRAGEDY *and the* ATHENIAN EMPIRE

BY ANGELIKI TZANETOU

UNIVERSITY OF TEXAS PRESS
*Austin*

Requests for permission to reproduce material from this work should be sent to:
Permissions
University of Texas Press
P.O. Box 7819
Austin, TX 78713–7819
utpress.utexas.edu/about/book-permissions

♾ The paper used in this book meets the minimum requirements of
ANSI/NISO Z39.48–1992 (R1997) (Permanence of Paper).

LIBRARY OF CONGRESS CATALOGING-IN-PUBLICATION DATA
Tzanetou, Angeliki
City of suppliants : tragedy and the Athenian empire /
by Angeliki Tzanetou. — First edition.
p.    cm. — (Ashley and Peter Larkin series in Greek and Roman culture)
ISBN 978-0-292-75432-4
1. Greek drama (Tragedy)—History and criticism.    2. Aeschylus. Eumenides.
3. Euripides. Children of Heracles.    4. Sophocles. Oedipus at Colonus.
I. Title.    II. Series : Ashley and Peter Larkin series in Greek and Roman culture.
PA3131.T96    2012
882′.0109—dc23    2012007466

First paperback printing, 2013

*For Philip and Orestes*

# CONTENTS

# ABBREVIATIONS

The list of authors and works follows the abbreviations in Liddel-Scott's *Greek-English Lexicon*; the journals are abbreviated following the *Année Philologique*.

## JOURNALS AND WORKS

*AJA*     *American Journal of Archaeology*

*AJAH*    *American Journal of Ancient History*

*AJP*     *American Journal of Philology*

*ATL*     B. D. Meritt, H. T. Wade Gery and F. M. McGregor, eds. *The Athenian Tribute Lists*, 1–4, Cambridge: Harvard University Press. 1939–1953.

*ASNP*    *Annali della ScuolaNormale Superiore di Pisa. Classe di lettere e di Filosofia.*

*BICS*    *Bulletin of the Institute of Classical Studies*

*CA*      *Classical Antiquity*

*CAH*    J. Boardman and N. G. L. Hammond, eds., *The Cambridge Ancient History*, vol. 3, part 3. 2nd ed. Cambridge: Cambridge University, 1982.
J. Boardman, N. G. L. Hammond, D. M. Lewis, and M. Ostwald, eds., *Cambridge Ancient History*, vol. 4. 2nd ed. Cambridge: Cambridge University, 1988.
D. M. Lewis, J. Boardman, J. K. Davies, and M. Ostwald, eds., *Cambridge Ancient History*, vol. 5. 2nd ed. Cambridge: Cambridge University, 1992.

*CJ*      *Classical Journal*

*CP*      *Classical Philology*

*CQ*      *Classical Quarterly*

*CSCA*    *Californian Studies in Classical Antiquity*

| | |
|---|---|
| CW | *Classical World* |
| DK | H. Diels and W. Kranz, *Die Fragmente der Vorsokratiker*, 6th ed. Berlin: Weidmann, 1952. |
| FGE | D. L. Page, *Further Greek Epigrams before* AD *50 from the Greek Anthology and Other Sources, Not Included in "Hellenistic Epigrams" or "The Garland of Philip,"* revised by R. D. Dawe and J. Diggle. Cambridge: Cambridge University, 1981. |
| FGrH | F. Jacoby, *Fragmente der griechischen Historiker*, Leiden: Brill, 2005. |
| GRBS | *Greek, Roman and Byzantine Studies* |
| HSCP | *Harvard Studies in Classical Philology* |
| HTR | *Harvard Theological Review* |
| ICS | *Illinois Classical Studies* |
| IG | *Inscriptiones Graecae, 1873–* |
| JHI | *Journal of the History of Ideas* |
| JHS | *Journal of Hellenic Studies* |
| LIMC | H. C. Ackermann and J.-. Gisler, eds. *Lexicon Iconographicum Mythologiae Classicae*. Zurich: Artemis Verlag, 1981–1997. |
| LSGG | F. Sokolowski, *Lois Sacrése des cités grecques*. Paris: de Bocard, 1969. |
| MD | *Materiali e discussioni per l'analisi dei testi classici* |
| ML | R. Meiggs and D. Lewis, eds., *A Selection of Greek Historical Inscriptions to the End of the Fifth Century B.C.* Oxford: Clarendon, 1969. |
| PCG | R. Kassel and C. Austin, eds. *Poetae Comici Graeci*. Berlin: de Gruyter, 1983–. |
| PCPS | *Proceedings of the Cambridge Philological Society* |
| PMG | D. L. Page. *Poetae melici Graeci*. Oxford: Clarendon, 1962. |
| PP | *La parola del passato* |
| RE | A. Pauly and G. Wissowa, eds. *Realencyclopädie der klassischen Altertumswissenschaft*. Stuttgart: Metzler, 1894–1980. |
| REG | *Révue des études grecques* |
| RFIC | *Rivista di filologia e istruzione classica* |
| RHR | *Révue de l'histoire des religions* |
| RhM | *Rheinisches Museum* |
| RIDA | *Révue Internationale des droits de l'Antiquité* |
| TAPA | *Transactions of the American Philological Association* |
| TrGF | R. Kannicht, *Tragicorum Graecorum Fragmenta*, vol. 5. Göttingen: Vandenhoeck & Ruprecht, 2004. |
| WJfA | *Würzburger Jahrbücher für die Altertumswissenschaft.* |
| WS | *Wiener Studien* |
| YCS | *Yale Classical Studies* |
| ZPE | *Zeitschrift für Papyrologie und Epigraphie* |

| | | | |
|---|---|---|---|
| A. | Aeschylus | *IT* | *Iphigenia in Tauris* |
| *A.* | *Agamemnon* | Med. | *Medea* |
| *Ch.* | *Choephori* | *Or.* | *Orestes* |
| *Eu.* | *Eumenides* | *Ph.* | *Phoenician Women* |
| *Pers.* | *Persians* | *Supp.* | *Suppliant Women* |
| *Supp.* | *Suppliant Women* | *Tr.* | *Trojan Women* |
| Aeschin. | Aeschines | Hdt. | Herodotus |
| Antiph. | Antiphon | Hes. | Hesiod |
| Apollod. | Apollodorus | *Cat.* | *Catalogue of Women* |
| A.R. | Apolonius Rhodius | *Th.* | *Theogony* |
| Ar. | Aristophanes | *[Sc].* | *Shield of Heracles* |
| *Ach.* | *Acharnians* | Hsch. | Hesychius |
| *Av.* | *Birds* | Hom. | Homer |
| *Ec.* | *Ecclesiazusae* | *Il.* | *Iliad* |
| *Eq.* | *Knights* | *Od.* | *Odyssey* |
| *Lys.* | *Lysistrata* | Isoc. | Isocrates |
| *Th.* | *Thesmophoriazusae* | Lib. | Libanius |
| *V.* | *Wasps* | Lycurg. | Lycurgus |
| Arist. | Aristotle | Lys. | Lysias |
| *Ath.* | *The Constitution of the* | Paus. | Pausanias |
| | *Athenians* | Pi. | Pindar |
| *EN* | *Nicomachean Ethics* | *O.* | Olympian Odes |
| *Pol.* | *Politics* | *P.* | Pythian Odes |
| Ath. | Athenaeus | *N.* | Nemean Odes |
| D. | Demosthenes | *I.* | Isthmian Odes |
| Din. | Dinarchus | Pl. | Plato |
| D.S. | Diodorus Siculus | *Ap.* | *Apology* |
| D.H. | Dionysius of | *Cri.* | *Crito* |
| | Halicarnassus | *Lg.* | *Laws* |
| E. | Euripides | *Mx.* | *Menexenus* |
| *Andr.* | *Andromache* | *Prt.* | *Protagoras* |
| *Ba.* | *Bacchae* | *R.* | *Republic* (?) |
| *El.* | *Electra* | Plut. | Plutarch |
| *HF* | *Heracles* | *Mor.* | Moralia |
| *Hec.* | *Hecuba* | *Vit.* | *Parallel Lives* |
| Hel. | Helen | *Arist.* | *Aristides* |
| *Heracl.* | *Children of Heracles* | *Cim.* | *Cimon* |
| *Hipp.* | *Hippolytus* | *Dem.* | *Demosthenes* |
| *IA* | *Iphigenia in Aulis* | *Pel.* | *Pelopidas* |

| | | | | |
|---|---|---|---|---|
| Per. | Pericles | Tr. | Trachiniae |
| Phoc. | Phocion | Stesich. | Stesichorus |
| Publ. | Publicola | Str. | Strabo |
| Sol. | Solon | Th. | Thucydides |
| Them. | Themistocles | Xen. | Xenophon |
| Thes. | Theseus | Ag. | Agesilaus |
| S. | Sophocles | [Ath.] | Constitution of the Athenians |
| Aj. | Ajax | | |
| Ant. | Antigone | Hell. | Hellenica |
| El. | Electra | Lac. | Constitution of the Lacaedemonians |
| OC | Oedipus at Colonus | | |
| OT | Oedipus Tyrannus | Val. Max. | Valerius Maximus |
| Phil. | Philoctetes | Zen. | Zenobius |

# ACKNOWLEDGMENTS

My interest in political themes in tragedy began many years ago, and I owe thanks to many colleagues and institutions. Case Western Reserve University provided me with a leave, also supported by a grant from the Loeb Classical Library Foundation (Harvard University) in 2002–2003. The Illinois Campus Research Board of the University of Illinois at Urbana-Champaign supported a semester's leave in 2007–2008, when the project was well underway.

My colleagues both at Case Western Reserve and at the University of Illinois at Urbana-Champaign deserve warm thanks. From Case Western Reserve University, I would like to thank warmly the late Donald Laing, Martin Helzle, and Paul Iversen for many fruitful discussions and for their warm collegiality. Special thanks are due to Jenifer Neils for her generous friendship and always thoughtful advice. I would also like to thank warmly my colleagues at the University of Illinois, Maryline Parca, Kirk Sanders, David Sansone, Shannan Stewart, and Ariana Traill for their support and encouragement.

Portions of the book have been presented at the University of Chicago, Illinois Wesleyan University; at the annual Meeting of the Classical Association of Canada at Toronto in 2006; and at the "Why Athens? A Reappraisal of Tragic Politics" conference, held at Reading University in 2007. I am grateful to all these audiences for their valuable comments and suggestions.

Some of the material contained in the Introduction has also been published in "Supplication and Empire in Athenian Tragedy," in *Why Athens?: A Reappraisal of Tragic Politics*, edited by David Carter, 305–324 (Oxford: Oxford University Press, 2011); and a small part of Chapter 4 is replicated in "Does Oedipus Become a Citizen? (Sophocles' *Oedipus at Colonus*), in E. Karamalengou and E. Makrygianni (eds.), *Antiphilēsis: Studies on Classical, Byzantine and Modern Greek Literature and Culture In Honour of John-Theophanes A. Papademetriou*, 171–178. (Stuttgart: Franz Steiner Verlag, 2009).

Many colleagues have read portions of the manuscript at various stages.

I owe them all thanks for their generous comments and thoughtful suggestions: Antony Augoustakis, Aristoula Georgiadou, Marc Mastrangelo, Vassiliki Panoussi, Maryline Parca, Rachel Sternberg, and Polyxeni Strolonga.

Thanks are also due Corey Brennan, Kirk Freudenburg, Mary-Kay Gamel, Scott Garner, David Konstan, Bruce Lincoln and David Rosenbloom for their advice and discussions on a variety of issues.

I owe Antony Augoustakis and Vassiliki Panoussi special thanks for reading and commenting copiously on the manuscript in its entirety, and to Marc Mastrangelo for our discussions on Greek tragedy and for supporting this project from start to finish. I am deeply indebted to all three of them.

It is my great pleasure to acknowledge friends and colleagues for their steadfast support: Stratis Gallopoulos, Fred Hunter, Chryssoula Iatridou, Mika Kavetsou, Elizabeth Köll, Konstantinos Kourtikakis, Avra Papedemetriou, Villy Rouchota, Catherine Scallen, Maria Spiropulu, Angeliki and Natasha Tzanetou, and Vlassia Vassikeri.

I am especially grateful to the editorial team at the University of Texas Press: to Jim Burr, Humanities Editor, for his unfailing support and understanding during our collaboration; to Victoria Davis for shepherding the project through production; and to Nancy Moore for her painstaking and rigorous copy-editing efforts. Thanks are also due to Kelly Flessner and Adrielle Heath and especially Amy Oh for assistance with checking references and bibliography.

My family deserves my deepest thanks for helping and supporting me along the way: My parents, Anastasia and Panagiotis Tzanetos, for teaching me to persevere and for supporting my academic preparation. Apostolos Tzanetos, my brother, and Fani Giannaki, my sister-in law, for their unfailing support and thoughtfulness and for much more.

My greatest debt is owed Philip Phillips, my husband, and Orestes, our son, for many happy moments and for their adventuresome spirit. It is to them that this book is dedicated.

CITY OF SUPPLIANTS

# INTRODUCTION

In this book, I argue that the depiction of Athens as a city that welcomed suppliants from other cities lends insight into the Athenians' view of their empire. Athens' compassion and generosity toward suppliants became a topos in Athenian civic ideology and was employed to justify possession of her empire.[1] Athenian tragedy praised the city's altruism and denied that the pursuit of power was a factor motivating the Athenians' interest in helping others.[2] Yet Athenians outside the theater justified their rule over other Greek cities more bluntly, often by asserting that the strong rule over the weak or by claiming that ruling over others allowed them to maintain their own freedom.[3] My analysis traces the historical development of this ideology in the Athenian suppliant plays, Aeschylus' *Eumenides* (458 BC), Euripides' *Children of Heracles* (ca. 430 BC), and Sophocles' *Oedipus at Colonus* (ca. 407/6 BC).

Viewed as a group, these plays affirm the belief that Athens ruled justly and benevolently. Many of the memorable disenfranchised figures of tragedy, such as Orestes and Oedipus, are gravely defiled by crimes they have committed against their kin and unable to reclaim their ties with their native cities. Others, such as Heracles' children, lose their home and are relentlessly pursued by a tyrant. Athens earns her reputation for magnanimity repeatedly by surmounting successfully the obstacles that impede the reception of the suppliants into the city (e.g., heavy pollution or war by pursuers). Athens reaps significant benefits by incorporating these foreigners into the civic body, often as cult-heroes (e.g., Oedipus in Sophocles' *Oedipus at Colonus* or Eurystheus in Euripides' *Children of Heracles*), because they bring some special boon.

This book is not a study of all the plays that are grouped under the category of suppliant drama. Instead, it offers case studies of three plays, one by each of the major playwrights, which taken together contribute to a new understanding of supplication and its relevance to Athenian hegemony. Because most of the suppliant plays are staged in Athens, one of the objectives of this monograph is to demonstrate the significance of place. While other plays exist that contain elements relevant to this thesis, my idea that hegemony presents a unifying interpretive framework for the Athenian suppliant plays will be developed from a systematic study of *Eumenides*, *Children of Heracles*, and *Oedipus at Colonus*.

Other plays fit the pattern as well. Even though Euripides' *Medea* is staged in Corinth, the outcome of Medea's supplication of Aegeus in Euripides' play is reminiscent of the pattern that we find in the Athenian suppliant plays: she too is promised a home in Athens by Aegeus. Similarly, in Euripides' *Heracles*, Theseus persuades Heracles to follow him to Athens, though the bonds of friendship and hospitality offer a more appropriate context for relating this play to the familiar theme of Athens' generosity toward strangers. While these two plays pay tribute to Athens, they do not go further in their explication of Athenian hegemony. On the other hand, Aeschylus' *Suppliant Women* is the only suppliant play set in Argos, not Athens. For this reason, I discuss some aspects of the play programmatically in the introduction to establish some important differences between *Suppliant Women*, *Eumenides*, and the rest of the suppliant plays, which depict Athens as the hegemonic city of Greece. The many facets of Athenian hegemony cannot be exhausted within the small space of a single monograph, and in fact one encounters the complex character of Athenian hegemony in other plays as well. It is my hope that this book will pave the way for a broader examination of this topic.

Aeschylus' *Eumenides*, Euripides' *Children of Heracles*, and Sophocles' *Oedipus at Colonus* allow us to trace the development of the dramatic expression of Athenian hegemonic ideology, as it evolved from the height of Athenian imperialism to the end of the Peloponnesian War. Moreover, Euripides' *Suppliant Women* (424 BC) shares the characteristics of the other Athenian suppliant plays but is more briefly treated than the others (see Chapter 3). In studying Euripides' political plays—*Children of Heracles* (ca. 430 BC) and *Suppliant Women*—I opted for the former because it has been less studied in light of the workings of Athenian hegemonic ideology than has *Suppliant Women*. Finally, while both plays date to the first decade of the Peloponnesian War, *Children of Heracles* bears more clearly the imprint of the changes in the history of the empire that had come about between the production of Aeschylus' *Oresteia* in 458 BC and the beginning of the war between Athens and Sparta.

The portrayal of Athens as an inclusive city that provides support to those suffering undeservedly is shaped by the historical realities of Athens' empire.[4] Having fended off Persia, Athens first led the Delian League, a military alliance against the Persians, and soon after became an empire. Turning their former allies into subjects, the Athenians exacted military and financial contributions from them in the form of compulsory tribute. Even though the duration of Athens' rule was brief, it fostered its share of discontents. Her subjects protested bitterly against the loss of their independence even before the Peloponnesian War broke out, ending Athenian hegemony in 404 BC. Both Spartan propaganda and complaints from the allies painted a negative image of Athens as a tyrannical master, ruling over involuntary subjects.

The interpretation of the reception of foreign suppliants in tragedy is germane to the debate surrounding the political character of Athenian theater. Political interpretations of tragedy over the past thirty years have focused on the role that democratic political culture played in tragedy. Extending the insights of the French structuralist school (Vernant and Vidal-Naquet 1990), which emphasized negation of structure, transgression, and ambiguity as the salient features of the genre, the majority of critics have argued that the plays themselves can be shown to interrogate democracy and its institutions.[5] Simon Goldhill's article "The Great Dionysia and Civic Ideology," has had a long-lasting impact upon this debate, especially among Anglophone critics.[6] Emphasizing the pivotal role of the predramatic ceremonies in the context of the annual civic festival in the theater of Dionysus, Goldhill has demonstrated the ways in which the plays themselves can mirror and question Athenian civic ideology within the context of performance. It is now widely accepted that the plays explore Athenian democracy and its institutions and in so doing engage with gender and class disparities and with war and justice. Though some critics doubt whether Athenian civic institutions played as vital a role in tragedy,[7] as has been assumed, more recent work has expanded our awareness of the significance of this approach.[8]

Most notably, Richard Seaford argues that the destruction of the royal household—a typical feature of many plots in tragedy—is also representative of the negation of a pre-*polis* and pre-democratic past whose subversion exemplifies the process through which the democratic community came into being.[9] While Seaford emphasizes the centrality of ritual and civic cult in constructing and affirming community solidarity, Mark Griffith argues that the negotiation of class disparity within the ranks of Athenian citizens can yield a novel way of bridging the divide between aristocratic past and democratic present.[10] As he demonstrates, elite figures in tragedy act as models of authority, serving to mask disparities between mass and elite citizens. Identification with these elite figures yields an act of misrecognition on the part of the audience, who consent to a version of Athenian civic ideology, which promotes "solidarity without consensus."

A good illustration of the wide variety of approaches and perspectives on politics in tragedy is David Carter's *Why Athens: A Reappraisal of Tragic Politics*.[11] In his joint introduction with Mark Griffith, Carter offers a new working definition of historicist studies under the label of "audience studies."[12] Shifting from text to audience, as he argues, historicist critics ask what the plays meant to the original audiences of the plays, utilizing the text as evidence about the "performance that went on between the poet, actors, and audience," who attended and participated in the annual celebration of the religious festival of the Great Dionysia.

This body of work is especially valuable for crafting an approach to Athenian civic ideology in light of the historical realities surrounding the growth of Athens' power as well.[13] The study of empire, whose stamp is visible in the civic ceremonies that preceded the performance of the plays (e.g., the display of the tribute of the allies, the libations poured by the generals) at the festival of Dionysus, invites us to examine the ways in which the treatment of traditional myths furnished a tool for exploring the character of Athens' rule. Drama, like public art, glorified and monumentalized the Athenian achievement by celebrating Athens' prowess—encased in the city's mythical victories against the Persians and other Greeks, her defense of Panhellenic laws and customs, her openness to suppliants—and praised her democratic traditions by featuring her autochthonous origins, celebrating freedom of speech, and commemorating the Areopagus as revered bulwark of Athens' imperial democracy.

This process did not always unquestioningly reproduce Athenian civic ideology. The results of this inquiry in turn can be brought to bear upon the Athenians' self-understanding of their role and obligations as citizens and rulers of the empire. In this connection, it is important to take into account that the plays were performed before an audience of citizens and foreigners. The City Dionysia had acquired an international character through the presence of representatives from the allied cities, who after 454/3 BC made an annual trip to Athens in March to remit the tribute. Indeed, the presence of foreigners may have set limits, as Aristophanes claims that it did (*Ach.* 502–506), to what could be said in their presence. But the composition of the audience poses a different problem for tragedy, since the plays represent the realities of empire obliquely, unlike comedy, where Athenian imperialism is represented in a clear and unapologetic fashion.

The particular subject matter of the plays, historical background, and their religious and social settings also account for the divergent ways in which different plays represent the historical realities of empire. For example, we see that Euripides' political plays *Children of Heracles* and *Suppliant Women* deliver the core message of Athens' openness and generosity (see further, Chapter 2), distancing the city's ideal image from the realities of Athens' rule. To be sure, these plays afford the possibility of questioning Athens' motives, but they do not outwardly undercut the theme of Athenian benevolence toward others. Euripides' *Trojan Women*, which dates to 415 BC, on the other hand, depicts the suffering of war through the endless laments of Troy's women, the razing of the city, and the enslavement of its population as a way of commenting on the Greeks' accountability from which the Athenians are not excluded.[14]

In tragedy, the coexistence of positive and negative statements about the empire may also reflect a certain degree of ambivalence on the part of the Athenians toward their achievements, as Tonio Hölscher notes in his discussion of the public art of the empire:[15]

> . . . artistic intensity was a result of the "adventure" on which Athenian society had embarked in the fifth century. Their path led them, almost irresistibly, into a political order without precedent and into dominion over an empire of incomparable extension; theirs was a balancing act without net that must have created an ambivalent state of collective psychology, between euphoric self-assertion and profound self-doubt, in which all themes of social import were discussed, represented, celebrated, and questioned without end.

Recent approaches on the topic of empire attempt to come to grips with the process by which the plays convert history to drama. Some of the most representative studies have engaged specifically with the representation and actions of particular characters onstage, using them as templates for evaluating the positive and negative portrayals of Athens' power.[16] Sophie Mills and Rebecca Futo-Kennedy examine the roles assigned Athenian characters—the Athenian king Theseus and Athena, the city's divine patron—and demonstrate how each came to represent distinct facets of Athens' political identity.[17] Mills says that Theseus served as the model of the quintessential Athenian hero and as the embodiment of the Athenians' idealized civic ethos along the lines presented also in the surviving funeral speeches. The characteristics ascribed to Theseus—courage, justice and an eagerness to remedy the suffering of others—typified the ideal standards of conduct, expected of all Athenians, and were used to articulate Athens' distinctiveness, military and cultural, not only over barbarians but also over other Greeks. As Mills writes, Thucydides' narrative provides a counterpoint to this fixed, unchanging and ideal image of Athenian excellence. Such built-in ideological constraints contributed to an exaggerated image of the Athenian achievement, which precluded a more dynamic engagement with the realities of Athens' power.

Yet the presence of Athenian characters onstage did not always guarantee a straightforward affirmation of Athens' imperial ideals. As Rebecca Futo-Kennedy argues, Athena's characterization as patron of the city in the tragedies of Aeschylus and Sophocles refers more readily to the historical realities of Athens' rule. Futo-Kennedy maintains that the plays do not in effect conceal Athens' imperial conduct, given its sure and early signs already by the 470s and 460s BC. Athena furnished a powerful symbol of imperial rule by way of advertising onstage the superiority of the Athenian justice system, which was used to justify her military dominance. The fault lines between the ideal and the reality of imperial power, however, begin to emerge, as she contends, in later plays, such as Sophocles' *Ajax*, where Athena wields her power in an authoritarian manner and is no longer vested in advocating the cause of justice on behalf of others, as she did in Aeschylus' *Eumenides*. Athena's connections with the empire are well documented in the ancient sources, and the study of her character demonstrates the ways in which tragedy begins to represent the harsh realities of Athenian imperialism more overtly over time.

David Rosenbloom argues that Aeschylus' *Persians* and *Agamemnon* represent Xerxes' and Agamemnon's demise as foils for Athens' empire.[18] By staging the failure of great leaders, Aeschylus' plays prompted Athenians to reflect upon the negative consequences of their continuing expansion in Greece and upon the political and moral costs of their military undertakings. The lesson of Aeschylean tragedy, Rosenbloom writes, is Solonian, urging Athenians to adopt a stance of "looking to the end" and admonishing them to take political lessons from tragedy about the eventual demise of their own power.

Critical efforts to determine the extent to which tragedy attempts to legitimate Athens' rule unavoidably face the difficult question of answering definitively what Athenians thought of their empire and how they went about representing their dominion to others. Did playwrights lend voice to the Athenians' moral discomfort with their rule over their fellow Greeks by warning them about its inherent limits, as Rosenbloom suggests? Or were they content to celebrate it by commemorating the worthy and valorous deeds of illustrious mythical heroes and by creating a separate space where Athens' ideal civic self could remain intact, immune from any critique, as Mills argues? Alternatively, did the plays lend voice to the two faces of Athens' power and undercut its legitimacy by exposing the fissure between hegemonic and imperial justice, as Futo-Kennedy suggests?

Taking my cue from these approaches, I submit that undertaking an inquiry into the manifestations of the ideology of hegemony in the Athenian suppliant plays allows us to situate the perceptions that Athenians held about their power against the historical setting of the empire. The statements that the Athenian suppliant plays make about empire are ideological, offering an image of Athens' relations with other Greeks not as they actually were but as the Athenians purported them to be. Accordingly, the plays converge in representing Athens as a hegemonic city, that is, a city that led others on the basis of consent and on the strength of her moral commitments. The plays offer variations on the idealized portrait of the city as protector of the weak and the oppressed, each representing Athens as a city of justice (*Eumenides*), a "free city" (*Children of Heracles*) and as a "pious and reverent city" (*Oedipus at Colonus*).

The need to defend and consolidate Athens' hegemony over Sparta began in the 460s BC, when Athens' foreign policy changed, challenging profoundly the relationship between the two major powers, Athens and Sparta. *Eumenides* sets in relief the need to endorse the legitimacy of Athens' leadership after Athens broke away from the Spartans' anti-Persian League and began to pursue her military interests on her own, in the early 450s BC. The depiction of Athens as a "free city" in *Children of Heracles* in turn can be read as a defense of her conduct toward the allies against the claims that the Spartans were making around the time of the beginning of the Peloponnesian War, when they proclaimed themselves as the liberators of the cities that the Athenians ruled. *Oedipus at Colonus*, composed ca. 407/6 BC (and produced after Sophocles' death in 401 BC), also defends Athens' conduct and advertises her pious and humane treatment of strangers close to the end of the war when Athens still had the opportunity to answer for her ruthless use of force against other Greeks. By testing and probing Athens' moral leadership, the plays showcase the potentialities and limits of this ideology.

The cluster of issues that I have set out to examine in these plays conveys a new understanding of supplication in tragedy that sets this study apart from recent treatments of the topic. My study differs from those of Suzanne Gödde, who concentrates on ritual and rhetoric in the suppliant plays, and of Jonas Grethlein, who also emphasizes the significance of the exchanges between Athens and foreigners in the suppliant plays. For Grethlein this exploration is by-and-large limited to how Athenians perceived themselves as citizens in the democracy, not as rulers of an empire.[19] Athenian myths of supplication offer sophisticated political commentary on Athenian attitudes toward the status of the empire. The study of ideology in these plays does not fit neatly into the categories of "ideology as questioning" or "ideology as creed," proposed by Christopher Pelling.[20] The book's focus lies in explicating the ideological strategies employed in the texts, with particular attention to ideology as a process of legitimization.

My approach to ideology in the Athenian suppliant plays is indebted to Nicole Loraux's[21] major study of the Athenian funeral oration and to Christopher Pelling's contribution to the study of tragedy and ideology. It also draws upon ideas current in political theory, religion, and anthropology (Gramsci 1971; Bell 1992; Honig 2003). The goal of the present study is twofold: first, it seeks to establish the historical and ideological parameters that shape supplication in tragedy. Second, it develops a theoretical framework for reading the Athenian panegyric with attention to the workings of hegemonic ideology, especially as defined by Gramsci (see below, "Hegemony and Ideology").

## CONTEXTS OF SUPPLICATION

Supplication, an important religious and civic institution in Greece, commanded the attention of poets and artists alike. My own discussion here is limited to an overview of some aspects of supplication in epic and tragedy that shed light on its historical development and clarify my thesis on supplication and Athenian hegemony. Both Homer and tragedians accorded prominence to this theme, which threads through the epics and provides the focal point of plays devoted to the perilous predicament of suppliants. Indeed, some of the most famous depictions of supplication scenes in art were inspired by Homer, such as Priam's supplication of Achilles, Nausicaa's of Odysseus, or Cassandra's of Ajax.[22] They also reproduced scenes familiar from tragedy, such as Iphigenia's supplication of Agamemnon (Euripides' *Iphigenia at Aulis*), Alcmene's supplication (Sophocles' *Amphitryon*), the supplication of Heracles' children (Euripides' *Children of Heracles*), and numerous others.[23] A number of these scenes, especially those depicting supplication at the altar, captured the intense pathos of the situation and elicited pity from the viewers.

Because epic and tragic scenes of supplication stage the act from beginning to end, they furnish a fuller understanding of the process of supplication. Thus, both epic poetry and tragedy offer a repertory of gestures, words, and arguments that suppliants used to persuade their addressee to grant their request; crucial to the representation of the process in both genres was the evaluation of the petition by its recipient. In representing this process, however, epic and tragedy differed in a variety of respects. The main difference between the two lay in the decision-making process, which in epic emphasizes individual responsibility, while in tragedy the decision also involves the participation of the community.[24] We can account for the shift from the personal to the collective sphere of activity by tracing the development of practices of supplication historically, from epic to tragedy.

In Homer, suppliants direct their plea to an individual (a god or a mortal) and make a personal plea to their addressee, who then decides its outcome. Supplication is embedded within the power networks of the aristocratic society the poems by and large depict. Like *xenia* ("guest-friendship"), supplication constituted one of the avenues available to outsiders for gaining access to a community, and this avenue, too, was also closely tied to warfare.[25] The suppliant would accordingly supplicate an individual able to grant his request but whose executive power did not necessarily derive from his political authority (as it does in tragedy). Rather, the choice of whom to supplicate depended upon the specific circumstances of the request and took place in a variety of locales. There are numerous examples of supplications by the vanquished to the enemy on the battlefield[26] or at a military camp, pleading for the release of prisoners of war—of which those of Chryses' supplication of Agamemnon in the *Iliad* (1.8–32) and Priam's supplication of Achilles (*Il.* 24.485–506) are perhaps the most famous ones.

Suppliants, however, especially exiles who had fled their own country on account of homicide or who were strangers in need of assistance, could also approach either the palace of the king or the house of a powerful nobleman. Thus, arriving as a stranger in Phaeacia, Odysseus receives detailed instructions from Nausicaa on how to enter the palace of King Alcinous and supplicate Queen Arete (*Od.* 6.303–315). Telemachus accepts the seer Theoclymenus, now an exile from Argos, as a suppliant aboard his ship at Pylos and takes him home with him to Ithaca (*Od.* 15.256–281). Thus, aside from supplications in battle, Homeric supplication was by and large regulated within the sphere of the *oikos* ("the household"), often serving as preamble for establishing relations of guest-friendship or, in the case of exiles seeking a new home, as a path toward reintegration.[27] Similarly, some of the exchanges occurring in the context of supplication involved transactions of an economic nature, such as the suppliant's offer of gifts or ransom, to ensure a positive outcome.[28] Since gifts were markers of honor and prestige, their bestowal links supplication to the network of exchanges binding an aristocratic society. Within this context, their use illuminates the ways in which supplication could be deployed to call attention to, or consolidate, the recipient's status and authority.[29]

Although scholars acknowledge the continuity in the practice of supplication in the post-Homeric period,[30] tragedy also reflects the significant historical developments that took place in the archaic and classical periods and caused supplication to come under the purview of Athenian civic institutions. The practice of supplicating at the sanctuaries of the gods is scarcely attested in Homer.[31] Tragedy mirrors this development—all plays are staged at the altars of the gods[32]—and renders supplication largely a matter for the *polis*, with the king and the people as the parties to whom suppliants directed their pleas. Following this initial tableau, the evaluation of the suppliants' request in tragedy, as in real life, was placed in the hands of the civic authorities.[33]

Thus, apart from examples of individual supplication,[34] the pattern whereby suppliants direct their plea to the entire city by supplicating the king and the *demos* is present in all suppliant plays.

From Pelasgus in Aeschylus' *Suppliant Women* to Demophon and Acamas, Theseus' two sons, in Euripides' *Children of Heracles* to Theseus in Euripides' *Suppliant Women* and Sophocles' *Oedipus at Colonus*, the king of the city is in charge of deciding the supplication after consulting with the citizens of mythical Athens, while Athena in Aeschylus' *Eumenides*, the only divine *supplicandus* (recipient/addressee) in the suppliant plays, is addressed by Orestes in her capacity as civic leader (A. *Eu.* 289, ἄνασσα). Dramatically, supplication in the city calls attention to the personal and collective accountability of king and *demos*, who together share the responsibility in deciding its outcome. Thus, Pelasgus in Aeschylus' *Suppliant Women* is very reluctant to decide the case of the Danaids by himself and refers the decision to the Argive Assembly (*Supp.* 468–479, 516–523). Similarly, Athena expressly states that Orestes' guilt is too weighty a matter for her to decide, and she therefore calls for a trial and selects citizens to judge the outcome (A. *Eu.* 470–484). In suppliant drama, the participation of the community and its representatives frames concerns about moral agency in light of collective practices of decision-making and in so doing offers judgments on the moral character not only of individuals but also of the city as a whole.

## DRAMA AND COMMUNITY

In suppliant drama, the decision to accept or reject the suppliant is part of a process of political deliberation, which underscores the ethical responsibility of the city's agents by dramatizing scenarios of conflict that render the outcome of the supplication doubtful. Comparison between Homer and tragedy is instructive in this respect as well. In Homer, the *supplicandus* makes a choice between accepting or rejecting the suppliant, based on the context and circumstances of the appeal, and wavering in reaching a decision is rare. When Menelaus, for example, hesitates whether to spare Adrastus' life on the battlefield, Agamemnon intervenes and tells him to kill him (*Il.* 6.45–65). By contrast, the action of suppliant drama revolves around the difficult decision of accepting the suppliants into the city, a choice that involves going to war against the suppliants' enemies.[35] Such obstacles surface in all the suppliant plays, and the risk that their reception entails for the fortunes of the city is the object of debate, often protracted, between the suppliants and the king, on the one hand, and the enemy, on the other.

The threat of war acts as a deterrent to granting the request, and the kings to whom the suppliants address their plea do not readily accede to such requests. Instead, they exhibit hesitation and uncertainty (Pelasgus) or initially even deny the request (Theseus in Euripides' *Suppliant Women*, 247–249).[36] In Aeschylus' *Suppliant Women*, to take one example, Pelasgus is overcome by feelings of indecision and faces a significant moral quandary, being forced to decide between his obligation to act piously toward the suppliants and the gods and his duty to protect his city (*Supp.* 376–380, 387–401, 407–417, 438–454).

Pelasgus' predicament differs from that of other characters such as Agamemnon or Medea whose decisions prove ruinous for their family and city. Unlike them, the king does not view his choice as a personal one but stresses his accountability to his city and its people (*Supp.* 365–369, 397–401).[37] Since the test to which Pelasgus is put constitutes a trial of his competence as a leader, he makes a sensible choice by relegating the decision to the Assembly of the Argives (516–523). The overall moral evaluation of the principles underlying the dilemma of accepting the suppliants in the rest of the plays of this group, similarly extends beyond the agency ascribed to individual actors by presenting the decision as a matter of collective responsibility, shared by the people and their representatives. Like Pelasgus, Theseus argues that the Assembly must decide the supplication (E. *Supp.* 350–353) and Demophon conducts an assembly meeting to judge the herald's demand that the city expel the suppliants sitting at the altar of Zeus Agoraios (E. *Heracl.* 130–133).[38]

Suppliant plays then constitute dramas about the community—a fact Richmond Lattimore recognized in his analysis of Aeschylus' *Suppliant Women*, in which he highlights the key role the king's dilemma plays in deciding the Danaids' supplication.[39] As Peter Burian points out, however, Lattimore perhaps overstates its importance for the suppliant drama, since only Pelasgus presents this choice as a dilemma.

## BETWEEN RITUAL AND LAW

In her book on Homeric supplication, Manuela Giordano aptly shows that supplication was a human institution with divine authority.[40] Indeed, there were clear limits to the authority of the mortal *supplicandus*, since all suppliants were placed under Zeus' protection, and those who harmed a suppliant or violated the established rules were liable to divine sanctions.[41] While the divine imperative afforded the suppliant protection against wrongdoing, the success of his petition lay in the discretion of the *supplicandus*. Though in many cases divine and human custom could work in tandem, tragedy presents situations that create uncertainty about the motives of the suppliant and in so doing set in doubt the legitimacy of his claims. To understand further the dramatic representation of such ambiguities and the manner in which they were negotiated in the plays, we must turn next to some of the major scholarly interpretations on this subject.

The large body of literature on supplication has elucidated the code of gestures, acts, and words that suppliants employ.[42] Crucial for an understanding of the dynamics of the exchange that took place between the suppliant and his addressee is the discussion of whether supplication constitutes a ritual in the proper sense of the word, as John Gould argues in his influential article "*Hiketeia*," published in 1973.[43] Gould maintains that the success of supplication was largely a matter of the proper execution of the ritual gestures, which, once properly performed, engendered the obligation on the part of the *supplicandus* to grant the request.[44] Additionally, the efficacy of the suppliant's approach consisted in establishing and maintaining contact by touching either literally or figuratively a part of the body, usually the knee or the chin of the *supplicandus*.[45] Maintaining contact during the performance of supplication highlights the ritual dimension of the practice and explains its efficacy, which Gould and others attribute to establishing physical contact.[46]

Critics of the ritualist approach point out its limitations for an analysis of supplication in epic and tragedy, where speeches and arguments are instrumental for the suppliants' act of persuasion.[47] With his study of Greek and Roman practices of supplication, Fred Naiden has broken new ground by showing that ritual gestures play a secondary role in determining the outcome of the suppliant's request. Based on an exhaustive examination of the available evidence, he contends that the success or failure of supplication stems from the legal or quasi-legal elements of the institutional practices associated with supplication. His four-step schema illustrates that the process of supplication unfolds from the suppliant's initial approach, followed by appropriate gestures and words, which introduce arguments germane to the request, culminating in the final and most important step, the decision to accept or reject the suppliant.[48] Naiden identifies the two main components of any supplication, ceremony and judgment, and thus clarifies the discrete roles performed by suppliant and *supplicandus*.[49] He thereby boldly demonstrates that the structural elements of supplication underlie the variations and adaptations of this practice across different cultures in the Mediterranean.

Naiden acknowledges the significant variations in local practice and ascribes differences to historical and political changes that occurred over time.[50] He further discusses the historical evidence on practices of supplication in classical Athens and demonstrates that suppliant plays incorporate aspects of historical practice, as it relates to Athenian democratic institutions.[51]

## SUPPLICATION AND DEMOCRACY
## (AESCHYLUS' *SUPPLIANT WOMEN*)

Thinking about supplication along these lines brings into sharp focus the resonance of Athenian institutions in the drama of supplication for ancient audiences, who were familiar with these practices. In this connection, Naiden has shown that in Athens suppliants first presented their request before the Council; then, after the preliminary hearing, the Council would make the recommendation for the petition to be heard by the Athenian Assembly.[52] Individuals bringing their petitions before the Assembly presented themselves as suppliants at the altar of the Twelve Gods in the *Agora* before the opening of the proceedings. After the deliberations over the case in the Assembly, the decision was taken by vote, and (successful) outcomes were recorded on Assembly decrees.[53]

In Aeschylus' *Suppliant Women* we encounter the closest approximation between dramatic and actual practices of supplication as it was practiced in Athens.[54] In this play, the Argive Assembly, not the king, decides the supplication by a popular vote (609–612). Pelasgus' jurisdiction mirrors the role served by the Athenian magistrates of the Council, while his later instructions to Danaus to come before the Argive *demos* to petition for asylum on behalf of the group replicates the process of deliberation in the Athenian Assembly to decide a variety of requests from foreigners.[55] Like other metics ("resident aliens") who petitioned for tax exemption on the basis of their merits, Danaus' successful petition results in the award of metic status to the Danaids and a guarantee for asylum protection (*Supp.* 605–612).

## (RE)LOCATING SUPPLICATION IN ATHENS

Critics have focused on the dramatic motifs and themes common to all suppliant plays. In this vein, they have suggested that suppliant drama conforms to a uniform pattern of confrontation and resolution, involving a three-party exchange between the suppliants, their savior, and the enemy; savior and enemy fight against each other, and the host city wins the war and receives praise and blessings.[56] However, Naiden's emphasis on the mirroring of Athenian norms and practices in the suppliant plays offers a starting point for rethinking the parameters that underlie the pattern of suppliant drama.

The setting of the majority of the plays in Athens is significant in its own right. All of the suppliant plays, but Aeschylus' *Suppliant Women*, are set in Athens, as are his fragmentary *Eleusinioi* (ca. 470s) which probably predated his *Suppliant Women* (463 BC) and *Children of Heracles* (ca. 456 BC).[57] Though this is admittedly a limited corpus, the playwrights' predilection for staging plays in Athens deserves further attention.

BATTLE FOR HEGEMONY?

The military challenge that typically features in plots of suppliant drama can be explained against the backdrop of the intense hegemonic rivalry between Greek cities in the course of the fifth century. We have already seen that suppliant drama was a *polis* drama and that the test of the city's piety revolved around a military confrontation between host and enemy city. The decision to support the suppliants by going to war, however, also furnished a trial of the city's strength and of her capacity to oppose her foes successfully. More specifically, the host city's willingness to accept foreigners, despite the threat of war, advertised her military superiority no less than her reverence for the suppliants and the gods. To be sure, the justification for going to war varies widely among the suppliant plays. In Aeschylus' play, in particular, the king never explicitly mentions Argos' military superiority among the reasons compelling him to go to war,[58] as do, for example, King Demophon (E. *Heracl.* 243–246, 284–287) or Aethra (E. *Supp.* 315–333). Even so, military antagonism is a feature of *Suppliant Women* as well, and the ensuing engagement is a measure of Argos' military capabilities.

The suppliant plays point out the connections between supplication and hegemony. Both Argos in Aeschylus' *Suppliant Women* and Athens in the later suppliant plays lay specific claims to hegemony. In Aeschylus' play, King Pelasgus proclaims that Argos' dominion extends to the ancestral territory of the Pelasgians (*Supp.* 250–270).[59] The suppliant plays set in Athens called attention to Athens' military superiority in varied ways, not least by emphasizing that this city alone was able to shelter and abet strangers (e.g., E. *Heracl.* 329–332, *Supp.* 339–342).

But Argos and Athens do not share equal claims to hegemony.[60] Argos' dominion is weak compared to that of Athens.[61] Pelasgus' rule is short-lived and proves inconsequential. According to the reconstruction of *Aegyptioi*, the second play of the Danaid trilogy, the war ends badly: the king dies in the course of the battle, and Danaus, a foreigner, takes over the throne and rules Argos as a tyrant.[62] The Danaids are forced to marry their cousins, and Danaus orders them to murder their husbands in the last play of the trilogy, bringing pollution to the city. Conversely, the Athenian suppliant plays make a show of Athens' power: not only does the city prove her foes to be inferior but Athens also reaps military benefits from the suppliants, who help secure her ascendancy in the future (e.g., the Argive alliance in Aeschylus'

*Eumenides*). Compared with his Athenian counterparts, Pelasgus emerges as a weak leader.[63] The suppliants, powerless foreigners, exert tremendous pressure upon the king to their advantage and threaten to bring indelible pollution upon the city (*Supp.* 455–465). Argos falls short of attaining the stature of Athens, for even though Pelasgus insists on relegating the decision to his citizens (*Supp.* 368–369, 398–401, 517–519), the king does not act altogether from a position of power. In the Athenian plays, kings negotiate shrewdly with the suppliants and do not accede to their demands unconditionally. Unlike Pelasgus, they take steps to ensure positive outcomes and effectively neutralize the threat that the suppliants pose for the city, as they do, for example, when they accept Eurystheus and Oedipus, who promise to protect Athens against her enemies.

These differences lend support to the argument that the historical realities of the mythical city's power conditioned her image as *supplicandus*. Argos is divested of the trappings of hegemonic power, which typically define Athens' role in tragedy. While Athens had achieved ascendancy in Greece by the 460s BC, Argos had been eclipsed by Sparta's rise to power.[64] Athenians were sympathetic toward the Argives, the Spartans' main contenders in the Peloponnese, and they became their allies in 462/1 BC. This may account in part for the positive depiction of Argos' mythical constitution;[65] but, as we have seen, Argos can lay only partial claims to the idealized image of Athens as a city of suppliants. While the clear references to Athenian practices and institutions of supplication in Argos may lend the impression of a shared civic landscape with Athens, the depiction of Athens as a hegemonic city differentiates the two city settings of suppliant drama.

Because this study examines the interdependence between hegemony and supplication against the historical backdrop of Athens' rise to power, I do not treat Aeschylus' *Suppliant Women* as fully as the rest of the plays in this book. However, the play's affinities with, and differences from, the model that Athens represents in the later plays are germane to the book's thesis. As the earliest of the extant suppliant dramas, Aeschylus' *Suppliant Women* may have furnished a preliminary representation of the pattern we find in the later suppliant plays, which celebrated myths of Athenian political mythology. Admittedly this is not conclusive, and we can speculate further whether Athens had come to be regarded both as the ideal and as the prototypical *supplicandus* of the suppliant plays. Even so, if discrete meanings are attached to particular city settings in tragedy, as Froma Zeitlin and Suzanne Saïd have argued, then the depiction of Argos in Aeschylus' *Suppliant Women* could also have served as a foil to that of Athens. More specifically, while the prevalence of tyranny, violence, and civil discord typified Thebes as an "anti-Athens" in tragedy,

Argos offered the middle ground between Athens and Thebes, in part because it is portrayed as a city of returns (e.g., the Danaids in Aeschylus' *Suppliant Women*; Orestes in Aeschylus' *Eumenides*).[66]

More specifically, when the Argive Assembly facilitates the suppliants' reception through a grant of *metoikia* ("the status of foreign resident") to the Danaids (*Supp.* 605–620), the play points to realities familiar to an Athenian audience and further suggests, as scholars have noted, that mythical Argos stands as a metonymy for contemporary Athens. In Aeschylus' *Suppliant Women*, as Geoff Bakewell notes, the suppliants' petition for asylum and the difficulties that emerge in this context set in relief tensions and anxieties over Athens' metic population.[67] Even though the Danaids offer praise and blessings to the city and its people at the end of the first play, the adverse consequences of the Danaids' acceptance for the city (war and, later, pollution) suggest that Aeschylus' trilogy may have explored the threat that outsiders or foreign settlers posed for Athens but also for any other city. As Athens' counterpart, Argos furnishes the only other setting of suppliant plays where Athenian concerns can be examined. In the Athenian suppliant plays, the playwrights also entertain and negotiate negative possibilities, but Athens' hegemonic leadership emerges unchallenged.

## SUPPLICATION AND EMPIRE

Attention to the actual practices of supplication, combined with critical engagement with tragedy as a civic performance and as a forum for reflecting upon Athenian democracy and its institutions, has shaped the direction of recent criticism on suppliant drama.[68] The strong focus on Athens in the suppliant plays provides an especially apt exploration of Athenian beliefs, values, and ideals, set in relief through the city's encounters with outsiders who sought her protection.[69]

Further probed, however, the position of strength, which Athens commands in the eyes of the suppliants as the only city able to arbitrate and defend their claims and differences against other Greeks, offers a portrait that is representative of Athens' character as an imperial power. Specifically, my claim is that supplication in the Athenian suppliant plays offers a blueprint for examining Athens' relations with her imperial allies and concentrates on the affinities that obtain between supplication and empire. To begin with, in actual practice, the rules of the ritual dictated that the roles between suppliant and *supplicandus* be unequal: one party put forward a request; the other had the power to approve or reject it. In the Athenian suppliant plays the distribution of roles between Athens, who plays the part of powerful *supplican-dus*, and the non-Athenian suppliants, who are consistently depicted as weak and defenseless, renders the plight of the suppliant parallel to that of Athens' tribute-bearing allies in significant respects. This analogy furnishes a concrete basis for considering the suppliants' reception in light of political issues and concerns pertinent to the character of Athens' leadership.

Among the suppliant plays, those staged in Athens, Aeschylus' *Eumenides*, Euripides' *Children of Heracles* and Sophocles' *Oedipus at Colonus*, feature dramatic scenarios of Athens' successful intervention on behalf of non-Athenian suppliants. Each of these plays explored different facets of the central theme of Athens' panegyric, the city's openness toward suppliants, and celebrated the city's unique character. Her compassion and generosity toward suppliants were distinctive features of her portrayal as protector of suppliants along with other values also felt to be distinctively Athenian, such as piety, freedom, justice, and moderation.[70] Athens' distinctive portrayal as a city open to suppliants served as a platform for articulating a series of political and ideological arguments that affirmed Athens' leadership. This debate was not confined to the plays but also extended beyond the theater to the arena of politics, where Sparta and Athens had been waging ideological wars against each other already before the Peloponnesian War began.

The historical context sheds light on the ideological purpose served by the suppliant plays. The positive portrayal of Athens therein is expressly removed from the unpalatable realities of the allies' enforced subjection, which had emerged by the 460s and early 450s BC. Instead, the plays model Athens' rule upon the template of a hegemonic alliance, that is, they represent Athens' interactions with foreign suppliants as a partnership between mutually consenting parties. In casting the suppliants as assuming the role of willing allies, beholden to Athens by gratitude, they underplay the true character of Athens' rule. This positive depiction offered a response to the criticism leveled against the empire for its treatment of the allies, by rivals and discontents alike.[71]

Another purpose served by Athens' depiction as protector of the rights of the suppliants in tragedy was to garner support and recognition of her hegemonic position among Greek cities. Tragedy defined such leadership in moral terms. The portrayal of Athens as open to suppliants, who were victims of tyrannical persecution, injustice, and actions in violation of Panhellenic laws, is consistent with this aim. There was, nonetheless, a crucial disjunction between the professed and actual motives, that is, between drama and real life. More specifically, the plays depict Athens as pursuing a more liberal foreign policy than she did in actuality. Athenian diplomacy was based on pragmatism and self-interest; and Athenians exercised their dominance over the allied cities forcibly as well: by intervening in their affairs, with or without their consent, to install democracies, to punish recalcitrant allies, and to restore the balance of power to their favor if their interests were challenged in any way.[72]

My discussion of the Athenian suppliant plays sets out to explore this discrepancy by concentrating on the process whereby tragedy builds the concept of hegemony. In modern theoretical discussions, hegemony is used to distinguish leadership exercised through consent from leadership exercised by domination.[73] The representation of Athens as a hegemonic city affirms her values and power. The reception of the suppliants, however, is fraught with obstacles that preclude a straightforward affirmation of this self-professed commitment toward suppliants and outsiders. The eventuality of war against the receiving city or the risk of contagion, if the suppliants were polluted, posed barriers to entry, thereby diminishing the suppliants' prospects of success.[74] Such contingencies reflect generic constraints, imposed by the plot, which served as a vehicle for dramatizing the *peripeteia* ("reversal") of the suppliant plot. Yet the difficulties entailed in accepting foreign suppliants also disclose the dialectical process through which tragedy negotiated Athens' depiction as a hegemonic city.

Broadly defined, this dialectic explores the interstices between morality and power. On the one hand, the dilemma of the *supplicandus*, whether to accept or reject the suppliant's petition, served as a test of his piety.[75] On the other, the risks that the city underwent to accept the suppliants signal the necessity of imposing limits on Athens' openness and compassion for the suffering of others. Such limits are represented as valid and justified, emanating as they do from the contingencies surrounding supplication. Yet, closely probed, the conditions that the city imposed upon the acceptance of suppliants replicate the obligations that Athens enjoined upon her allies. Mirroring the role of allies, the suppliants prove eager and able to reciprocate the city's offer of protection by repaying her generosity in kind.

Similarly, by juxtaposing Athens' role as *supplicandus* with the power she wielded as *hegemon* ("leader"), the plays mobilize a complex dialectic surrounding the aims and methods of Athenian hegemony. On the one hand, Athens' gestures of acceptance toward outsiders affirm her portrait of benevolent *hegemon*. On the other, the crisis of supplication sheds light on the operations of power by reinforcing the hierarchies that ensured Athenian dominance over her allies. By annexing foreigners who bring significant military and political benefits to Athens, the plays contrive solutions that address the requirements set by Athens. Athens' power is then affirmed in the most concrete terms possible. The acceptance of the suppliants at the end of these plays serves to naturalize the contributions, which the allies made to the city by maintaining the fiction that these were generated spontaneously out of gratitude and loyalty toward a generous protector.

## THE TOPOS OF SUPPLICATION: POSSIBLE ORIGINS?

It is difficult to trace the origins of the special relationship Athenians claim to have enjoyed with foreigners in their mythical past. Thucydides provides the earliest mention of Athens as a haven for foreigners in his "Archaeology," noting that the city had enjoyed political stability in her early days, owing to the barrenness of her soil (1.2.5–6). This protected her from incursions, thus allowing the original inhabitants to dwell in Attica undisturbed and grow over time in numbers "on account of migrations" (διὰ τὰς μετοικίας), by receiving and enfranchising prominent exiles fleeing war or strife in their own cities.[76] Athens was also atypical by the standards of other Greek cities in that a very large number of foreigners lived and worked in Athens and the Piraeus by the fifth century. Even though after 451/0 BC, with the passage of Pericles' citizenship law, non-Athenians could no longer be enfranchised, their presence in the city was significant; metics, in particular, contributed to the cultural and financial life of the city and also served in her armed forces.[77] Thus, in Thucydides' own experience of Athenian civic life, dealings with foreigners were common.[78]

The wide and varied range of interactions between Athenians and foreigners—metics, visitors, and diplomatic envoys—furnished an obvious point of contrast with the Spartans' well-known distrust of outsiders. In the section of his funeral oration dealing with military preparation, Pericles contrasts the easy access that Greeks from other cities are said to have enjoyed in Athens with Sparta's stringent measures against foreigners, as evinced by the practice of *xenelasiai* ("expulsions of foreigners"):

διαφέρομεν δὲ καὶ ταῖς τῶν πολεμικῶν μελέταις τῶν ἐναντίων τοῖσδε. τήν τε γὰρ πόλιν κοινὴν παρέχομεν, καὶ οὐκ ἔστιν ὅτε ξενηλασίαις ἀπείργομέν τινα ἢ μαθήματος ἢ θεάματος, ὃ μὴ κρυφθὲν ἄν τις τῶν πολεμίων ἰδὼν ὠφεληθείη . . . (2.39.1–2)[79]

We also differ from our opponents in our military training. Our city is open to all, and we never engage in deportations to prevent anyone from seeing or learning something from which any of our enemies might derive profit, were we not to guard it as secret.

---

The comparison with the Spartans, who are not mentioned, is obvious. In seeking to promote Athenian claims of superiority, Pericles argues that Athens led the charge in military affairs as well. To this end, he credits the Athenians for their openness[80] and for avoiding concealment, an overt criticism of the Spartans' insularity, aimed at undercutting their much-touted reputation in military matters among the Greeks.[81] The speech, an *encomium* of Athens, delivered after the first year of the war, acknowledged Athens' military exploits in the sphere of the empire but also depicted Athens as a source of benefits for her allies, not least by highlighting her generosity on behalf of others:

καὶ τὰ ἐς ἀρετὴν ἐνηντιώμεθα τοῖς πολλοῖς· οὐ γὰρ πάσχοντες εὖ, ἀλλὰ δρῶντες κτώμεθα τοὺς φίλους. βεβαιότερος δὲ ὁ δράσας τὴν χάριν ὥστε ὀφειλομένην δι' εὐνοίας ᾧ δέδωκε σῴζειν· ὁ δὲ ἀντοφείλων ἀμβλύτερος, εἰδὼς οὐκ ἐς χάριν, ἀλλ' ἐς ὀφείλημα τὴν ἀρετὴν ἀποδώσων. καὶ μόνοι οὐ τοῦ ξυμφέροντος μᾶλλον λογισμῷ ἢ τῆς ἐλευθερίας τῷ πιστῷ ἀδεῶς τινὰ ὠφελοῦμεν. (2.40.4–5)

In doing good, we are also unlike others; we make our friends by bestowing rather than by accepting favors. Now he who confers a favor is a firmer friend, because he keeps alive the gratitude of those indebted to him through his goodwill; but the one who must pay it back is more detached in his feelings, because he knows that in repaying another's generosity, he will not be incurring gratitude but instead be paying a debt. We alone do good to others not through a calculation of interest but by acting without fear with the confidence we possess on account of our freedom.

Athens' numerous acts of generosity (τὰ ἐς ἀρετὴν) also set the city apart from all others, argues Pericles, who thereby represents the realities of the allies' dependency in idealized terms as an exchange of *charis* ("favor") among *philoi* ("friends"), adding that the benefactor is more likely to secure a return if the beneficiary responds out of gratitude rather than from a sense of duty or obligation.[82] Pericles paints a positive image of Athens' interventions, which are distanced from the pursuit of interest (καὶ μόνοι οὐ τοῦ ξυμφέροντος μᾶλλον λογισμῷ . . . τινὰ ὠφελοῦμεν).[83]

In the suppliant plays, openness and generosity toward foreigners are also the key traits of Athens' panegyric. The plays highlight the Athenians' unique sense of pity and justice that prompt them to help the marginal and the disadvantaged (women, children, and the old) as well as outcasts from other cities, fleeing blood pollution. Athens' ability to shelter and protect them against all odds, and even incorporate them into the civic body, exemplified her unswerving resolve to intervene for the purpose of remedying the suffering of others. Athens' other-regarding conduct was meant to inspire trust in her moral leadership. The template of a hegemonic alliance, that is, a coalition of voluntary members, organized under the leadership of a single city, which joined forces for the purpose of confronting a common military threat, is useful for thinking about the relationship between Athens and the foreign suppliants. Its salient elements—the duality of power, mutual consent, and the exchange of military benefits—emerge as the defining traits of the exchanges between Athens and the mythical suppliants as well. The foreign suppliants' dependency upon Athens is represented as voluntary, as each of them offers and receives military and political benefits from Athens.[84]

The image of Athens as benevolent *hegemon* in the extant Athenian suppliant plays dates to 458 BC, when Aeschylus' *Oresteia* was performed. But the origins of the topos of supplication are to be sought earlier, during the period of the Persian Wars, which set the stage for Athens' increasing involvement in Greek affairs. The covenant of voluntary submission to a powerful protector, which has left its imprint on the depiction of Athens as protector of suppliants, reflects the circumstances pertaining to the founding of the Delian League in 478/7 BC. Founded at the request of the Ionian states, whose supplication the Spartans had previously ignored, the Delian League was a defensive military and political alliance, led by Athens with the voluntary participation of the original member states that joined forces with Athens to furnish protection against the Persians and punish Greek cities, which had pledged loyalty to the Persians (Th. 1.96–97.1).[85]

If Herodotus and Thucydides are to be believed, Athens' imperial designs were present from the beginnings of the league.[86] Cimon's victory at Eurymedon in 467 BC furnished proof of the change in the character of the alliance whose military operations could no longer be regarded as defensive, once the Persian threat had been removed (Th. 1.100).[87] Instead, the Athenians led the allies on extensive campaigns first in northeast Greece and the Aegean, and then they sought to expand their influence in the East by fighting wars against Cyprus and Egypt (Th. 1.104–105).[88] The imperial character of Athens' rule, however, can be documented even more clearly over time not only by continuous warfare and expansion but also through the harsh treatment of the allies. The use of force first against Naxos (Th. 1.98.4) and then against Thasos (Th. 1.100.2) in the 460s set the precedent for treating the allies as subjects by enforcing payment of the tribute.[89] Following Cimon's victory at the naval battle at Eurymedon, the Persian threat weakened significantly; nevertheless, Athens' punitive measures against the allies offer evidence that the tactics of the empire were soon at variance with the founding principles of the league.

Unlike the histories, tragedy and funeral speeches consistently depicted Athens as a benevolent *hegemon* who sheltered the weak and the oppressed and punished their enemies.[90] The most celebrated among these were the mythical supplications of Adrastus and Heracles' children dramatized by Aeschylus in the now lost *Eleusinioi* and *Heraclidae* and in Euripides' *Children of Heracles* and *Suppliant Women*. These political myths, which celebrated Athens' protection of suppliants, her commitment to freedom and justice, and her legendary victories against formidable foes, provided ideological justification for Athens' position of leadership after her victories against the Persians.[91] The surviving evidence does not allow for an exact dating of these myths. The earliest that we can date the Athenian panegyric in tragedy is in the early 470s, the probable date of the *Eleusinioi*.

We also lack firm evidence on the dating of the funeral oration, whose beginnings scholars place anywhere between 506 and 465 BC.[92] The funeral speeches celebrated Athens' military superiority and situated its beginnings in the distant mythical past. The catalogue of the deeds of the ancestors, which was a fixed element of the later fourth-century funeral speeches, included not only the mythical wars fought on behalf of suppliants and the battle against the Amazons but also Athens' early victory against Eumolpus, culminating in her more recent victories against the Persians at Marathon and Salamis. Though the surviving sample of fifth-century speeches is meager,[93] Loraux and others have argued that the address to the dead had acquired its fixed form in the fifth century, and the fourth-century speeches reproduce, though not unoriginally, the topoi that had been established over a century ago.[94]

Among these, the examples of the suppliants who flocked to Athens from every part of Greece, in particular, proved her worthy of the power she wielded.[95] Protection for the weak was the prerogative of the powerful, and the supplications that others had made to Athens in the past confirmed that her power was widely recognized among the Greeks. As Isocrates (4.57) puts it: ἐκ δὴ τούτων [i.e., the supplication of Heracles' children] ῥᾴδιον κατιδεῖν ὅτι καὶ κατ' ἐκεῖνον τὸν χρόνον ἡ πόλις ἡμῶν ἡγεμονικῶς εἶχεν ("from these events, it is easy to understand that our city already at that time held the position of leader"). Similarly, in Herodotus (9.27) the Athenians are said to have sought and earned the position of honor in leading the army on the battlefield before the battle of Plataea by claiming, as proof of their superiority, the supplications that Heracles' children and Adrastus had made to them in the past, as well as their victory against the Amazons.

These political myths further constructed a portrait of Athenian leadership from which the arbitrary use of force and violence is expressly absent. Athenians went to war to defend their city against Eumolpus of Thrace or the Amazons or to punish offenders, such as Eurystheus or the Thebans, who refused to recognize the rights of suppliants or denied the dead their due honors. As Mills has shown, Athens gained recognition in the eyes of those whom she led as a civilizing power because she upheld the moral standards that were binding for all Greeks.[96] Furthermore, the funeral speeches highlight the contrast between Athens' morally principled leadership and violent domination, ascribed to despotic and tyrannical Greek kings or uncivilized barbarians. This antithesis also serves to define hegemony against despotism.[97] The former is defined as leadership based on consent; the latter, as the exercise of domination against states or entities that oppose it.

Both generic and historical conditions contributed to the constant and unchanging depiction of Athens in the funeral speeches. The praise of Athens' hegemonic leadership, which we find in the surviving funeral speeches, is at odds with her style of leadership, which progressed rapidly from hegemonic to imperial. As we have seen, Athens began to annex other cities by force and tighten her control over the allies already a decade after the Delian League was formed, and by the 450s Athenian imperialism had reached its final phase of development.[98] Once this change became palpable, it engendered strong feelings of disaffection among Athens' allies and mobilized serious resistance on the part of the Spartans and their allies, for whom the growth of Athenian power presented a serious threat (Th. 1.88, 1.118.2). We get a sense of the growing anti-Athenian sentiment from Athenian sources, notably Thucydides, whose history offers a penetrating account of the rise and fall of Athens' power.

Thucydides demonstrates compellingly that the Athenians' appeal to a hegemonic past was inconsistent with their current practices of empire.[99] For example, when the Athenian envoys in Sparta (1.75.2–4) take the stand, they argue that Athens acquired the empire through the allies' and the Spartans' consent, even as they admit that they must now restrain their rebellious allies in the interest of preserving their rule. The paradoxical collocation of consent and force in this context lays bare the incongruity between hegemonic and imperial power. Thucydides demonstrates that this favorable image of Athens' rule was not tenable in the post-Periclean phase of the war, as the empire continued to consolidate its power by subjugating other Greek cities. Thus, Cleon's speech in the Mytilenaean debate (3.37.1–3) squarely condemns the cherished Athenian value of pity as inappropriate for ruling an empire; and the Athenian speaker in the Melian debate summarily rejects any attempt at putting a good face on Athens' motives either by referring to earlier victories against the Persians or by claiming that they had been wronged (5.89.1). Similarly, Euphemus in his speech to the Camarinians also rejects typical justifications of Athens' power by embellishing his speech with her victories on behalf of Greece during the Persian Wars (6.83.2). As Mills puts it: "Such speeches are not renunciations of the claims of Athens to others' gratitude: they are rather admissions that Athens' power is such that the city can and will do what it likes anyway, and that the justifications which we find implicit in the speech of the Athenians in Book 1, in the funeral oration and, I suggest, in the mainstream of fifth-century Greek thought, are therefore irrelevant."[100]

Panegyric literature did not engage with the harsh realities of Athenian imperialism and least of all with the atrocities perpetrated by the Athenians against Scione, Melos, and other cities during the course of the Peloponnesian War. The image of Athens as a benevolent *hegemon* in the Athenian suppliant plays remained distanced from the thorny issues of force and domination.[101] Instead, orators and playwrights remained committed to representing Athens as acting in concert with allied interests, even as Athenians secured their imperial stronghold through continued expansion.

### TRAGEDY AND THE FUNERAL ORATION: TWO DIFFERENT KINDS OF PANEGYRIC?

Tragedy and funerary oratory also differed in the way in which they justified Athens' power. The arguments made by orators on the occasion of the state-sponsored funeral in support of Athens' rule are qualitatively different from those heard in the Theater of Dionysus. The orators of the funeral speeches defend the legitimacy of Athens' empire by praising above all her military prowess and by advertising her moral and cultural superiority, but they do not mention the contributions that foreigners, metics, and allies made to Athens' wars. In part this was due to funeral speeches themselves being primarily addressed to the Athenians and their families. Additionally, the funeral oration, which commemorated the city of Athens and the exceptional courage of the Athenian citizen-soldiers, also cultivated an image of Athenian democracy, aligned with the civic purpose of the speech.

As Loraux argues, however, the orators omitted mention of the allies and their contributions so as not to detract from the praise of Athens' excellence, which alone stood as proof of Athens' right to hegemony.[102] Pericles in his funeral oration (Th. 2.39.2–3.1), for example, compares the Spartans to the Athenians, claiming that the former always fought with their allies, while the latter prevailed against those defending their native territory by fighting alone. Lysias (2.23–24) claims in his funeral oration that the Athenians had earned the victory at Marathon by themselves since they did not expect to win any war with the allies' assistance that they could not have won themselves, nor did they want to be indebted to them for their safety. This view is in accord with the exaggerated praise of Athens' hegemony in the speeches of the orators. Metics or allies come into view occasionally in the speeches to pay tribute to Athens' greatness. As Loraux puts it, Athens' dependents exist in the speeches to endorse the city's hegemony.[103]

The majority of the extant funeral speeches postdate the empire, which could explain why they praised Athens unilaterally, that is, without paying tribute to the allies. They may have represented Athens' rule favorably and nostalgically in the wake of Sparta's rule, which followed the demise of the empire in 404 BC and was admittedly far more cruel than that of Athens. Thus, the fourth-century speeches (and perhaps the fifth-century ones), I would argue, provided a more monolithic or one-sided representation of Athens' rule than tragedy did. Playwrights pursued a different strategy; the acceptance of the suppliants suggested that their contributions were understood by the Athenians to be part and parcel of advancing her power and securing the promise of benefits.

The ideological tenor of these arguments was to a large extent shaped by the distinct occasions and settings in which they were performed. The occasion of the public commemoration of the Athenian dead at the cemetery in the district of the Ceramicus focused on praise of the *arete* ("excellence") of the city and those who had served it. Though foreigners were not prevented from attending the speech, both metics and allies who had fought in the same battles were not commemorated in the public oration. In the theater, however, the predramatic ceremonies—which included the pouring of libations by the generals (Plut. *Cim.* 8.7–9), the voting of honors to citizens (D. 18.120), the display of the tribute of the allies (Isoc. 8.82),[104] and the parade of orphans who had been raised at the city's expense (Aeschin. 3.154; Isoc. 8.82)—endorsed Athens' imperial power, not least by acknowledging the contributions made by the allies.[105] Furthermore, performances at the City Dionysia took place before a mixed audience of citizens and foreigners; among them were foreign dignitaries, who were accorded seats of honor (*prohedriai*; Aeschin. 3.76; D. 18.28). The dignitaries were representatives from members of the Delian League who after 454 BC (when the treasury was moved from Delos to Athens)[106] made the trip to deposit their share of the annual tribute.

The presence of foreigners at the Dionysia conditioned the image of themselves that Athenians sought to promote before an international audience and was strengthened through the celebration of Athenian openness toward suppliants.[107] Dicaeopolis in Aristophanes' *Acharnians* (502–506) implies that poets at the Lenaia enjoyed greater freedom of expression because foreigners were absent. Yet the strictures against which he protests prove an important point: that the Athenians took stock of the presence of foreigners, and their inclusion in the festival suggests that Athens' image as a hegemonic city in the suppliant plays took into account the perspective of the allies.

## THE ATHENIAN SUPPLIANT PLAYS:
### NEGOTIATING CONSENT

We have seen so far that the image of Athens, as harboring suppliants and outsiders seeking refuge from other cities, affirmed her imperial enterprise by celebrating her generosity, openness, and compassion. Athens gains specific reference as a haven for foreigners in the majority of the extant suppliant plays. Many of these are staged in Athens:[108] Aeschylus' *Eumenides*, Euripides' *Children of Heracles* and *Suppliant Women*, and Sophocles' *Oedipus at Colonus* all dramatize the plight of non-Athenians to whom Athens offers assistance. This theme also surfaces in Euripides' *Medea* and *Heracles*, which are staged away from Athens. Both plays feature the intervention of Athenian kings, Aegeus and Theseus respectively, who offer a refuge to Medea and Heracles, both soon-to-be exiles on account of the murder of their children (though Heracles is not a suppliant, and Medea's supplication to Aegeus is part of the revenge plot).[109] This theme has also left its imprint on tragedies that are not concerned with supplication, such as Euripides' *Electra* and *Orestes* and perhaps to a lesser extent on *Iphigenia in Tauris*.[110] The first two mention Athens in their aetiologies in connection with the trajectory of the exiled Orestes (*El.* 1238–1275, *Or.* 1644–1652), while the last links Orestes and Iphigenia with existing Attic cults of Artemis in the coastal sanctuaries of Brauron and Halai Araphenides upon their return to Greece (*IT* 1435–1474).[111]

In all the suppliant plays, the initial request for asylum is always followed by an urgent situation, typically arising from the risk of war or pollution for the receiving city, which jeopardizes the suppliants' acceptance, even when they are deemed worthy of acceptance.[112] The pattern of request followed by crisis is treated in a particular manner in the Athenian suppliant plays, which consistently resolve the crisis through the offer of benefits on the part of the suppliants. This gesture, an expression of the suppliants' gratitude toward their protectors, further ensures that the terms of asylum are advantageous for Athens. By contrast, Pericles' portrait of Athens' benefactions in his funeral oration (Th. 2.40.4–5) represents the allies' contributions as spontaneous acts of gratitude and underplays the economic benefits of the empire.

Supplication in these plays mobilizes a pattern of reciprocal exchanges that substantiate the city's representation as benevolent *hegemon*. Dramatically, the conclusion of this pattern culminates in some form of integration, engineered by Athens, for those excluded from their native city. Thus, with the exception of Euripides' *Suppliant Women*, in which Adrastus and the Argive mothers seek Theseus' intercession on their behalf in settling their conflict with Thebes,[113] exiles and foreigners such as Oedipus in Sophocles' *Oedipus at Colonus* or Eurystheus in Euripides' *Children of Heracles* gain acceptance and acquire a new standing as Attic cult-heroes.[114] Similarly, in *Heracles* and *Medea*, Theseus brings Heracles to Athens, while Medea is also promised a safe haven by Aegeus.

As a group, the Athenian suppliant plays offer a broad and comprehensive understanding of the evolution of the ideology of Athenian hegemony, which can be documented from the earlier plays, Aeschylus' lost *Eleusinioi* (probable date in the 470s) and *Eumenides* (458 BC), to Sophocles' *Oedipus at Colonus* (407/6 BC; performed in 401 BC), spanning roughly the rise and fall of Athens' empire.[115] The historical realities of empire affect Athens' hegemonic image. Plutarch (*Thes.* 29.4) suggests that in the *Eleusinioi* Theseus assisted Adrastus by negotiating a truce with the Thebans to facilitate the recovery of the bodies.[116] In *Eumenides*, on the other hand, Orestes offers Athena and her people a political and military alliance with Argos in return for their advocacy. Exemplifying one of the core elements of this ideology, his role as friend and ally of Athens derives from the historical context of the alliance between Argos and Athens, concluded in 462/1 BC. Correspondingly, in the wake of the breach of diplomatic relations with Sparta, spearheaded by Ephialtes and the radical democrats, the play promotes Athens' sole hegemony in the Greek world.[117]

The later suppliant plays register the tensions that Athenian imperial policy had yielded more overtly by the 450s, setting in relief the increasingly heavier financial and military burdens facing the allies. Significantly, they depict the benefits that suppliants promise as necessary for their acceptance and, as a result, pose limits to the acceptance of non-Athenians. At the same time, they represent the suppliants as willing to offset the risks entailed by their reception by promising Athens lasting advantages in their capacity as heroes after their death. For example, in Euripides' *Children of Heracles* and Sophocles' *Oedipus at Colonus*, the integration of the suppliants meets with significant resistance—in the former, on account of the divine demand for a human sacrifice; in the latter, due to Oedipus' pollution—that complicates the image of Athens as helper of suppliants and registers a shortfall between ideology and practice.

The dramatic framing of these issues may take a variety of forms. *Children of Heracles* explores volition in the face of compulsion by situating the sacrifice of Heracles' daughter against the prospect of the suppliants' expulsion. In a similar vein, Oedipus' pollution does not allow for his ready acceptance, as the chorus' initial impulse is to drive him out (118–164, 226–236). Theseus receives him as a permanent resident (631–637), thanks to his deep sense of compassion, justice, and moderation but also in recognition of the great boon that Oedipus brings Athens as a guardian and protector of Attica against his native Thebes.

## HEGEMONY AND IDEOLOGY

The examination of supplication under these parameters also draws upon a theoretical framework that is germane to Athens' depiction as a hegemonic city. I use the term "hegemony" in the sense of moral leadership, designed to elicit broad consent on the part of the audience with the policies of the empire. This definition of hegemony derives from the work of Antonio Gramsci, who first used the term "hegemony" to denote the control exerted by the dominant class over subordinate groups by representing its point of view as "natural."[118] Hegemony, however, was not exercised as a form of dominance. The fundamental characteristic of hegemonic discourse is the production and negotiation of consent. This process involves an active and continuous struggle between the beliefs, ideas, and values that the dominant class seeks to impose and the social reality that exposes the disadvantages of subordination. At the root of hegemonic discourse then is a constant tension between ideology and reality that "makes this interface into an inevitable site of ideological struggle."[119]

In this sense, hegemonic discourse is at its core dialogic and dynamic, not monolithic and static. Ideology for Gramsci is primarily aimed at the dominant class and seeks to promote internal self-understanding. The subordinated classes consent to a negotiated version of ideology in the absence of other articulated alternatives. To this effect, hegemony attempts to counter resistance by opposing or even assimilating competing voices. An important corollary of hegemony is that "it must be continually renewed, recreated, defended and modified. It is also continually resisted, limited, altered, challenged by pressures not all its own."[120]

The Athenian suppliant plays offer fresh insights into the complex process whereby ideology is produced in tragedy. The tension between hegemony and domination is expressed through complex scenarios of negotiation and acquiescence that suggest a dynamic interplay between competing voices. In this regard, the interaction between drama, politics, and ideology in the Athenian suppliant plays partakes in the polyphony that is a hallmark of the genre. This is not the case, for example, in funerary speeches, which offer a straightforward affirmation of Athenian ideals. Tragedy instead constructs the relationship between ideology and historical reality in terms of a dialectic between the ideal and the real instantiations of empire. The realities of Athens' domination do not surface directly but through scenarios of conflict between Athens and the suppliants, which set in relief the ideological tension between force and consent and between resistance and acquiescence. The resolutions of these conflicts, in turn, can be shown to employ strategies typical of the operation of ideology at large.[121] The plays contrive illusory, albeit dramatically appropriate, solutions that attempt to eliminate the apparent discrepancy between the ideal and the reality. Even so, the dialectical process in which they are engaged lays bare the contradictions that underlie the exercise of Athenian power and lend voice to the Athenians' increasing anxieties regarding the preservation of the empire.

The Athenian suppliant plays construct the realities of imperial subjection in positive terms, fashioning the image that Athenians wanted to project to their allies. Although the tragedies engage multiple and at times conflicting points of view, the inclusion of the voice of the "weak and the oppressed" exposes the asymmetry of power between Athens and her allies and constitutes an important aspect of the image of the imperial city, which the plays project for Athenians and foreigners in the theater. Though the ideological stance of the Athenian suppliant plays towards empire may ultimately appear to lie closer to legitimization than dissension, the plays underscore the divergence between hegemony and empire. In this way, the ideological negotiation, which they help mobilize, offered alternatives to violent domination by privileging consent over force and by envisioning Athens' leadership in moral terms.

The individual chapters explore the manifestations of Athens' hegemonic power by tracing its progress from the earlier to the later days of the empire. In Chapter 1, I demonstrate that the double reception of Orestes and the Furies by Athena in Aeschylus' *Eumenides*, read against the background of Athens' breach of diplomatic relations with Sparta in 462/1 BC, helped articulate the hegemonic rivalry between the two most powerful cities in Greece. Orestes' acquittal and the reception of the Furies—polluted outsiders who find a refuge in Athens—support Athens' hegemonic ambitions by affirming her military superiority and advertising her judicial authority. Orestes' offer of the Argive alliance acknowledges and expands Athens' military reach. The Furies' integration as Athenian divinities further strengthen Athens' hegemony by representing the city as direct beneficiary of the powers that these chthonic divinities had wielded in the distant past in the sphere of justice.

In Chapter 2, I offer a brief historical overview on the growth of Athenian imperialism and explain the varieties of tragic hegemony in the suppliant plays. In Euripides' *Children of Heracles*, which was performed at the beginning of the Peloponnesian War (ca. 430 BC), the plight of Heracles' suppliant children brings into sharper focus the realities of imperial subjection at the beginning of the Peloponnesian War. While the play's *encomium* of Athens' imperial freedom validates the ideal image of Athens as protector of the weak, the demands placed subsequently upon the suppliants register a significant tension between the ideal and the reality. The sacrifice of Heracles' daughter sets in relief the limits that the play builds into Athens' ideal image. Forced to remit a heavy tribute in return for asylum, the suppliants acquiesce to the burdens of empire. The sacrifice exposes the disparity of status between Athenians and their allies, maintaining all the while the fictional premise that the allies' contributions were not compulsory but rather a token of loyalty in recognition of Athens' magnanimity.

In Sophocles' *Oedipus at Colonus* we witness signs of an ideology in crisis. Athens' pity toward the suffering of others in this play does not augment Athens' praise but instead attempts to defend her ideals at the end of the Peloponnesian war by offering proof of her commitment to morality. The significant obstacles that Oedipus' integration entails, however, preclude an easy affirmation of these ideals. The process of Oedipus' integration negotiates the threat of contagion for the city against the promise of future benefits that his annexation as savior-hero will bring. The traits that Oedipus embodies as a hero, at once dangerous and beneficial, become a matter of civic concern. Oedipus' pollution serves to articulate the type of limits imposed upon foreigners who took up residence in Athens. Although Theseus awards Oedipus an honorary type of citizenship, the play clearly distinguishes between foreigners' standing and that of Athenian citizens, even when they become fully assimilated as "Athenians." For when Oedipus chooses the grove of the Furies as his residence, he embraces with gratitude a status equal to, but separate from, that of his hosts.

## CHAPTER I

# AESCHYLUS' *EUMENIDES:* HEGEMONY *and* JUSTICE

Aeschylus' *Eumenides* was performed in 458 BC, shortly after the reorganization of the Areopagus under Ephialtes and the new alliance between Athens and Argos in 462/1 BC. Against this background, the play paints a singular portrait of Athens' hegemony both military and judicial. The image of Athens as protector of suppliants in this play among others challenges Sparta's much-touted military superiority by celebrating the mythical alliance between Athens and Argos, which Orestes formalizes at the end of his trial.

*Eumenides* calls attention to Athens' distinctive ability to assimilate what is "foreign" and to forge relationships of mutual advantage even among opposing parties. Athens' gestures of acceptance are realized through two different forms of civic integration: Orestes' repatriation in Argos and the Furies' incorporation as cult divinities in Athens. Both Orestes and the Furies return the favor of their reception by making contributions to Athens that augment her power. Orestes' offer of the Argive alliance expands Athens' military reach, while the Furies play an equally important role in ensuring Athens' dominance by serving Athena and her people. The advantages, which accrue to Athens as a result of the incorporation of these foreigners, jointly advertise her military and her judicial superiority.

## ORESTES AND THE ARGIVE ALLIANCE

"Tragic allusions to contemporary events are not as a rule, taken on trust, but *Eumenides* contains three notable exceptions," notes J. H. Quincey, in his discussion of the dramatic representation of the historical alliance in Aeschylus' *Eumenides*.[1] Scholars now agree that *Eumenides* furnishes a mythical aetiology for the Argive alliance of 462/1. Led by Ephialtes and the radical democrats, the alliance with Argos was emblematic of the new course in Athens' foreign policy.

In the late 460s BC, the Athenians withdrew from the Hellenic League formed in 481 BC against the Persians, renouncing their diplomatic ties with Sparta, and concluded a military and political alliance with Argos, Sparta's avowed enemy in the Peloponnese.[2] The rift was prompted by the conduct of the Spartans, who requested the Athenians' assistance in quelling the uprising of the helots and the *perioikoi* during the Messenian War.[3] Cimon had proposed the motion to dispatch an Athenian contingent, which Ephialtes and many democrats opposed. The Spartans later dismissed the Athenian force, led by Cimon, fearful and suspicious of their potential involvement in the revolt.[4] It was this incident that led the Athenians to dissolve their alliance with the Spartans against the Persians (Th. 1.102.4). Concurrently, Cimon's involvement afforded Ephialtes and many democrats who had originally opposed his motion the opportunity to ostracize Cimon while he was away (Plut. *Cim.* 17.3).[5] For despite his military successes in northwest Greece and the Aegean, Cimon had maintained friendly relations with the Spartans out of personal conviction and as a matter of strategy.[6] The Argive alliance put an end to Cimon's philo-Laconian politics and defined Athens' foreign policy through open enmity to Sparta.

The Argive alliance in *Eumenides*, which is mentioned three times in the course of Orestes' trial on the Areopagus (287–298, 667–673, 762–777), is granted such prominence because it was "part and parcel of the democrats' program of reforms in domestic and foreign policy."[7] For critics, the two mythical aetiologies of the play, Orestes' inauguration of the alliance and Athena's foundation of the Areopagus as a homicide court in Athens, relate the new direction in foreign policy with the reforms of 462/1 BC, which the democrats pushed ahead, thereby dismantling the aristocrats' stronghold on the Areopagus Council.[8]

My discussion further demonstrates that the depiction of the mythical alliance with Argos strengthens Athens' image as a hegemonic city.[9] The protection that Athena affords Orestes against the all-powerful Furies affirms Athens' reputation for helping those in need. The play adapts the coordinates of myth and plot to the requirements of hegemonic mythmaking, tracing its origins in the distant past. Orestes pays tribute to Athena's leadership by offering the goddess an alliance with Argos as a token of his gratitude.

The dramatic configuration of supplication acquires specific relevance in the context of the historical antagonism between Athens and Sparta that led to the breach of diplomatic ties in 462/1 BC. For while Sparta's authority was widely recognized among the Greeks due to her leadership of the Hellenic League, Athens' power continued to grow with the result that neither was Sparta ready to cede first place to Athens nor could Athens curb her hegemonic ambitions any longer to avoid Sparta's displeasure.[10]

Orestes' return to and burial in Argos elicits the hegemonic rivalry between the two cities.[11] The well-known story of the "return of Orestes' bones" from Tegea to Sparta (Hdt. 1.65–68) had supplied the Spartans with their own myth of hegemony already in the sixth century and had been used to justify Sparta's claim of the right to leadership over the Peloponnese at Argos' expense. Within these parameters, the location of Orestes' tomb cult in Argos, prefigured in the aetiology of the mythical alliance, rivals the Spartan cult of Pelopid Orestes and challenges Sparta's claims to hegemony. The political and ideological motives, which underlie the dramatic depiction of the alliance between Athens and Argos, emerge by exploring the rival mythical and religious traditions rather than by directly mirroring the historical events.

Situated broadly within the realm of power politics, the relocation of Orestes in Argos can be seen as affording Argos the opportunity to claim its revenge against Sparta. It is Athens, however, who benefits from the hero's figurative transfer, as Orestes vows that as a hero he will ensure Athens' military superiority against her foes in perpetuity.

## SUPPLICATION IN A CITY OF JUSTICE

Orestes' trial at the homicide court of the Areopagus has been broadly regarded as the basis for the glorification of Athens in *Eumenides*. Athena and her city receive credit for their role in resolving a family feud arising from kin murder and for releasing Orestes from the guilt of the matricide. Unlike previous analyses of the play, which interpret the Athenian panegyric primarily through the contemporary reforms of the Areopagus, I argue that the homage paid Athena and her city is linked with the dynamics of Orestes' supplication in Athens. Adapting the familiar pattern of the arrival of a foreign suppliant whose supplication Athens accepts, Orestes' supplication in *Eumenides* allows us to consider the relationship between drama, myth, and politics from the vantage point of hegemonic politics.

Orestes' supplication of Athena shares significant similarities with that of other mythical suppliants such as Heracles' children and Adrastus, who seek Athens' assistance in settling their claims against their enemies. In this play, Orestes arrives in Athens from Delphi, takes his seat at Athena's image and delivers his initial supplication (235–243), followed by a prayer to Athena (276–298). As in the other Athenian suppliant plays, the progress of the supplication is not smooth. The presence of the Furies who surround their victim, uttering threats of reprisal and gruesome violence (244–275), places his supplication at risk (258–260). Their hostility and aggression mobilizes the conflict between the suppliant and his opponent, typical of supplication plots.

While Orestes prays to Athena for protection, the Furies track him down like hounds, following the scent of blood, demanding retribution, and oppose his request for Athena's judgment (αὐτοῦ φυλάσσων ἀναμένω τέλος δίκης, "I keep watch here and await the end of my trial," 243; ὑπόδικος, "brought to trial," 260). They strike an even more threatening pose, as their pursuit of Orestes turns into a hunt for their human quarry (246–252, 265–266). Blurring the boundaries between human and animal and between sacred and profane, they threaten to reanimate the cycle of sacrificial violence by committing outrage against a suppliant.

The suppliant's powerlessness in the face of violent retribution, embodied by the Furies, acquires ideological valence, as it typifies the contrast between the weak and outraged suppliant and his powerful inimical pursuers — one of the key features of Athens' characterization as protector of the weak and the defenseless. Accordingly, the Furies' attempt to subvert Orestes' supplication prompts Athena's mediation of the crisis. Athena first lends both parties the opportunity to present their claims.[12] After both parties advance preliminary arguments (415–469), Athena is faced with the task of deciding the legitimacy of Orestes' supplication against the risk of incurring the wrath of the Furies. Athena pronounces the matter too grave for her to decide (470–479).[13] She then proceeds to institute a trial by jury, composed by a select group of Athenian citizens (482–489).[14] Arguably, her decision deviates from the procedures in other suppliant plays. Pelasgus' decision to relegate the decision over the supplication of the Danaids to the Argive Assembly in *Suppliant Women* furnishes the closest parallel to Athena's refusal to judge the case on her own. More importantly, as in Aeschylus' *Suppliant Women*, so in *Eumenides* the participation of the citizens alludes to democratic practices or institutions.[15]

The import of democracy in *Eumenides* derives predictably from and bears the imprint of the reforms that Ephialtes and the democrats had passed a few years earlier to curtail the aristocrats' political power.[16] The trial of Orestes furnished the charter myth for the homicide court of the Areopagus,[17] and to this extent his supplication is closely linked to this major innovation, which Aeschylus introduced to the tradition surrounding Orestes' trial.[18]

Aeschylus' depiction of the court is not at odds with the representation of Athens as a hegemonic city. Athena's foundation of the court in response to the suppliant's plea for protection highlights the city's primacy in the sphere of civic justice. The mythical court comes into existence for the purpose of settling a conflict, which arises among parties with no prior ties or allegiance to Athens. This process highlights in programmatic fashion Athenian hegemony through Athena's leadership. The play portrays political discord as issuing in disputes among external parties and Athena's arbitration of Orestes' claims against those of the Furies fosters stability and concord, not discord and strife. Furthermore, when the Furies accept Athena's offer, they agree to serve Athens, praising and offering benefits that lend support to the city's hegemony (see below, "Hegemony Revealed"). Accordingly, the combination of supplication followed by trial brings the subsequent founding of the court in line with Athens' role as protector of suppliants in the suppliant plays.

## AN IDEAL ALLIANCE: ATHENS AND ARGOS

The alliance with Argos that Orestes offers Athena for her help, presented as a debt of gratitude, highlights military benefits that issue from the exchange of supplication. Furthermore, the dramatic depiction of the mythical alliance serves not only to reflect the traditional enmity between Argos and Sparta but also to promote Athens' claims to hegemony against Sparta.[19]

Apollo establishes Athens' hegemonic benevolence early in the play, when he enjoins Orestes to travel from Delphi to Athens as a suppliant:[20]

. . . μολὼν δὲ Παλλάδος ποτὶ πτόλιν
ἵζου παλαιὸν ἄγκαθεν λαβὼν βρέτας·
κἀκεῖ δικαστὰς τῶνδε καὶ θελκτηρίους
μύθους ἔχοντες μηχανὰς εὑρήσομεν
ὥστ' ἐς τὸ πᾶν σε τῶνδ' ἀπαλλάξαι πόνων. (79–83)

. . . when you come to the city of Pallas, sit holding her ancient image in your arms. There we will have judges to judge these matters, and words that will charm, and we will find means to release you from this misery altogether.

Apollo's speech renews his commitment to his protégé, after he fails to release him from his bondage to the Furies. He presents Athens as the only city able to end Orestes' suffering (ὥστ' ἐς τὸ πᾶν σε τῶνδ' ἀπαλλάξαι πόνων, 83–84). Though the god here speaks in his dramatic persona, that is, as Orestes' protector and ally, it is also worth noting that as divine patron of Delphi, Apollo was a recognized authority on interstate affairs and was wont to dispense advice on military matters as well. Accordingly, his mandate that Orestes go to Athens further marks his recognition of Athena's power.[21]

The political implications of the god's mandate emerge more clearly in Orestes' prayer to Athena (276–298):

καὶ νῦν ἀφ' ἁγνοῦ στόματος εὐφήμως καλῶ
χώρας ἄνασσαν τῆσδ' Ἀθηναίαν ἐμοὶ
μολεῖν ἀρωγόν· κτήσεται δ' ἄνευ δορὸς
αὐτόν τε καὶ γῆν καὶ τὸν Ἀργεῖον λεὼν
πιστὸν δικαίως ἐς τὸ πᾶν τε σύμμαχον. (287–291)

Now, therefore, from a pure mouth I call reverently on Athena, sovereign of this land, to come to my aid; and she will thereby, without any use of force, have myself, my land, and my Argive people as loyal and righteous allies for all time.

Holding the goddess' image, Orestes declares that he is no longer a polluted suppliant, seeking purification.[22] His suppliant seat emphasizes his inferior standing to his powerful *supplicanda*, as he abases himself in proper ritual manner to seek her assistance.[23] The performance of the ritual calls attention to Orestes' abject plight and makes Athena's intervention imperative to avert the harm that the Furies intend to visit upon him. Orestes' plight, a suppliant mired in crisis, brings home the political message of supplication by affirming the city's hegemonic position, which, like Apollo, Orestes deems worthy of Athens, as he places his perilous predicament in Athena's hands. The suppliant's initial approach thus tailors his request for deliverance and restoration to the play's Athenian panegyric.

The suppliant's submission to Athena is hereby envisioned as a military and political partnership between the two cities, led by Athena. Though Orestes appeals to Athena's authority and competence in the realm of justice, he also pays tribute to Athens' military superiority overtly, when he summons Athena to come to his aid:

ἀλλ' εἴτε χώρας ἐν τόποις Λιβυστικῆς
Τρίτωνος ἀμφὶ χεῦμα γενεθλίου πόρου
τίθησιν ὀρθὸν ἢ κατηρεφῆ πόδα
φίλοις ἀρήγουσ', εἴτε Φλεγραίαν πλάκα
θρασὺς ταγοῦχος ὡς ἀνὴρ ἐπισκοπεῖ,
ἔλθοι, κλύει δὲ καὶ πρόσωθεν ὢν θεός,
ὅπως γένοιτο τῶνδ' ἐμοὶ λυτήριος. (292–298)

But whether she is in a region of the Libyan land, close near the waters of her native stream of Triton, planting a straight or covered leg, helping her friends, or whether she is surveying the plain of Phlegra like a bold commander of an army, let her come here—a god can hear even from away—so that she may be my deliverer from these troubles.

In his invocation to Athena, Orestes prays to the goddess to come to him from afar and situates her in two separate locales that are distinctively associated with the goddess.[24] He first locates the goddess in the vicinity of the river Triton, Athena's birthplace, according to one tradition (Hdt. 4.180), and next on the plain of Phlegra, the site of the mythical battle between the gods and the Giants. Both describe the goddess as discharging military duties by taking the lead in military operations. The first reference to Athena's presence in Libya has been associated with the Egyptian campaign of 460/59 BC, which the Athenians and their allies undertook at the request of the Libyan king Inarus (Th. 1.104).[25] The second reference to the plain of Phlegra has not been as successfully tied to any particular event or campaign, but it may allude to Athenian involvement in military operations in the area Chalcidice or Thrace.[26] What is more, Athens' imperial presence can be documented in both regions. As such, the coordinates of the two geographical references—the river Triton is the southernmost place with which Athena was associated just as Phlegra is the northernmost—establish Athena's hegemony over a broad region, corresponding roughly with the reaches of the empire at that time.[27]

Taken together, I would argue, these references promote a positive portrait of Athenian interventionism, shaped largely by the play's Athenian panegyric. In a manner reminiscent of the *encomia* of tragedy and the funeral orations, Orestes specifically praises Athena's leadership by envisioning the goddess either as "helping friends" (φίλοις ἀρήγουσ', 295) in the land of Libya and or as "a military leader" (θρασὺς ταγοῦχος ὡς ἀνὴρ, 296).[28] The goddess' military accomplishments emblematize not only her own martial prowess but also that of the city, which she leads.[29] To be sure, mortals often addressed a particular divinity by praising the specific aspect of the god's sphere of influence, which would be most beneficial to them. Orestes addresses Athena as civic leader (ἄνασσ', 235) and as military *hegemon*, deeming both relevant to the goddess' praise and in turn to the success of his petition.

The appeal to the goddess' military prowess underlines the recognition that the city had deservedly earned in the eyes of other Greeks. As a suppliant, Orestes specifically takes on the role of ally and professes eternal loyalty to Athens on Argos' behalf (289–291). He declares that Athens will obtain an ally in Argos without exercising any force (289).[30] Both the expression "without force" (289) and the term "ally" (291) allow the audience to envision this new military alliance in positive terms as a hegemonic alliance, led by Athens. The expression ἄνευ δορός ("without a spear," 289) characterizes the alliance as freely given, thereby emphasizing Orestes' voluntary association with Athens. Similarly, the term σύμμαχος, which in the fifth century characterized the military and political relationship between Athens and her allies, underscores the political character of Orestes' supplication, signaling Argos' acceptance of Athens' hegemonic standing.[31]

His supplication typifies a relationship of political dependency; but Orestes' promise of the Argive alliance casts the exchange between the city and the suppliant as an ideal partnership, based on an agreement that is voluntary and reciprocal. In his prayer to Athena, Orestes stresses reciprocity as the basis for the military and political association between Athens and Argos. The alliance stands as an acknowledgment of the debt of gratitude he owes Athena. His loyalty, moreover, demonstrates that Athens earned constant allies by intervening on behalf of those who suffered undeservedly. The idea that Athens acquired her allies through acts of benevolence finds its most clear demonstration, as I argued in the introduction, in the ideal of *charis* ("favor") in Pericles' funeral oration in Thucydides (2.40.4–5).

Pericles in that passage presents a positive image of Athenian interventionism by describing the relationship between Athens and her allies as a non-obligatory exchange, governed by *charis*. In the context of the funeral oration, the reciprocity of *charis* serves to mask relationships of unequal advantage between Athens and her allies by stressing the recipient's obligation to repay the favor incurred.[32]

In the context of the play, the tenor of this relationship is different. Orestes' offer of the alliance emphasizes the mutual advantages that both parties would derive from the alliance. Consent and reciprocity represent the military and political alliance with Argos as an ideal exchange. Set against the historical context of the Argive alliance, Orestes' offer to Athena promotes and advertises Athens' superior leadership at the expense of Sparta.

### AN ATHENIAN HERO

Orestes' homecoming is closely linked with his role as founder of the Argive alliance. His acquittal brings his exile to an end, and, as he departs for his home, Orestes thanks Athena, Apollo, and Zeus[33] for reinstating him in his patrimony and helping him to reclaim his citizenship in his native city (754–761). Having established his rightful claim as king of Argos,[34] he formalizes the alliance with an oath that the alliance will be binding for his descendants in perpetuity. The formal conclusion of the alliance also contains the rationale for Orestes' heroization as he vouches to protect Athens against her foes for all time:

ἐγὼ δὲ χώραι τῆιδε καὶ τῶι σῶι στρατῶι
τὸ λοιπὸν εἰς ἅπαντα πλειστήρη χρόνον

ὀρκωμοτήσας νῦν ἄπειμι πρὸς δόμους,
μή τοί τιν' ἄνδρα δεῦρο πρυμνήτην χθονὸς
ἐλθόντ' ἐποίσειν εὖ κεκασμένον δόρυ.
αὐτοὶ γὰρ ἡμεῖς ὄντες ἐν τάφοις τότε
τοῖς τἀμὰ παρβαίνουσι νῦν ὁρκώματα
†ἀμηχάνοισι πράξομεν† δυσπραξίαις,
ὁδοὺς ἀθύμους καὶ παρόρνιθας πόρους
τιθέντες, ὡς αὐτοῖσι μεταμέληι πόνος·
ὀρθουμένων δὲ καὶ πόλιν τὴν Παλλάδος
τιμῶσιν ἀεὶ τήνδε συμμάχωι δορὶ
αὐτοῖς ἂν ἡμεῖς εἶμεν εὐμενέστεροι.
καὶ χαῖρε καὶ σὺ καὶ πολισσοῦχος λεώς·
πάλαισμ' ἄφυκτον τοῖς ἐναντίοις ἔχοις,
σωτήριόν τε καὶ δορὸς νικηφόρον. (762–777)

I return to my home now, after I swear solemnly to this land and to your
people, for the future and all time to come, that no helmsman of my land,
will ever come, well equipped with arms, will ever come to bring war
against this place. For I myself, then in my tomb, will act against those
who violate my present oath, by misfortunes that lack remedy, making
their marches dispirited and their paths ill omened, so that they repent
of their effort; but if my oath is properly maintained, and if they always
honor their obligations to this city of Pallas by fighting at its side, we shall
be more well-disposed to them. Now farewell to you and to the people of
your city: you have a means to success that your enemies will be unable to
escape, which will bring you safety and victory in war.

Pledging as a representative of Argos his own loyalty and that of his descendants, his oath links the mythical alliance with his hero-cult in aetiological terms (762–774).[35] Furthermore, the oath links Orestes' future standing as a hero to the historical and political background of Athenian-Argive
relations.[36]

The historical realities surrounding the cult of the hero are significant for
understanding the particular purpose that it served.[37] Among the varied functions of hero-cult, the transfer of a hero from one city to another[38] enabled
the city that claimed him to obtain military gains, as the hero's power was
thought to reside with his tomb.[39] An array of examples exists of the transfer of heroes from one city to another; Orestes' heroization is modeled after
the pattern of the annexation of the foreign hero.[40] The most prominent
examples in this category are those of the Theban Oedipus and the Argive
Eurystheus, both of whom pledge to defend Athens against her enemies

in the future in exchange for their acceptance and burial within the city.[41] Eurystheus in *Children of Heracles* promises to defend Athens against the descendants of Heracles' children, the Spartans, while Oedipus in Sophocles' *Oedipus at Colonus* vows to protect the city against a future attack from the Thebans. Though Orestes is not buried in Athens like the other two, Athens appropriates his protective powers in a similar way, as he promises to be loyal and favorable to the Athenians and hostile toward their enemies.[42]

Orestes' designation as an ally (290–291, 670–671) prefigures the association that he envisions between the alliance (συμμάχωι δορὶ, "with the spear of allies," 773) and his future service to Athens as a hero (775–777). Like the other heroes whom Athens accepts, Orestes vows to protect the city in perpetuity (291, 670, 763). The *Eumenides'* connection of the mythical alliance with his hero-cult, however, renders the interplay between the dramatic fiction and the corresponding historical realities even more precise. Both Oedipus and Eurystheus promise to protect Athens against her enemies, alluding, albeit in vague terms, to future attacks from Thebes and Sparta respectively (S. *OC* 583–589; E. *Heracl.* 1032–1037).[43] Orestes' pledge establishes a clear link between past and present: through his parting words (775–777) he presents the alliance as a conduit for his heroic powers by vowing to strengthen Athens' military capacity.[44] The link between the alliance and Orestes' hero-cult highlights its relevance for Athens' hegemony: Orestes pronounces the mythical alliance a blessing for Athena and her people (775–777), as he predicts its future success, calling it "an inescapable wrestling trick" (πάλαισμ' ἄφυκτον, 776) against Athens' enemies and stresses its contribution to Athens' safety and victory.

The reception of foreign suppliants as cult-heroes is specific to the way tragedy develops the Athenian panegyric.[45] In their capacity as heroes, they act as guardians and saviors:[46] they protect Athens' territorial integrity or grant the city the military advantage over her foes, strengthening both her defensive and offensive capabilities.[47] At the same time, Athens' appropriation of their protective powers is represented as issuing from an agreement that is at once voluntary and reciprocal, albeit predicated upon the exchange of benefits between parties of unequal standing. The foreign heroes whom Athens annexes function paradigmatically:[48] the plays draw on the analogy between foreigner and ally to present the hero in the guise of a constant and loyal ally. Like Oedipus and Eurystheus, Orestes offers tangible benefits in return for Athena's assistance.

Heroes were by definition ambivalent in that they could use their powers to good or harmful ends, if they were not properly propitiated. Orestes defines his heroic powers in a manner congruent with Athens' military interests. Thus, when he enlists his protective powers to Athens' service, Orestes vows to punish those who transgress his oath, "making their campaigns ill fated," and to be favorable to those who honor his pledge (764–774). The agreement, which he broaches in his capacity as hero-ally, however, does not represent an exchange among equals, as the oath he takes is sworn unilaterally and highlights Argos' acceptance of its subordinate role, as was customary for cities that entered into agreements with a hegemonic power.[49]

## RELOCATING ORESTES FROM SPARTA TO ARGOS

A number of publications have drawn attention to the way in which tragedy, a genre steeped in Athenian civic customs and institutions, adapts the rich tradition of Panhellenic myth by representing the Athenians as its chief heirs.[50] Homer's and Hesiod's poetry had contributed to the creation of a large repository of myths and religious beliefs, shared by all Greeks. Access to this heritage helped forge a sense of a shared Hellenic identity, defined by common rituals, language, and myths that characterized Panhellenism in the archaic period.[51] While Panhellenic poetry deemphasized local lore and rituals, already in the eighth century we find the opposite trend, whereby individual cities began to cultivate their ties with Panhellenic figures by worshiping them locally.[52] This process in turn documents the functions that hero-cults assumed over time within the context of the *polis*—notably by defining its political, religious, and territorial affiliations with other cities.[53]

The cults of Agamemnon and Orestes in Sparta offer a good illustration of the appropriation of figures of Panhellenic standing to serve political aims.[54] The Spartans, in particular, justified their leadership over the Peloponnese and Greece by claiming that their kings were descendants of Agamemnon and Orestes[55]—presenting themselves as the rightful heirs of the *kleos* ("glory," "renown") of the Achaeans who had fought at Troy. The dramatic aetiology of Orestes' cult in Argos in *Eumenides* suggests a reversal to the Panhellenic tradition, which located Orestes and the Atreids in Argos. Upon meeting Athena, Orestes emphasizes his Argive civic identity (Ἀργεῖός εἰμι, "I am an Argive," 455) and presents himself as the son of the victorious leader of the Greek naval force (456–458). Similarly, in his farewell speech, Orestes emphasizes his ties with his native Argos (γαίας πατρῴας ἐστερημένον, "deprived of my native land," 755) and proclaims himself a citizen again (Ἀργεῖος ἀνὴρ αὖθις, "I am an Argive again," 757), giving thanks to Athena, Apollo, and Zeus for restoring him to his patrimony (757–760).

The location of Orestes' cult in Argos is also ideologically motivated, as his depiction as an Argive hero subverts Sparta's established claims on Orestes. The play thus defines his standing as an Argive hero through recourse to his

Panhellenic identity. For implicit in Orestes' spatial relocation to Argos is his restoration to his Panhellenic inheritance, a reversal that allowed Athens to claim for herself the prestige of the association with the last of the Atreids.

Typologically, Orestes' hero-cult in Argos in *Eumenides* shares some similarities with accounts that cast the transfer of heroic cults from one city to another as the "return of the local hero."[56] Theseus' relics are brought home from Scyros to Athens (Plut. *Thes.* 36.1–2, *Cim.* 8.6; Paus. 3.3.7); Orestes', from Tegea to Sparta (Hdt. 1.66–69; Paus. 3.3.6–7); those of Tisamenus, from Helike in Achaea to Sparta (Paus. 7.1.8). The hero's "homecoming" enables the city that claims him as her own to be victorious against her foes: Athens conquers Scyros after settling Theseus in Athens,[57] and Sparta is victorious in the protracted war against her Tegean neighbors in 560 BC. In the case of Tisamenus, the transfer aimed to facilitate an alliance between Sparta and Helike, the most important Achaean city in the sixth century, but did not succeed in its aim.[58] Orestes' resettlement in Argos does not present an exact parallel with the examples of the transfer of the relics of heroes. Within the dramatic context, his association with Argos facilitates his conversion into an Athenian hero. His declaration of allegiance to Athens also makes his hero-cult somewhat of an amalgam: though presumably his tomb is located near Argos, Orestes himself vows eternal loyalty to Athens.

### ARGIVE-SPARTAN RELATIONS

The background of Argive-Spartan relations is vital for interpreting Orestes' future functions as a hero, as Argos was an avowed enemy of the Spartans. Consequently, Orestes' declaration of the alliance as a blessing for Athena and her people and as an affliction for her foes acquires even greater potency.[59]

Sparta had eclipsed Argos by the middle of the sixth century, when the Spartans began pursuing their interests in the Peloponnese strategically. Integral to Sparta's rise to hegemony was her victory in the war against Tegea and the cult the Spartans established in Orestes' honor after allegedly bringing back his bones to their city (ca. 560 BC). Sparta was able to conclude an alliance with her Arcadian neighbors after ending the war. This was the first in a series of alliances that Sparta made with other cities in the Peloponnese, forming the basis for the coalition that came to be known as the Peloponnesian League.[60]

Herodotus inserts the story to explain how Sparta in the time of Croesus had come to acquire her position of supremacy in the Peloponnese after defeating her neighboring Tegea in a prolonged frontier war (1.66–69). After sending representatives to Delphi for a second time, the Spartans were advised to bring back the bones of Orestes to gain mastery over Tegea. Herodotus recounts how a certain Lichas, a Spartan noble, came to discover the bones of Orestes and how by employing a ruse, he was able to exhume them and bring them back with him to Sparta. After that time, the Spartans were able to defeat the Tegeans and conclude an alliance with them. Sparta's military influence in the Peloponnese grew significantly after their victory. Herodotus notes that because of the Spartans' military superiority at that time, Croesus sought them as his allies over the Athenians (1.69.1).

Historians have argued that the transfer of the bones of Orestes also signaled a change in Sparta's foreign policy in the middle of the sixth century. Ending her earlier tactics of dominance via conquest, Sparta began pursuing alliances with other cities.[61] The story of Orestes' "return" thus served to legitimize Sparta's dominance over her Arcadian neighbors.[62] Being of Achaean stock,[63] Orestes served to validate the Spartans' claims to hegemony (at least as far as the Spartans were concerned) by emphasizing their shared ties with their Arcadian neighbors.

The Spartans had established their association with the Pelopids as early as the eighth century BC.[64] To be sure, the existence of numerous heroic memorials was a testament to the Spartans' fascination with genealogy and a mark of their religiosity. But political motives attached to their interest in a specific hero as well. For example, the cult of Menelaus at Therapnae, established during the Iron Age, acquired renewed prominence when a temple of Menelaus was built there in the eighth century. As Sparta's legendary king, Menelaus served to assert and legitimize her territorial sovereignty over Laconia and Messenia.[65] Agamemnon in turn played a significant role in asserting Spartan hegemony. Agamemnon's leadership of the army of the Panhellenes and victory at Troy made him the most apposite choice for Sparta's role as protector of Greece during the Persian Wars. In Herodotus, when Gelon of Syracuse demanded to lead the Greeks against the Persians, the Spartan Syagros replied that "Pelopid Agamemnon would wail loudly if he heard that Sparta had been deprived of hegemony by Gelon of Syracuse" (Hdt. 7.159).

The influence of Spartan lore surrounding the Pelopids has also left its mark on the poetry of the archaic period. Departing from Homer, for whom Agamemnon is king of Mycenae and "lord of Argos and many islands" (*Il.* 2.108),[66] Stesichorus sets his *Oresteia* in Sparta and eclipses altogether Agamemnon's and Orestes' ties with Mycenae and Argos.[67] Pindar says that Agamemnon died at the town of Amyclae, where a tomb of his is said to have existed.[68]

Aeschylus, on the other hand, follows Homer in setting the action of the first two plays of the trilogy in Argos, but he introduces a variation by representing both Agamemnon and Menelaus as ruling Argos jointly. The setting of *Agamemnon* is the palace of the Atreids (στέγαις Ἀτρειδῶν, "at the home of the Atreids," *A.* 399–402),[69] and the chorus specifically ask the messenger whether Menelaus has arrived home with the Greek army (*A.* 617–619). This is a departure from Stesichorus.[70] The transfer of Menelaus from Sparta to Argos also deviates from Homer. This is a telling departure and appears to be modeled on the Spartan tradition, according to which Agamemnon and Menelaus had ruled jointly. The territorial affiliation of both Atreids with Argos thus reinforces Orestes' ties with Argos and in this light can be read as a challenge to Orestes' Spartan cult.

Furthermore, Orestes' cult in Argos furnishes a rationale for promoting Athens' claims to leadership. The *Oresteia* aligns temporally the aftermath of Agamemnon's victory at Troy with the beginnings of the city's hegemonic history. When Athena first appears in *Eumenides*, she arrives from the banks of the river Scamander, where she received her share of the spoils of the Trojan war from Theseus' sons (398–402). Athena's role as military *hegemon* situates the city's hegemony within the mythical continuum, stretching back to the end of the great war with Troy. *Eumenides* shows Athena as already wielding her power in Greece in the aftermath of the demise of the leader who led the Greeks against Troy.[71]

Athens' acquisition of military hegemony is not a direct bequest of Argos' mythical kings—a distinct departure from the Spartan model of hegemony, which was based on claims made through genealogy.[72] Orestes pays tribute to Athens' power by establishing a new alliance with Argos. While his annexation as a foreign hero underpins the play's hegemonic message, his Panhellenic pedigree[73] as son and successor of the leader of the Panhellenes lends Athens access to this shared past, enabling her to advertise her hegemonic ambitions in the present. Orestes' figurative transfer from Sparta to Argos and his promise to serve Athens as her ally for all time served to articulate the historical struggle for supremacy between the two major powers in Greece.

## FROM VENGEANCE TO POLLUTION

Pollution in *Eumenides* serves a key role in showcasing Athens' ability to shelter Orestes and offer a home to Orestes and the Furies. The play offers the most detailed rationale for Athens' treatment of pollution among the extant plays and could conceivably have served as a model and precedent for the tragic topos of Athens as protector of the polluted.

The process of signification associated with pollution, however, is complex.[74] First, after Orestes' arrival at Delphi, Apollo undertakes his purification.[75] The ritual falls short of ridding Orestes from bloodguilt and instead reanimates the hostility of the Furies, who continue to hunt down their quarry, guided by the sight and smell of blood (*Eu.* 244–253). This shortfall between the ritual and its outcome punctuates the movement of the plot and redirects it, as Apollo now enjoins upon his protégé to travel to Athens to seek Athena's assistance (74–84, 221–224). Orestes' ambiguous ritual standing, partially pure and partially polluted, raises questions about what constitutes the proper means to redress crimes against the family.

Pollution emerges as the primary consequence of blood vengeance in *Choephori*, the second play of the *Oresteia* trilogy, only after Orestes kills Clytemnestra and Aegisthus. Here, the consequences of kin murder begin to be treated outside the purview of the family vendetta of the house of Atreus, since Orestes must leave Argos to be purified by Apollo at Delphi (74–79). In *Agamemnon*,[76] neither Agamemnon nor Clytemnestra suffers the consequences of pollution arising from homicide; neither is banished nor purified.[77]

In *Choephori*, the effects of pollution are palpable. The chorus refer to Clytemnestra and Aegisthus together as polluted (ὑπὸ δυοῖν μιαστόροιν, "by the two defilers," 944); recognizing that pollution has festered, they hope that ritual remedies will restore order in the royal household (ὅταν ἀφ᾽ ἑστίας/ μύσος ἅπαν ἐλαθῆι/καθαρμοῖσιν ἀτᾶν ἐλατηρίοις, "when the entire pollution has been driven from the hearth by cleansing rites that drive out destruction," 966–968).[78] Defilement signaled the disruption of the social order and the need to remedy the infraction ritually and by applying penalties commensurate with the injuries inflicted. The effects of pollution in connection with the murder of Agamemnon are now acknowledged, but they begin to take effect only after Orestes' matricide. In *Choephori*, pollution expresses the profound crisis caused by vengeance against one's own kin.[79] Pollution appears to be a stage removed from the law of vengeance, which dictates that blood shed can only be requited through the shedding of new blood (400–402). The consequences of reciprocal vengeance now extend beyond the family, and Orestes must therefore leave the city.[80]

In *Agamemnon*, the murders externalize the inbred violence of the house and typify the impasse that such violence brings about.[81] In *Choephori* pollution appears as the middle stage in the progression from retributive justice of the *oikos* to the judicial institutions of the *polis*.[82] The dramatic representation of this process is anachronistic and sets the stage for the foundation of the court and the Furies' reception in Athens. Orestes' vengeance for his father is still represented as an act of requital, one that Apollo enjoins upon him to undertake (εἰ μὴ μέτειμι τοῦ πατρὸς τοὺς αἰτίους/τρόπον τὸν αὐτόν, ἀνταποκτεῖναι λέγων, "if I do not take vengeance against the murderers of my father, telling me to kill them in the same fashion," 273–274),[83] even as he warns Orestes of the dire consequences in store for him, should he not avenge his father (κἀξορθιάζων πολλά, καὶ δυσχειμέρους/ἄτας ὑφ' ἧπαρ θερμὸν ἐξαυδώμενος, "and proclaims aloud calamities that chill the warmth of my heart," 271–272).[84]

Retribution is associated with the chthonic realm and expresses the belief that compensation for the dead man is necessary and unavoidable. For this reason, failure to avenge the victim's anger engenders consequences that mirror the psychological and physical symptoms of pollution—madness and disease—and further necessitate exclusion from society (278–296).[85] Clytemnestra, on the other hand, warns Orestes of the wrath of the mother's Furies (ὅρα, φύλαξαι μητρὸς ἐγκότους κύνας, "watch out for your mother's wrathful hounds," 924). Orestes overtly links the matricide with pollution, when he pronounces his victory an unenviable one on account of his defilement (ἄζηλα νίκης τῆσδ' ἔχων μιάσματα, "bearing the inenviable pollution of this victory," 1017). Orestes exacts vengeance against his closest of kin,[86] but he displays a different understanding of how killing affects the killer and the community.[87] His tragic quandary, to neglect his duty toward his father or fulfill it by killing his mother, demonstrates the impasse that kin-killing engenders.[88] Aware of the consequences, Orestes submits to Apollo's command and avenges his father. As Orestes reveals after the murder, the divine seer had promised to purify him and save him from the Furies (1029–1039).[89] Thus, at the end of the *Choephori*, the effects of pollution are vividly represented in the guise of the Furies of the mother (μητρὸς ἔγκοτοι κύνες, "the mother's wrathful hounds," 1054) who drive Orestes out of the city. The chorus attributes the terrifying visions and the mental disturbance that Orestes reports to the blood that taints his hands and concur with him that only Apollo's purification can relieve him of his suffering (1055–1060).

Purification, then, pronounced as the remedy for matricide, is dramatically realized, as Orestes chased by the Furies leaves Argos and arrives at Delphi to be cleansed by Apollo. In the prologue of the play, the Pythia reports that Orestes has taken his seat at the god's altar (40–45), holding his sword still dripping with blood and a branch of olive, crowned with a tuft of white wool in the pose of a suppliant awaiting purification (θεομυσῆ/ἕδραν ἔχοντα προστρόπαιον, 40–41).[90] She also reports that the Furies are inside the temple, lying on the ground asleep. As living embodiments of Orestes' pollution, their presence intimates the consequences of the matricide in the starkest terms possible. The execution of the ritual and its efficacy, however, are a more complicated matter, since there is no clear textual indication of when it is performed. Though Orestes later proclaims that he is ritually pure, since Apollo cleansed him from the pollution of homicide with the sacrificial blood of a pig (282–284), the purification is never described. Furthermore, its efficacy is further set in doubt by the Furies, who regard him as still being polluted and, led by the smell of blood, pursue him beyond Delphi to Athens (225, 244–253).

STAGING PURIFICATION

Most scholars consider the ambiguities surrounding Orestes' purification as intentional due to the immense social and ethical consequences surrounding the matricide.[91] In this context, it seems fruitful to discuss the staging of Orestes' purification at Delphi.[92] At what point could the ritual have taken place? Oliver Taplin argues that "there is no trace whatsoever in the words that Orestes was purified on-stage during this play." He asks further, "So do we presume that he was purified at some unspecified time before the play began, or at least before line 64?"[93] I do not find the first alternative plausible, namely, that he was purified before the play began, because the Pythia describes him as seated at the altar in the pose of a polluted murderer seeking purification (40–45). Taplin does not develop the second alternative, namely, a scenario of purification that takes place offstage during the play but before Apollo enters, presumably since no character makes explicit reference to the performance of the ritual.

My own position is that Orestes is purified before Apollo's entry in line 64, while the Furies are asleep and not privy to his purification being underway. This helps explain the failure of purification in ritual terms or alternatively why its performance is never acknowledged by the Furies, who stand opposed to any kind of restitution, ritual or otherwise. My reading of the staging of the scene, beginning with Apollo's first appearance, after the Pythia leaves the stage, and leading up to the dispute between Apollo and the Furies, sets out to demonstrate that the central scene of the Delphic episode represents the aftermath of Orestes' purification by Apollo. There are, however, a number of critical issues associated with the staging of this scene.

When examining this scene, most scholars infer that after the Pythia finishes her speech and goes inside, the doors of the *skene* ("stage building") open and the *ekkyklema* ("wheeled platform") is rolled out to reveal the tableau that the Pythia has just described, that is, the blood-stained Orestes seated at the navel surrounded by the Furies (39–63). There are deictic references (67–68, 140), which appear to argue in favor of the use of an *ekkyklema* and suggest that the scene is taking place inside the temple.[94] Probably the strongest argument in favor of the use of the *ekkyklema*, however, is that it does away with the problem of having Clytemnestra's ghost address an empty stage when she speaks to the Furies. For though there are parallels for the chorus' presence onstage conversing with a character who is indoors, in *Medea, Ajax*, and *Philoctetes*, it is unusual for a character to deliver a speech on an empty stage, with the exception of prologue speeches. Taplin, who argues against the use of the *ekkyklema* in this scene (and for that matter in the *Oresteia* as a whole), points out that the chorus of the Furies could not have appeared on stage before the *parodos*. Others postulate that only a few of the Furies are visible onstage.[95]

The next question concerns the staging of Apollo's entrance. As Taplin argues, Apollo enters accompanied by Orestes, not alone, as is generally assumed. I agree with Taplin that Orestes and Apollo must appear together. If we assume that Orestes is still seated at the altar when the *ekkyklema* is rolled out, that would seem to indicate that he is still awaiting purification. To suppose that Orestes and Apollo converse before the ritual had taken place would contravene ritual custom, which required that a polluted suppliant observe ritual silence.[96]

I suggest that Orestes leaves just as Apollo orders him to do before Clytemnestra's ghost appears to rouse the Furies from their sleep. For, upon awakening, the Furies anxiously protest that they have lost their quarry (οἴχεται δ' ὁ θήρ. / ὕπνωι κρατηθεῖσ' ἄγραν ὤλεσα, "The beast has escaped *from our net and is gone*. Conquered by sleep, I have lost my prey." 147–148), presumably because Orestes is no longer seated at the altar. Angered by the seer's interference, they blame Apollo for attempting to wrest Orestes away from them and attack Apollo twice verbally, calling him a thief (149–150, 153). Thus, the brief exchange between Apollo and Orestes, followed by the Furies' remonstrations, taken together convey to the audience that Orestes' ritual status has changed. The Pythia's parting words at the end of the prologue indicate that purification by Apollo is imminent (τἀντεῦθεν ἤδη τῶνδε δεσπότηι δόμων/ αὐτῶι μελέσθω Λοξίαι μεγασθενεῖ/ ... καὶ τοῖσιν ἄλλοις δωμάτων καθάρσιος, "the rest ought to be a concern for the mighty Loxias, the master of this house ... and purifier of others' homes," 60–61, 63). It is possible, then, that the ritual could have been administered by Apollo while the Furies were asleep, during the Pythia's second address to the audience. Ordinarily, this type of ritual, which involved animal sacrifice, would have taken place offstage, as in Euripides' *Heracles* (922–940). Instead in *Eumenides*, the audience is given a combination of visual and dramatic cues for inferring that it has been performed (as reported later by Orestes [281–283]). What the audience probably saw onstage when Apollo and Orestes enter is different from the scene that the Pythia has just described.

The Furies' silence about purification is consistent with their dramatic role and identity. As personifications of the dead victim's anger, the only type of compensation that they recognize is blood vengeance, as evinced by their opposition to Apollo (149–154).[97] Yet the audience's familiarity with the rules for purification for homicide provides an additional avenue for explaining why mention of the ritual is postponed until Orestes reaches Athens.

## PURIFICATION: RITUAL AND AUDIENCE

If the scene in which Apollo and Orestes appear together represents the aftermath of Orestes' purification, the ensuing conflict between the Furies and Apollo, representatives of the old chthonic regime and the new order of the Olympian gods respectively, can be understood as issuing from the particular way in which Apollo performs the ritual.

To place this argument within the broader context of the performance of ritual in tragedy, it is important to note that a variety of ritual scenarios were regularly staged within the plays. Playwrights oftentimes presented failed rituals to express the breach of social customs. For example, the consistent perversion of sacrificial norms in *Agamemnon* is emblematic of the corruption of familial and social norms. The improper performance of the purification at Delphi in *Eumenides* similarly fails to put an end to kindred violence, because the performance of the ritual by Apollo turns out to be ineffective. Athena's intervention after the trial and her offer of new cultic honors in Athens allows for a full restoration of the negative consequences of purification.[98]

For the original audience of the plays in the theater of Dionysus, the performance of rituals in religious and civic occasions was an essential part of their everyday experience, and as spectators they could decode more precisely the meaning of the rituals performed within the dramatic settings of the plays than modern spectators. Thus, their familiarity with the rules of purification would have allowed the audience to assess the anomalous outcome of the purification Orestes undergoes at Delphi.

Actual rites of purification for homicide appear to have included two discrete stages: the sacrificial procedure, aimed at cleansing the murderer's blood, and ritual offerings made to Zeus and the Furies as compensation for their pardoning the killer. Apollonius Rhodius provides the fullest description for the ritual for homicide, which Circe performs to cleanse Medea and Jason for the murder of Apsyrtus (A.R. 4.685–717). After Medea and Jason arrive at Aeaea, they take their seat as suppliants at the hearth of Circe's home. The goddess first performs the sacrifice; she slaughters a suckling pig by sprinkling its blood on the hands of the murderers and then also makes offerings to Zeus the Purifier. After the conclusion of the sacrifice, her attendants dispose of the offscourings, while she alone remains at the hearth and makes additional libations to Zeus and the Erinyes (the "Furies"). The rites of appeasement

---

complete the purification, setting to rest the anger of the Furies and ensuring Zeus' goodwill toward the murderers.[99] The ritual evidence, then, suggests that the two stages of purification sought to remove two sources of pollution: that of the murderer, who had to be cleansed by the shedding of new blood, and that of the Furies who personified the dead man's anger.[100]

We cannot ascertain whether propitiation of the victim through offerings made to the Furies was a typical concern in purification rites at large. Even so, the full ritual schema of purification is especially apt for interpreting Apollo's handling of Orestes' pollution. If we read the scene in the manner I have suggested, it follows that Apollo only cleanses Orestes, as he later confirms (Φοίβου καθαρμοῖς ἠλάθη χοιροκτόνοις, 283), but does not attempt to propitiate the Furies in any way. The absence of the second stage, the propitiation, intimates anew why the Furies angrily oppose Apollo.

To be sure, the circumstances of the dramatic purification are idiosyncratic. The Furies' presence onstage largely precludes successful performance of the second stage. Even so, the ritual schema serves as a guide for structuring the audience's understanding of the performance of the purification, which Apollo presumably administers stealthily offstage, while the Furies are still asleep.

Apollo's disregard for the Furies provides a dramatic motive for their wrath against him. The ritual process prescribed that amends be paid to the slain victim by propitiating the spirits of the Underworld. The Furies protest against Apollo's depriving them of their divinely allotted dispensations (παλαιγενεῖς δὲ μοίρας φθίσας, 172; τιμή, 209; τιμάς, 227–228) and their loss of honor. Their honor was intimately bound with the obligation to retaliate against the killer of one's kin to rehabilitate family honor.[101] In the *Oresteia*, inbred violence engenders an enduring stigma, difficult to remove. The Furies' anger is consistent with their role as avengers of slain kin (208).

Apollo's neglect to take heed of the Furies clarifies why Orestes' ritual standing is placed in doubt or, alternatively, why the Furies continue to regard him as polluted. Pointing to the blood that stains the altar, the Furies also insist that these are visible signs of Orestes' pollution (164–167). Their insistence that Orestes' pollution is still alive denies any legitimacy to Apollo's attempt to use purification as a substitute for retribution. There are further indications that the process of purification has been undermined as well. Clytemnestra's offerings to the Furies (106–109) suggest that the purification is not a welcome substitute to blood vengeance.[102]

Orestes' ambiguous ritual standing can be explained both in ritual and symbolic terms. Familiarity with the actual rules of ritual helps guide the audience's understanding of the claims regarding its efficacy. Orestes says truthfully before Athena that he has been cleansed (276–285), while the

Furies continue to track his movements from Delphi to Athens, guided by the smell and sight of blood (244–253). His anomalous purification at Delphi motivates Orestes' journey from Delphi to Athens. But beyond its dramatic purpose, the symbolism of the failed ritual highlights the new impasse in the cycle of vengeance and so points ahead to the foundation of the lawcourt as the final, viable solution to the problem of bloodguilt.

## WHY DOES PURIFICATION FAIL?

The dramatic divergence from the rules of purification that helped structure the audience's understanding of the ambiguous outcome of the ritual does not sufficiently explain why the ritual is engineered to fail, despite Apollo's assurances. According to fifth-century practice, ritual cleansing, though necessary for protecting the community against pollution, was not adequate to release the murderer from bloodguilt. The *polis* obtained restitution through a formal trial at the lawcourts, as prescribed by Athenian law,[103] with purification customarily following the trial.[104] Bloodguilt in most cases was subject to penal and ritual measures, though legal sanctions did not constitute a substitute for purification.[105]

In *Eumenides*, purification is followed by a period of purificatory exile, as Parker has argued, before Orestes' trial and acquittal in Athens (235–243).[106] This sequence reverses contemporary fifth-century practice whereby the trial precedes the killer's exile; purification takes place either upon the killer's arrival abroad to enable his reception by his hosts or upon his return (Dem. 23.72). But since Orestes' crime dramatically predates, as it were, the foundation of the court, his disputed ritual standing can be explained as a way of representing the eventual bifurcation between ritual and penal restitution, which developed over time. Its partial success then can suggest an anachronistic understanding of the original function that purification and exile had served before the introduction of penal sanctions for homicide in Athenian law.[107]

Within the dramatic context, purification punctuates the transition from reciprocal vengeance to the institution of the first homicide court in Athens. The temporal sequence that unfolds does not mirror the actual process of the evolution of legal history. Rather, it reconstructs the past in a manner that lends support to the primacy of Athens' judicial system. This evolutionary schema presupposes the eventual establishment of the first lawcourt of homicide in Athens toward which the drama hastens, once purification fails (79–84).

The appearance of pollution presupposes a society in which the community had begun imposing sanctions for killing outside the family. Historically, purification for homicide appears to have postdated recourse to self-help. We do not know when pollution actually emerged.[108] The first instance of purification for blood pollution occurs, according to Proclus, in the *Aethiopis*, when Achilles goes to Lesbos to be purified after the murder of Thersites. Homer makes no mention of the killer's pollution. In the sixth century, Draco's laws on homicide appear to take pollution into consideration.[109] Once homicide laws are established, ritual compensation becomes consequent upon the severity of the crime, and, though necessary, it usually does not precede legal redress. As such, unintentional homicide was punished with temporary exile, which served a purificatory function.

Parker's view, that *Eumenides* reverses the sequence of trial, followed by exile and purification, explains the role of pollution in the play from a synchronic perspective. Demosthenes' discussion of the legal provisions for unintentional murder (23.71–73) also clarifies the way in which compensation toward the family of the victim and ritual restitution remained part of the process even after legal redress had superseded these earlier measures. After a period of purificatory exile, the murderer was to seek pardon from the dead man's relatives and was expected to perform sacrifices and be purified before being readmitted into the community (καὶ φεύγειν ἕως ἂν †αἰδέσηταί τινα† τῶν ἐν γένει τοῦ πεπονθότος. τηνικαῦτα δ᾽ ἥκειν δέδωκεν ἔστιν ὃν τρόπον, οὐχ ὃν ἂν τύχῃ, ἀλλὰ καὶ θῦσαι καὶ καθαρθῆναι καὶ ἄλλ᾽ ἄττα διείρηκεν ἃ χρὴ ποιῆσαι, "and to remain in exile until he is pardoned by one of the relatives of the aggrieved party. Then the law permits him to return not in an arbitrary manner, but it specifies that he must make sacrifices and purify himself and also gives other instructions that he must complete," 23.72).

The ritual steps that Demosthenes describes in the context of the murderer's return from exile combine compensation to the victim's family with ritual measures—sacrifices and cleansing—as appropriate for his return. In Orestes' case, however, his heavy pollution necessitates that purification take place before his arrival in Athens.[110]

As we saw in Apollonius Rhodius' account, the ritual of purification acknowledged the necessity of making amends to the victim by propitiating the gods of the Underworld. To ensure this, the purification addressed the killer's duty to compensate the dead person and his family ritually, that is, in addition to the legal sanctions he faced. The provisions Demosthenes outlines also acknowledge the significance of the family and underscore the exile's obligation to seek their pardon and be ritually purified as part of the process of his reintegration. These measures may also reflect the collective memory of earlier practices, which the advent of the law had in part supplanted and in part redefined. Restitution to the family was part of the ritual process whose role legal redress had by then replaced.

In conclusion, the evolutionary conception of justice in the trilogy may be based on the collective memory of the historical past that survived in later ritual practices. By positing that contemporary ritualized practices allow us to gain insight into the way in which the audience understood the legacy of their collective past, we have a far more secure basis for explaining the synoptic treatment of the evolution of justice in the trilogy. Anachronism plays a crucial role in shaping the mythical past against the historical present as a process leading from vengeance, through the failure of purification, to the establishment of the homicide court in Athens. Undoubtedly, recent historical memory as well—the legacy of the Cylonian affair as well as Ephialtes' murder—may have prompted Aeschylus to reflect on the consequences of protracted strife for the community by underscoring the profound disruption pollution caused.[111] Concerns surrounding pollution remain central in the play, when polluted outsiders, Orestes and the Furies, arrive at Athens. The reception of the Furies offers an additional and novel way of looking at the connections between Athenian hegemony and justice. The foundation of their cult by Athena merges their religious functions with the political and ideological outlook they espouse as Athenian deities in the play.

## THE FURIES IN ATHENS: JUSTICE AND HEGEMONY

As instigators of pollution, a role that they come to inhabit as dramatic characters in *Eumenides* as Clytemnestra's avengers, their actions set in relief the necessity of deterring pollution and containing ritual violence by placing limits to and redefining their powers. This process also calls for the redefinition of the Furies' close ties with the *oikos*, which comes about through their physical relocation within the realm of *polis* cult.

The Furies' dramatic characterization in *Eumenides* problematizes their affiliation with the chthonic realm. Their presence among the living emphasizes the necessity of articulating anew the boundaries that separate the chthonic and Olympian realms. Athens benefits greatly from settling the generational dispute between the old ministers of Justice and Apollo. Athena's successful resolution of the crisis augments the city's hegemonic reputation by highlighting her distinctive role in shaping the course of the cosmic history of justice.

The annexation of the goddesses presents Athena and her city as rightful heirs to the Furies, primeval agents of justice, and conveys to the audience the significant legacy that Athens receives by way of this new divine and mortal partnership. The identification of the Furies with the *Semnai Theai* ("Dread Goddesses") of the Areopagus[112] whose shrine was known as a place of refuge, plays a key role in this process (see below, "Power Play at Delphi"). As such, the Furies' annexation offers a model and precedent for the city's depiction as a haven for the polluted and objectifies Athens' claims to hegemony.

## POWER PLAY AT DELPHI

The Furies' trajectory as exiles from Delphi to Athens brings their reception in Athens into congruence with the hegemonic topos of Athens as a city that assists the polluted, the marginal, and the dispossessed. The Furies' forced exclusion from Delphi is the outcome of a political struggle in the course of which Apollo progressively devalues the Furies' powers. The dynamics that inform this hostile encounter resemble those between other suppliants and their opponents in the Athenian suppliant plays. For example, in *Children of Heracles*, Eurystheus' abuse of tyrannical power forces Heracles' children to abandon Argos as refugees in search of asylum. Similarly, the strife between Eteocles and Polyneices over succession in the city of Thebes also suggests a strong motive for his banishment in Sophocles' *Oedipus at Colonus*. The Athenian suppliant plays typically deploy the exile's experience to effect a sharp contrast with the fair treatment, which outsiders receive in Athens.

The conflict that erupts between Apollo and the Furies at Delphi quickly escalates into a full-blown strife in the course of which Apollo weakens the Furies' standing. The Furies vigorously protest against Apollo's patent violation of their honors (149–177). Though powerful in their capacity to inflict harm, the Furies are nonetheless placed in a disadvantageous position from the outset. Throughout the trilogy, their relationship with the upper world is always presented as an anomaly. In *Agamemnon*, their close ties with the *oikos* casts them in the role of bad guests, a drunken company of revelers, who abuse hospitality and corrupt the proper code of *xenia* ("guest-friendship").[113] Lacking as they do any normative type of associations within the religious and civic structure of the *polis*, the Furies are imagined as dangerous interlopers at Delphi: Apollo and his priestess represent them as unfit for any kind of civilized interaction (55–59, 193–195).

Apollo, more specifically, systematically undermines the Furies' power. He not only undercuts their claims to their primordial rights but also demeans their habits and way of life as primitive and uncivilized. He offers as examples their participation in acts of violence, bloodshed, and torture, practices that negate the Greek standards of civilized conduct (185–190). Apollo degrades them further by likening them to a pack of wild animals. He pronounces their nomadic way of life to be more akin to that of feral beasts than of domesticated animals, insinuating that the Furies do not conform even to the lowest forms of the definition of culture (191–197). He associates them, not incidentally, with the ferocious bloodthirsty lion whose lair he identifies as their natural habitat. Roaming in the wild, they remain untamed, undomesticated, and dissociated even from the rudimentary norms of social organization.

Dramatically, the altercation between Apollo and the Furies is reminiscent of the generational battle of the gods in Hesiod's *Theogony*. Old versus new, male versus female, Olympian versus chthonic, these distinctions surface distinctly in the course of the quarrel at Delphi.[114] The power dynamics at work can be suitably analyzed according to the following set of polarities:

| | |
|---|---|
| Power | Impotence |
| Young | Old |
| Civilized | Uncivilized |
| Olympian | Chthonic |
| Purity | Pollution |
| Inclusion | Exclusion |

These oppositions reflect hierarchical distinctions already present within the religious system of the Greeks, which accorded higher value to those gods who belonged to the upper realm, relegating in turn those associated with the realm of the dead to an inferior position. But Apollo manipulates their standing in the divine hierarchy so as to denigrate and marginalize his opponents. He treats the Furies with great contempt and hostility: he describes them scornfully as old hags, virgins for life, too dangerous and too revolting for man, god, or beast to consort with (67–70). Next, he exaggerates their marginality by locating them in the outer limits of the Underworld, the Tartarus, the lowest and darkest region under earth (71–73). The reference to the Tartarus evokes the conflicts over divine succession in Hesiod's *Theogony* and alludes to the defeat and imprisonment of Cronus and the Giants by the Olympians. Apollo's veiled threat that he will imprison them is not carried out; their defeat results in eviction from Delphi.

The charge of pollution, however, proves effective in turning the Furies into pariahs. Apollo thus adheres to his promise to Orestes that he will be cruel to his enemies (64–66). The political antagonism between Apollo and the Furies provides a motive for their reception in Athens. The new honors

Athena grants the Furies redefine their negative attributes: a move that exemplifies Athens' capacity to gain friends and partners through such singular gestures of acceptance.

## RECONFIGURING THE CHTHONIC REALM

In the trilogy the dramatic role of the Furies becomes progressively redefined. The evolution of justice dictates their subordination to the *polis*, which is realized through their conversion from avenging spirits to the benevolent goddesses of Athenian cult.[115] Their characterization first as avengers and then as instigators of pollution goes hand in hand with the momentous transition of transferring the punishment for homicide from the *oikos* to the *polis*. The subordination of the Furies' functions to the judicial institutions is represented as the positive outcome of their reception as cult divinities in Athens.

References to the Furies in *Agamemnon* suggest that they performed the roles they were also assigned in Homer.[116] They punish offenses against the family, but they are also more broadly associated with justice, punishing those who deviate from its proper course. For example, in the *parodos* they are responsible for punishing the robbers of the vultures' nest (A. A. 54–59); in the first *stasimon* their presence at the ill-omened wedding of Helen and Paris is consistent with the punishment of wrongdoers (A. *Ag.* 744–749); as ministers of Justice, the black Erinyes punish the one who is fortunate but not just (A. A. 461–468).[117] As the play progresses, however, their function becomes more restricted, and they are primarily involved in murders perpetrated within the family. Thus, the Furies become implicated in the ritual corruption that ravages the house of Atreus, as each murder triggers the next one and replicates the pattern of sacrificial violence, frustrating any hope for ending violence.[118]

Cassandra sees them clinging to the house, wreaking havoc in their own way. She paints a gruesome picture of the Furies as a band of revelers, drunk with the blood of their victims, unseemly guests who transgress the rules of hospitality in an extreme manner (1186–1190). Their physical presence at the royal palace typifies the erosion of kinship norms that they paradoxically support: the Furies appear as sole participants and guests at the after-dinner drinking party that accompanies the feasts of blood vengeance in Atreus' house (1188–1193). Their song of revel reveals the origin of the murders, Atreus' transgression against Thyestes, and links them with the impending murder of Agamemnon.[119] In *Agamemnon*, then, the Furies are drawn into the pattern of ritual corruption, symptomatic of the perpetuation of violence within the family.[120]

In the next two plays, the depiction of the Furies is consistent with their earlier function as avengers of kin-killers,[121] though after the matricide is performed, they act of their own accord, not through human agents, to instigate new killings.[122] When they appear at the end of *Choephori*, visible to Orestes alone, it is to activate the effects of pollution. Orestes ascribes the onset of his madness to the Furies, whom he describes as monstrous Gorgon-like figures, clad in dark-red robes with snakes densely wrapped around them, a description that intimates their chthonic attributes and prefigures their appearance in *Eumenides* (1048–1050, 1053–1054).[123] Their attacks on Orestes cause him to suffer mental delusions, signs of his pollution (1055–1056). Clytemnestra's warning that Orestes should guard himself against his "mother's angry hounds" (924) is now confirmed (1054). The Furies torment him, yet Orestes and the chorus pronounce Apollo's purification at Delphi to be the only remedy for his pollution (1059–1060).

The emphasis on defilement is consistent with contemporary religious ideas surrounding the Furies' association with pollution. As chthonic divinities, they are able to inflict harm by instigating pollution; their association with defilement stems from the belief that the slain victims continued to pursue the killer if they were not properly appeased.[124] In Greek religion, they were associated with the victim's anger and regarded as a source of pollution,[125] as Parker explains:

> The Erinyes, above all, are animate agents of pollution who embody the anger of one slain by a kinsman. Although they are not formally identical with pollution (rather they "arrive where a man hides bloody hands [*Eu.* 316–20]"), there is no difference between its effects and theirs, and the operations of the two are normally co-extensive; even where, in the exceptional poetical conception of Aeschylus' *Eumenides*, they continue their assaults after the murderer's hands are clean, the evils which they threaten Athens for harbouring the murderer are familiar effects of pollution. This co-extensiveness of pollution and the victim's anger is implicit in the formal rites of purification, in which "washing off the blood" is followed by appeasement.

Parker sets out clearly how pollution binds the murderer to his victim and vice versa. In *Eumenides*, the Furies' association with vengeance and pollution reveals the harmful side of their chthonic nature. Each of these traits demonstrates the negative impact of their agency. First, they destroy ties within the family by perpetuating violence among kin. In the next stage, their capacity to defile also affects the *polis*, threatening to destabilize the obligatory segregation of the chthonic realm from that of human and divine interactions.

---

Vengeance and pollution provide the two poles of the Furies' dramatic persona, when they appear onstage as the chorus of the final play. Previously unseen, now visible, terrifying apparitions, harbingers of death and pollution, the Furies lie asleep around Orestes by the altar:

πρόσθεν δὲ τἀνδρὸς τοῦδε θαυμαστὸς λόχος
εὕδει γυναικῶν ἐν θρόνοισιν ἥμενος.
οὔτοι γυναῖκας ἀλλὰ Γοργόνας λέγω·
οὐδ' αὖτε Γοργείοισιν εἰκάσω τύποις
εἶδόν ποτ' ἤδη Φινέως γεγραμμένας
δεῖπνον φερούσας· ἄπτεροί γε μὴν ἰδεῖν
αὗται μέλαιναί τ', ἐς τὸ πᾶν βδελύκτροποι,
ῥέγκουσι δ' οὐ πλατοῖσι φυσιάμασιν,
ἐκ δ' ὀμμάτων λείβουσι δυσφιλῆ λίβα·
καὶ κόσμος οὔτε πρὸς θεῶν ἀγάλματα
φέρειν δίκαιος οὔτ' ἐς ἀνθρώπων στέγας.

. . . . . . . . . . . . .

τἀντεῦθεν ἤδη τῶνδε δεσπότηι δόμων
αὐτῶι μελέσθω Λοξίαι μεγασθενεῖ·
ἰατρόμαντις δ' ἐστὶ καὶ τερασκόπος
καὶ τοῖσιν ἄλλοις δωμάτων καθάρσιος. (46–56, 60–63)

In front of this man there is an extraordinary band of women, asleep, sitting on chairs—no, I won't call them women, but Gorgons; but then I can't liken their form to that of Gorgons either. I did once see before now, in a painting, female creatures robbing Phineus of his dinner; these ones, though, it is plain to see, don't have wings, and they're black and utterly nauseating. They're pumping out snores that one doesn't dare come near, and dripping a loathsome drip from their eyes. And their attire is one that it's not proper to bring either before the images of the gods or under the roofs of men. . . . From now on, let this be the concern of the master of this house himself, mighty Loxias, since he is a healer and seer, a diviner, and a purifier of the houses of others.

The Pythia, like Orestes in the earlier play, likens them to Gorgons and Harpies and calls attention to their foul breath and the bloody discharge that oozes from their eyes (52–54). The Furies themselves invoke Night and Darkness as their mother (416–417);[126] this common ancestry with the *Keres* (Hes. *Th.* 211, 217–220),[127] spirits of the dead, suggests that Aeschylus may have derived from Hesiod the idea of representing the Furies as gory, bloodthirsty creatures.[128] Other aspects of their physique, specifically, their serpentine hair, also intimate a near-identification with the spirits of the dead, since ghosts were known to appear in the guise of snakes.[129]

The Pythia deems the intrusion of these gruesome and terrifying creatures in the realm of the living pernicious and ill-omened and calls attention to the need to guard against the significant risk of incurring pollution, which is caused by the Furies' presence at the seat of the god who, above all others, embodied purity. Clad in black, these gore-filled ministers of death are ill suited for any kind of contact within the realm of civilization. No land, she says, can boast to have nurtured them unharmed (ἀνατεί, 59). In the eyes of Apollo's priestess, then, they must not be allowed to haunt either sacred or profane spaces. Indeed, the Furies' association with the realm of the dead and the shedding of blood by kin made them unsafe for contact on account of their pollution against which the *polis* protected itself through apotropaic or purificatory rites. In a similar vein, the Pythia concludes her speech by suggesting that Apollo in his capacity as seer-healer and purifier of men's houses will attend to the defilement of the Furies (61–63).

The Pythia's introduction of the Furies grounds their dramatic identity within the context of religious beliefs, which inspired dread about their capacity to inflict harm. The Erinyes embodied the negative aspects of the duality of chthonic powers and, unlike their positive counterparts, the Eumenides and the *Semnai*, they did not have a cult (see the next section). As the Pythia explains in detail, their presence disturbs cosmic balance, once they begin to intrude upon the realm of the living.

The Pythia exaggerates their harmful potential by describing their hideous and revolting physical traits, posing thereby the Furies' chthonic character as a problem in need of a resolution. In this way, their association with defilement articulates a programmatic concern of the play. The various strands of conflict and opposition between Apollo and the Furies, that is, the clash between old and new justice, purity and pollution, chthonic and Olympian gods, can be ascribed to the same process of signification, that is, they stem from the need to assign boundaries between the chthonic on the one hand, and the human and divine realms of existence on the other. Athens plays a significant role in negotiating the evolving cosmic and civic hierarchies. The Furies' integration into a new cult by Athena becomes part of the play's hegemonic history of Athenian justice and its institutions. To this end, the incorporation of the Furies is modeled upon the Athenian cult of the Athenian *Semnai*. As a result of this process of assimilation, Athens is able to claim these primeval agents of Justice as her own.

In setting out to interpret the trajectory of the Aeschylean Furies, who leave Delphi, shunned by gods and men alike, and eventually settle permanently in Athens, it is important to bear in mind that the Furies' anger and relentless persecution of Orestes instantiate the negative facets of their chthonic nature, not the totality of their identity. As Albert Henrichs has shown, the mythical conception of the Erinyes as angry, polluting, avenging spirits exemplifies the negative traits characteristic of the duality and ambivalence associated with chthonic divinities and heroes.[130] While the Furies embody only the negative aspects of the chthonic in myth,[131] they were thought of as delivering blessings and benefits, once propitiated.[132] In cult, these divinities were invoked through euphemistic titles and epithets as *Semnai* or Eumenides,[133] or remained nameless and received propitiatory offerings in the form of wineless libations and sacrifices, appropriately called "appeasements" (107) in the play.[134] The differences between the mythical Furies and the Eumenides/*Semnai* of Attic cult similarly exhibit the inherent antinomy of their character as chthonic divinities, which can be summarized through the following paired opposites: curse/blessing, prosperity/blight, famine/nurture.[135]

*Eumenides* accounts for the duality of the Furies' powers in aetiological fashion by dramatizing their eventual incorporation into the Athenian cult as a movement from crisis to resolution. The failure of purification activates a familiar process whereby an offense against a deity causes him/her to retaliate before the infraction is restored when the offender founds rites on his/her honor. Apollo's failure to propitiate the Furies supplies the motive for the Furies' anger. Viewed in this light, the new cultic honors that Athena later bestows upon the Furies remedy Apollo's undermining of their privileges.

Following their defeat in the trial, the Furies turn against the city and threaten to contaminate the soil, to damage the crops and harm the process of reproduction by spreading polluting growth all around (781–785). A curse to Athens, as they were to Atreus' house earlier, they now threaten "manslaughtering" destruction, caused by infectious disease (785–788). By placing the fertility and prosperity of the community at risk, the Furies' threat of pollution exemplifies the negative aspects of their chthonic nature.

The subsequent redefinition of their functions as benevolent goddesses is conceived of as compensation for the loss of their previous honors; to the Furies' complaints that their honors have been abrogated and trampled upon, Athena responds that they will receive their own distinct honors in their new cult (795–796, 804–807, 824–825). To this end, she sums up their new prerogatives by indicating that no household will fare well without the aid of the Furies (895)—redefining in this way their function as purveyors of fertility and reproduction (831–836, 907–909). The Furies' beneficent side is externalized as a result of Athena's effective use of persuasion (ἀλλ' εἰ μὲν ἁγνόν ἐστί σοι Πειθοῦς σέβας,/γλώσσης ἐμῆς μείλιγμα καὶ θελκτήριον, "but if you have holy reverence for Persuasion, the sweetness and charm of my tongue," 885–886), which succeeds in propitiating the Furies' anger (θέλξειν μ' ἔοικας, καὶ μεθίσταμαι κότου, "you are winning me over with spells and I appear to be relenting my anger," 900) and echoes the propitiatory offerings mentioned earlier (χοάς τ' ἀοίνους, νηφάλια μειλίγματα, "wineless libations, sober appeasements," 107) that they will receive from here on now in the realm of cult.[136]

Athena turns their curses into blessings, persuading them not to harm the land and its people with blight and sterility (800–803, 829–831). In return, she offers them new seats of honor, situated at their underground cave shrine, next to their altars (ἕδρας τε καὶ κευθμῶνας ἐνδίκου χθονὸς/λιπαροθρόνοισιν ἡμένας ἐπ' ἐσχάραις/ἕξειν ὑπ' ἀστῶν τῶνδε τιμαλφουμένας, "you will have a cavernous sanctuary in a righteous land, where sitting on shining thrones at your hearths, honored by the citizens," 805–807). She further promises to them that they will be the recipients of first-fruit offerings (τἀκροθίνια, 834), of sacrifices preliminary to marriage, and thank-offerings for successful births (θύη πρὸ παίδων καὶ γαμηλίου τέλους, "sacrifices for childbirth and weddings," 835). It is reasonable to assume that the Furies' association with marriage and birth, otherwise not attested for the *Semnai*, arises from the broad association of the *Semnai* and of the Eumenides with fertility on account of their affinities as deities associated with the earth.[137]

Thus, the kinship between the Furies and the *Semnai* informs the process of the Furies' reception in important respects. In particular, the duality of the Furies deploys the negative/positive polarity that they embodied as chthonic divinities in the context of Greek religion, to account for the origins of their Athenian cult. The instantiation of the Furies' beneficial side is thereby depicted as the outcome of their inclusion within the realm of cult. Dramatically, the positive attributes of their agency are externalized through the role ascribed the Furies within the *oikos* as protectors of fertility and procreation.[138]

## HANDMAIDENS OF CIVIC JUSTICE

Dramatized as a progression from relegation to restoration, the Furies' civic integration as cultic divinities in Athens calls attention to the physical location of their cult, situated in the vicinity of the Areopagus (833, 854–855, 916, 1022–1027). Scholars now largely agree that the cult that Athena founds in honor of the Furies is based on the Athenian cult of the *Semnai Theai*, whose sanctuary was located in a cave under the Acropolis, situated at the side closer to the Areopagus.[139] The shrine of the *Semnai* was known primarily as a place of refuge for those fleeing persecution.[140] *Eumenides* traces the origins of the shrine's association with asylum by representing the mythical Furies as polluted outcasts.

The identification of the locale would have undoubtedly called attention to the connection between the existing cult and the homicide court of the Areopagus. This association had developed owing to the proximity of their shrine to the hill of Ares, where the court convened to judge homicide trials.[141] Historically, the Areopagus' authority in deciding asylum must have been significant before the court was assigned homicide trials. Before the trial began, sacrifices were offered to the *Semnai*, and witnesses, prosecutors, and defendants took a solemn oath against perjury in the name of the Semnai to bring down destruction (ἐξώλεια) upon themselves and their family if they committed perjury (Din. 1.47).[142] Similarly, those who had been acquitted at the trial were known to offer sacrifices to the *Semnai* (Paus. 1.28.6).

The role the *Semnai* discharged in their capacity as cultic ministers of the court provides an additional framework for understanding the progressive relegation of the Furies' powers. The kinship between the mythical Furies and the *Semnai* emerges more clearly if we compare the functions that each group assumes: the former as chief purveyors of justice within the *oikos* in the distant mythical past, the latter as auxiliaries to homicide trials at the Areopagus in the present. The association of the *Semnai* with the Areopagus as overseers of oaths and recipients of sacrifices strengthens the argument of the Furies as avengers, and their self-identification as "Curses" (417; A. *Ch.* 406) also evokes the role that the *Semnai* served in connection to the court.[143] These connections are admittedly broad, but they are rooted in religious fears and beliefs pertaining to the powers of these chthonic divinities. The rituals that associated the *Semnai* with the Areopagus acknowledged their capacity to instigate harm and defilement and recognized the powers invested in them as representatives of the realm of the dead.[144]

Conversely, the aetiology of the new cult models the character of the court upon the role that the Furies had served until then.[145] Athena mentions the Furies when she includes in the court's charter the necessity that it inspire dread among the citizens (697–698). Thus, their earlier powers are not abrogated: Athena warns transgressors against incurring their wrath and hostility (928–937) and says that their power over gods and the dead alike is great (μέγα γὰρ δύναται πότνι' Ἐρινὺς/παρά τ' ἀθανάτοις τοῖς θ' ὑπὸ γαῖα, 950–955).

Historically, the emergence of the lawcourt dictated that it supersede the role of the family in redressing homicide.[146] The Furies' principal ties with family vengeance, when they adopt the role of prosecutors in Orestes' trial and act in the same capacity as the relatives of the deceased in actual homicide trials, also intimate the gradual erosion of their power. Like the *Semnai*, the Furies can no longer wield power within the new system directly and eventually agree to cede their original dispensations to the jurisdiction of the court. The relegation of their powers to the sphere of cult is represented as offering the Furies compensation for the loss of their earlier privileges. The Furies' dramatic identification with the Athenian cult not only clarifies the religious importance of their cult but also offers the scope for examining the civic discourse of their reception.

### HEGEMONY REVEALED

Athens can rightfully claim that her reputation as a just city is the direct bequest of Athena's partnership with the Furies. The charter myth of the Areopagus court and the reception of the Furies together promoted Athens' hegemonic justice. As such, the play's portrait of Athenian justice not only promotes the democrats' reforms but also furnishes a direct challenge to Sparta's authority as arbiter of the affairs of the Greeks. Sparta's reputation in the Greek world derived in large measure from the superiority of her legal system, the achievement of the lawmaker Lycurgus. As Herodotus explains in the Croesus narrative (1.53–69), Sparta had been badly governed and had no dealings with non-Spartans before Lycurgus. Providing a solid foundation for her growth, his constitutional changes enabled her subsequent rise to power, earning Sparta her reputation for *eunomia* ("good governance") (1.65–66). By the time of Croesus, the Spartans' military successes in the Peloponnese and their annexation of Tegea had established their leading reputation among the Greeks.[147] For this reason, when Croesus was making military preparations against the Persians, he chose the Spartans over the Athenians as his allies, recognizing Sparta's superiority (1.69.2: ὑμέας ... προεστάναι τῆς Ἑλλάδος, "that you ... held the power over Greece") while passing over the Athenians who at the time of the Athenian tyrant Peisistratus were heavily involved in civil strife (1.59–64).

The story is instructive because it provides insight into Greek perceptions of hegemony. Herodotus' comparison of Spartan and Athenian power at the time of Croesus reveals that constitutional stability was crucial for promoting her ascendancy and necessary for the confidence her leadership inspired in others. Similar concerns underlie the representation of Athenian hegemony in Aeschylus' *Eumenides*. Hegemony was a significant issue for the play's audience, who had experienced the consequences of the protracted strife between oligarchs and democrats in the wake of Ephialtes' reforms. *Eumenides* show-cases Athens' capacity to dispel quarrels, which originate outside the city, and thus places the danger of internal strife at a remove from the ideal image of the city. As we have seen, the Furies are depicted as outsiders, and the crisis, which Athena resolves, originates in Apollo's quarrel with the Furies. As mediator, Athena stands outside this conflict and prevents the outbreak of violence in the city. Thus, the reception of the Furies as exiles by Athena furnishes a paradigmatic case of conflict and resolution.

In addition, the Furies' integration celebrates a new civic partnership and enhances the Athenian panegyric in tragedy by highlighting the unique relationship that Athens enjoyed with non-Athenians. In welcoming the Furies, Athena brings home the message that their honors in Athens will be greater than in any other place (852–857), and they will partake in Athens' ascendancy still to come (851–854). The panegyric tenor of Athena's speech, as she promises the Furies that in time they will grow to love and desire this foreign land (851–852), echoes Pericles' later charge to the Athenians in the funeral oration to become "lovers of their city" (Th. 2.43.1).

Athena outlines the Furies' role as ministers of Athens' hegemony: she mandates them to ensure peace within the city by preventing the outbreak of civil strife (... ἐν τοῖς ἐμοῖς ἀστοῖσιν ἱδρύσῃς Ἄρη/ἐμφύλιόν τε καὶ πρὸς ἀλλήλους θρασύν, "and do not plant in my people the spirit of civil war and boldness against each other," 862–863). If strife does not arise, Athens can continue earning glory in external wars (θυραῖος ἔστω πόλεμος, οὐ μόλις παρών,/ἐν ὧι τις ἔσται δεινὸς εὐκλείας ἔρως, "Let their war be with foreign enemies, and not one in which there will be a terrible passion for glory," 864–865). Upon accepting Athena's offer, the Furies praise Athens' hegemony by naming Zeus and "all-powerful" Ares as witnesses and champions of her power and commending her above all as the protector of the altars of the gods in Greece (τὰν καὶ Ζεὺς ὁ παγκρατὴς Ἄρης/τε φρούριον θεῶν νέμει,/ῥυσίβωμον Ἑλλάνων/ἄγαλμα δαιμόνων, "which she, with Zeus the all-powerful and Ares, holds as a fortress of the gods, the ornament that guards the altars of the gods of Greece," 918–920). The Furies' panegyric echoes the ideology that emerged in the period of the Persian Wars, when Athens claimed to have exacted vengeance against the invaders as requital for their acts of impiety.[148]

The Furies' acceptance also partakes in the process of defining Athenian hegemonic ideology by negotiating the power differential between the *hegemon* and his subordinates. In accepting their new prerogatives, the Furies enter into a relationship of dependency with Athens, similar to that of other non-Athenians, by offering benefits in return for their incorporation. Athena uses the language of religious worship to describe the character of the interaction between the goddesses and her worshipers.[149] The reciprocal nature of the exchange between the city and the goddesses derives from the religious observances associated with their Athenian cult. But the element of reciprocity also carries ideological weight insofar as it allows Athena to script an idealized relationship between the Furies and her city that is both consensual and mutually advantageous. Athena's unyielding efforts to persuade the Furies to accept her offer of integration is consistent with the aims of hegemonic ideology, which emphasized the voluntary character of the agreement between Athens and those whom she led. Their integration is also spatially marked through the ceremonial procession that Athena leads at the end of the play. Dressed in crimson robes (1028), the Furies follow Athena, accompanied by priests and a group of Athenian women, to their new cultic abode under the Acropolis.[150]

At the same time, the Furies' reception is not altogether unconstrained. The Furies' resistance to Athena's offer proves difficult to surmount, and Athena is forced to set aside persuasion briefly and threaten compulsion (826–829).[151] Persuasion versus compulsion and consent versus force refer readily to the vocabulary of hegemony versus domination. Athena's momentary aside that she alone has access to Zeus' thunderbolt, which she will use against the Furies if they do not comply, clarifies the structure of power relations in no uncertain terms. The allusion to the use of force contravenes the idealized depiction of Athena's leadership and in turn allows a more complex picture of the Athenian panegyric to emerge.

The integration of the Furies by Athena deploys the panegyric depiction of Athens as a city open to foreigners to disguise the contemporary political realities of strife among the radical democrats and oligarchs in Athens.[152] The Furies' resistance, however, and Athena's resolve to force them into compliance acknowledge the fissure between ideology and historical reality, serving as a reminder that there were still many who opposed the new face of Athens' power. The play grapples with these realities within the parameters set by the Athenian panegyric. Athena takes stock of the Furies' opposition and subsequently defines the Furies' civic functions by placing them in charge of civic peace and prosperity. The crisis and resolution therefore defines the play's hegemonic discourse by acknowledging the dissonance between ideology and reality. The Furies' role as guarantors of civic concord provides a resolution, albeit a fictive one, to the problem of internal strife, enabling Athens to advertise her civic unity through the paradigmatic reception of the Furies as partners in the city's hegemonic enterprise.

## CHAPTER 2

# HEGEMONY *and* EMPIRE: PRESUMED ORIGINS

The image of Athens' ideal leadership is reassessed in Euripides' later suppliant plays, *Children of Heracles* and *Suppliant Women*, both of which date from the period of the Peloponnesian War and offer arguments in support of Athens' imperial democracy. By sketching discrete types of this ideology in the Athenian suppliant plays, this chapter offers a brief excursus on the development of Athenian imperialism; it also seeks to outline the evolution of the ideology of Athenian hegemony between 450 and 420 BC. Further, this chapter serves as a transition between Aeschylus' *Eumenides* and Euripides' *Children of Heracles*, produced almost thirty years later.

The beginnings of the ideology of Athens' moral hegemony can be traced to the beginnings of the Athenian alliance of 478/7 BC, when Athenians assumed the leadership of the allies, vouching to pursue the Delian League's anti-Persian objectives. The Athenians galvanized support for their leadership by calling on the allies to liberate the Greeks from the yoke of slavery.[1] In the wake of their victories at Marathon and Salamis, Athenians celebrated their unique achievements in the service of freedom. Touting their superiority, they now proclaimed themselves the defenders and liberators of all Greeks, presenting their leadership in the alliance as the deserved legacy of their earlier exploits.[2]

Thucydides casts doubt on the Athenians' sincerity toward their allies and notes that the Athenians' true motives were different from their professed aims to exact revenge from the Persians (Th. 1.96.1).[3] His narrative of the league's operations in the first decade shows Athens pursuing policies and exercising her power in a manner that contravened her original pledge to the allies (Th. 1.97–101).[4] However, Thucydides' appraisal of Athens' leadership is colored by his hindsight knowledge of a growing disparity between hegemony and empire that came later. Under Cimon, the Athenians led operations in the areas of the Chersonese, Thrace, and the Hellespont and secured control of the eastern islands of the Aegean, extending their reach to territories vulnerable to incursions from Persia. This is not to say that Athens did not pursue her own interests during this time. Athens' power also grew under Cimon's leadership of the league: the Athenians maintained control in areas formerly under Persia, annexed cities and islands of strategic importance to Athens (e.g., Carystos and Scyros), and used force to bring new members into the league or punish recalcitrant allies, such as Naxos and Thasos.[5]

It is therefore likely that when the league first came into existence, the arguments the Athenians used in support of their leadership served an ideological purpose, albeit limited. By advertising the moral character of their hegemony, Athenians sought to justify their leadership to other Greeks and enhance their own sense of civic superiority. The rift between alleged and real aims, which Thucydides imputes to the Athenians, emerged more clearly later, when Athens' imperial ambitions had become evident and unambiguous.

It is not possible to rehearse the arguments advanced in the long-standing debate of how and when the empire came into existence.[6] We can, however, point to particular events and developments that mark turning points in the history of the empire, as these are alluded to in tragedy's representation of imperialism in the post-Cimonian phase of the empire. Cimon's victory at Eurymedon in 467 BC marked the end of hostilities with Persia, though it remains doubtful whether their cessation led to the signing of the formal treaty between Athens and Persia, known as the Peace of Callias.[7] By 458 BC, the year of the production of the *Oresteia*, the empire had consolidated its reach in the northeast, and Athens and her allies were engaged in war in Egypt. *Eumenides* echoes Athens' military predominance through Athena's first appearance onstage.

## DEMOCRACY AND EMPIRE

Surviving decrees from the Athenian Assembly provide critical evidence for the growth of Athenian imperialism in the 440s. These decrees offer information on Athens' increasing interference in the financial, military, political and judicial affairs of the allies.[8] More specifically, the Athenians sought to control the internal administration of the cities they ruled by setting up garrisons, establishing Athenian officials as "supervisors" (ἐπίσκοποι) and by installing democracies in some cities to maintain a pro-Athenian basis. Hostility toward the Athenians was also caused by the allocation of land belonging to the allies to poorer Athenian citizens in the form of land grants (*cleruchies*) and the establishment of colonies in areas where Athenians had confiscated the land, following forced evacuations—a penalty usually applied to cities that had revolted. Athens' subjects also faced judicial compulsion, as particular lawsuits were referred to Athens, and the cities were similarly deprived of the right of holding trials for crimes involving the death penalty. In ignorance of Athenian law, the allies had no means of redress against the verdicts of the courts.[9] Last, but not least, the allies resented the imposition of the tribute, although quotas varied, depending on the wealth and resources of each city.[10]

The Athenian decrees make it clear that under Athens' imperial democracy, her rule over the allies became more rigid and harsher.[11] The decree of Erythrae ($IG^3$ I 14, ca. 460s–450s BC) makes mention of offerings at the Panathenaea, the establishment of a garrison, loss of judicial freedom, and the imposition of a constitution on the Athenian model. The "Coinage" Decree (ML 45, ca. 450–446 BC), which some consider a forgery, made the use of Athenian coins, weights, and measures mandatory in the cities under Athens' rule, while the decree of Cleinias ($IG^3$ I 34, ca. 447 BC) introduced new provisions aiming to tighten tribute collection and requiring all cities to send offerings to the Panathenaea. Lastly, the Chalcis decree ($IG^3$ I 40, ca. 446/5 BC) stipulates that trials of exile, *atimia* ("loss of civic rights") and death be judged by Athenian courts and provides evidence for an oath of loyalty to Athens.

The allies' loss of freedom became more palpable after the treasury of the league was moved from Delos to Athens in 454/3 BC, which formalized the allies' standing as dependents of an imperial metropolis: the treasury was now housed in the temple of Athena on the Athenian Acropolis; each city sent representatives to Athens to deposit their quota of the tribute and Athenians paid 1/60th of the tribute as first "fruit-offerings" (ἀπαρχαί) to Athena.[12] Following the transfer of the treasury, the Athenians also began recording the names of the cities and the amounts of the contributions each paid as tribute on marble *stelai*, erected on the Athenian Acropolis. These inventories, published in four volumes,[13] both furnish valuable information on the finances of the empire and allow us to document the allies' recalcitrance and disaffection, evidenced either through the absence of the names of particular cities in the tribute lists or alternatively through the record of late or partial payments.[14] Although the existence of common councils of the allies held on Delos (Th. 1.97.1) is far from certain, league councils would have been abolished, following the transfer of the treasury.[15]

TRAGEDY ON HEGEMONY

Euripides' suppliant plays adapt the model of Athens' moral hegemony in response to the growth of imperialism between 450 and 420 BC. *Children of Heracles* (ca. 430 BC) and *Suppliant Women* (ca. 424 BC) take up the challenge of defending the ideals of Athens' hegemonic leadership against the criticism of Sparta and her allies, who feared her power (Th. 1.23.6, 88, 118.2) and demanded that she should leave the allies' autonomous (Th. 1.139.3). The plays renew Athens' commitment to her hegemonic ideals by representing the city leading the charge against offenders of the common laws and customs of Greece and acting as an arbiter for justice for the benefit of all Greeks. Both plays emphasize the Athenians' commitment to moral ventures, taking up arms to fight against Eurystheus, when he sought to violate the supplication of Heracles' children, and against the Thebans to recover the bodies of the Argive Seven for burial.

The second distinctive feature of Athens' hegemonic ideology in *Children of Heracles* and *Suppliant Women* is the defense of democracy. Both plays present democracy as the mainstay of Athens' moral hegemony, echoing Pericles' ideal vision of Athens' imperial democracy. The plays negotiate the ideal image of Athenian democracy against the historical role that this very democracy served under the empire, and they fashion a portrait of Athens' ideal leadership that denies the allies' enforced subjection.

As Rosenbloom notes, the plays "emphasize in the manner of the funeral oration that democracy as an ideal and practice revolves around obedience to the laws, which serve against injustice, both written and unwritten to avoid shame."[16] In his funeral oration, Pericles represents democracy as the source of Athens' political, moral, and cultural superiority. The plays' emphasis on democracy furnishes the lynchpin of the dramatic representation of Athens' ideal leadership. Euripides' plays illustrate further that the two key facets of Athens' identity—democracy and empire—are organically related, and both tragedies represent democracy as handmaiden to, and true bulwark of, Athens' moral hegemony. For example, the decisions the kings of Athens (Theseus and Demophon) reach about the war against Thebes and Argos also involve either direct participation or some form of consultation with the citizenry.

As in Aeschylus' *Eumenides*, the later suppliant plays articulate Athens' ideal leadership on the basis of consent and reciprocity. Euripides' plays offer a more complex negotiation of consent versus force in that they promote Athens' claims to justice, specifically as they relate to democracy. Athenian democratic institutions—the Assembly and the courts—had played a key role in restricting the allies' independence over the two decades prior to the outbreak of the Peloponnesian War. Both plays paint a positive image of Athenian interference, representing Athens as undertaking limited and defensive wars against Argos and Thebes to uphold divinely sanctioned customs. To this effect, the suppliants' recourse to the law in Athens represents democracy not as an enforcer but as an arbiter of morality and justice in the service of Greece.

While assertions of righteousness aimed at defending Athens' conduct during the war, they also suggest that the distance between Athens' ideals and the realities of her rule had grown larger in the course of three decades since the production of the *Oresteia*.[17] Athenian ideals were subject to reevaluation and revision—a process determined by historical and generic parameters as well as tensions, internal and external, within this ideology, which crystallized the particular outlook of each of the suppliant plays.

# EURIPIDES' *CHILDREN of HERACLES*: HELPING THE WEAK *and* PUNISHING THE STRONG

In Euripides' *Children of Heracles*, the representation of Athens' generosity towards a group of weak and outraged suppliants addresses the relationship between imperial Athens and her subject allies more directly perhaps than do all other dramas, featuring Athens as a haven for foreign exiles. The suppliant plot is based on the story of the flight of children of Heracles,[1] who leave their native Argos as exiles to avoid execution by the tyrant Eurystheus. Expelled from every Greek city, they eventually arrive at Marathon, where they seek refuge at the altar of Zeus Agoraios.[2] Their supplication is, however, disrupted by the Argive herald, sent by Eurystheus to force them to return to Argos. The intervention of the Athenian king Demophon, who opposes the herald's violence (βία), predicates the acceptance of the suppliants upon the city's freedom (ἐλευθερία). Freedom is the key dramatic and ideological concept around which the play builds Athens' imperial portrait as defender of the weak and the oppressed.[3] The suppliants, moreover, act as well-disposed allies, supportive of Athens' policies, while Athens repays their trust by granting them protection.

But as soon as the supplication is decided in favor of the suppliants, the plot takes an abrupt turn: an oracle announces that Kore, Demeter's daughter, demands that a maiden be sacrificed in exchange for a fair outcome in the battle against Argos, which leads Demophon to retract his promise to fight on behalf of the suppliants. The king reneges on his promise to accept them, and the suppliants are on the brink of being expelled from the city until one of Heracles' daughters offers herself up for sacrifice. The Athenian army fights against Eurystheus, and with the help of an allied force, led by Heracles' oldest son, Hyllus, they win the war.

Unlike the funeral speeches, which celebrated Athens' victory against Eurystheus alongside the other great mythical wars against her foes, Euripides' introduction of the sacrifice of Heracles' daughter to the myth complicates the drama's panegyric. The sacrifice, a contribution to Athens' war effort on the part of the suppliants, recalls the responsibilities that Athens enjoined upon her allies.

The play was performed at the beginning of the Peloponnesian war (ca. 430 BC). Athens' successful protection of the suppliants, her victorious war against their tyrannical foe, and Eurystheus' unexpected pledge of loyalty to Athens just before Alcmene, Heracles' mother, kills him,[4] make this a play for its day.[5] Eurystheus prophesizes that the Spartans will attack Athens in the future. This prophecy provided a link between the mythical past and the present by contrasting Athenian generosity with the ingratitude of the Spartans, who attacked Attica repeatedly during the Archidamian War.[6]

Athens' image as a hegemonic city is further conditioned by the realities of the empire. The play negotiates Athens' idealized depiction against the demands the empire placed upon the allies. The suppliants' voluntary accession to the sacrifice—the condition that Athens sets for their reception—highlights the limits that underlie the city's generosity.


### DRAMA AND POLITICS

Earlier critics have criticized the play on aesthetic and dramaturgical grounds.[7] Many regard the praise of Athens as overtly patriotic or propagandistic.[8] Günther Zuntz's 1955 study of *Children of Heracles* and *Suppliant Women* under the rubric of "political" plays marked a modest turning point in twentieth-century scholarship. No longer dismissed as mere propaganda plays, both suppliant dramas began to be assessed more positively as a result of Zuntz's work. Yet despite his positive appraisal—Zuntz calls the play "a gem of concentrated dramatic action"—*Children of Heracles* has been judged the less successful of the two.[9] Its flaws, which some earlier critics explained away by relating specific traits in the plays to contemporary events,[10] were now interpreted by new critics through recourse to "internal" dramatic criteria.[11]

*Children of Heracles* has undoubtedly suffered critical neglect in the past, and it has also received less attention than it deserves in recent political interpretations of Greek tragedy. Only Daniel Mendelsohn's study of gender and politics and Jonas Grethlein's analysis of suppliant tragedies as loci for the construction of Athenian civic identity, which appeared in 2002 and 2003 respectively, probe further into the political character of this play.[12] Their approaches situate the civic discourse of the play within the political culture of Athens far more concretely than did earlier critics of the play. According to these critics, Euripides' praise of Athens reflects or reacts to values and beliefs largely underwritten by Athenian democratic civic ideology and its institutions. Athens in *Children of Heracles* is ruled by kings, Demophon and Acamas, sons of Theseus—the very symbol of Athenian democracy—and as a result features a more enlightened type of kingship compared to Argos, where Eurystheus wields power in the manner of a tyrant.[13] The comparison between Athens and Argos can easily be shown to highlight the superiority of Athenian democratic institutions, yet the enmity between the two cities sheds light more readily on the character of Athens' empire than on Athenian democracy.

Thus, respect for supplication, freedom, and justice are values deemed apposite for representing Athens' political superiority over her opponents both in the past and in the present by representing Athens as a free city rather than the tyrant city others thought it to be.[14] This reading of the play further seeks to tie the framework of supplication to the discourse of empire.[15] To achieve this, the play weds the proimperial discourse of the suppliants' voluntary subjection with that of Athens as a "free city" that resists tyranny. Athens becomes divested of the negative trappings of empire, which her enemies imputed against her: suppliants are converted into eager participants in the city's imperial democracy, and tyranny is kept at a safe distance from Athens. The play also pays tribute to Athens' imperial democracy by commending the city for upholding the Panhellenic custom of supplication. My reading of *Children of Heracles* thus concentrates on the ideological tropes—freedom and democracy—through which Euripides envisions Athens' image at the beginning of the Peloponnesian War.[16]

## SUPPLICATION: FREEDOM AND EMPIRE

### FREEDOM AND POWER

Freedom is the key trait of the dramatization of the topos of Athens as protector of the suppliants in this play. By this time, freedom was used in some contexts as a euphemism for Athens' rule over her allies, while in others it was used to justify her right to leadership among the Greek cities. The Spartans had sought to undermine the Athenian rhetoric of freedom already before the Peloponnesian War broke out, arguing that it was a mere cover-up for Athens' tyrannical treatment of her allies, by now reduced to subjects.[17] The play responds to this criticism by suggesting that a strong and free empire served as a guarantee for the protection that Athens was able to offer others.

Freedom is central to the city's praise in the prologue and the first *epeisodion*. Iolaus, Heracles' aged companion, singles Athens out from all other Greek cities because she alone is able to protect others from violence and persecution on account of her freedom (ἐλευθέρα τε γαῖ᾽, "a free land," 62; οὐκ οἶδ᾽ Ἀθήνας τάσδ᾽ ἐλευθέρας ἔτι, "I no longer regard Athens as being free," 198).[18] The circumstances surrounding the supplication of Heracles' children—that is, the threat of its disruption by Eurystheus' herald—set in relief the positive representation of Athens' power as it relates to her freedom. For no sooner have the suppliants taken their seat at the altar of Zeus Agoraios at Marathon than the Argive herald violates their sanctuary and attempts to drag them away by force and threats.[19] The herald for his part argues that Athens will not ally herself with worthless suppliants but will choose the powerful Eurystheus instead (55–62). Iolaus responds that Athens is the only city able to protect them on account of her freedom (62).

In the prologue, a stark contrast builds between Athens' freedom and power to help the weak and Eurystheus' tactics of coercion, which succeed time and again on two counts: to banish Heracles' children from the cities where they seek refuge and to force those same cities to accept an alliance with powerful Argos (15–22). Athens' characterization as a free city[20] also emphasizes the necessity of preserving both the city's sovereignty and her reputation. By demanding the removal of the suppliants, Eurystheus calls into question Athens' own freedom. For this reason, when the chorus first enters, they denounce the herald's transgression as an offense against both the gods and the city, because his actions violate Athens' own sovereignty (ἐλευθερία; 112–113).[21] Similarly, Demophon decides to fight on the suppliants' behalf, because Eurystheus' demand places his own city's sovereignty at risk (244–245).

Kurt Raaflaub's work on freedom in Greek thought during the archaic and classical periods is indispensable and serves as the point of departure for the discussion of freedom in this play.[22] As he shows, by the 430s Athenians had come to understand their own freedom as a consequence of their power, economic and military. This Athenian idea of freedom was explicitly associated with Athens' rule over others.[23] Political speeches, such as that of Diodotus in the Mytilenean debate in Thucydides, link freedom with imperial rule: καὶ ἡ τύχη ἐπ᾽ αὐτοῖς οὐδὲν ἔλασσον ξυμβάλλεται ἐς τὸ ἐπαίρειν· ἀδοκήτως γὰρ ἔστιν ὅτε παρισταμένη καὶ ἐκ τῶν ὑποδεεστέρων κινδυνεύειν τινὰ προάγει, καὶ οὐχ ἧσσον τὰς πόλεις, ὅσῳ περὶ τῶν μεγίστων τε, ἐλευθερίας ἢ ἄλλων ἀρχῆς, . . . ("Fortune too assists the illusion, for she often presents herself unexpectedly, and induces states as well as individuals to run into peril, however inadequate their means; and states even more than individuals, because they are throwing for a higher stake, freedom or empire," 3.45.6). In the context of the aftermath of the oligarchic coup in 411 BC, Thucydides also observes: χαλεπὸν γὰρ ἦν τὸν Ἀθηναίων δῆμον ἐπ᾽ ἔτει ἑκατοστῷ μάλιστα ἐπειδὴ οἱ τύραννοι κατελύθησαν ἐλευθερίας παῦσαι, καὶ οὐ μόνον μὴ ὑπήκοον ὄντα, ἀλλὰ καὶ ὑπὲρ ἥμισυ τοῦ χρόνου τούτου αὐτὸν ἄλλων ἄρχειν εἰωθότα ("For it was difficult about one hundred years after the dissolution of tyranny for the Athenians to lose their freedom, who not only had not been subject to anyone but also during more than half of this time been used to ruling over others," 8.68.4). In panegyric contexts such as this one, there was no explicit mention of Athens' rule over her allies.[24] In *Children of Heracles* the depiction of Athens' freedom suggests that Athens used her power not to rule but to protect those in need (61–62, 197–198, 243–246). Yet references to freedom in the play cannot be understood divorced from the reality of empire. Indeed, the suppliants' repeated appeals to Athens' freedom painted a positive image of its interventions.

It may be more apt to characterize Athens' designation as a "free city" in the play as a euphemism for Athens' rule. There is a notable progression from the claim that Athens was the liberator of other Greeks—Athens' expressed motive for assuming the leadership of the league in 478/7 (Th. 1.96–97.1)—and her depiction as a free city in *Children of Heracles*.

In Euripides' play, no Athenian character openly admits that Athens' rule over others had by now become necessary to her own freedom. Only Thucydides exposes the inconsistency between freedom and domination.[25] For example, Euphemus says to the Camarinians that Athens rules over other Greeks to avoid being dominated by them (φαμὲν γὰρ ἄρχειν τῶν ἐκεῖ ἵνα μὴ ὑπακούωμεν ἀλλοᾶ, "we say that we are in command there, so that we do not obey another," 6.87.2). The refugees' appeal to the free *polis* in *Children of Heracles*, however, downplays the incongruity of equating freedom with subjection.[26]

The suppliants' interactions with Athens, on the other hand, link freedom with Athens' power. For example, in the debate between Iolaus and Demophon, Iolaus challenges the Athenian king to prove Athens' freedom by highlighting the responsibilities that such power entails. Iolaus compares Athens to the other Greek cities that cowered before Eurystheus and presses Demophon to live up to the city's reputation by taking up the cause of the suppliants:

οὔκουν Ἀθήνας γ᾽· οὐ γὰρ Ἀργείων φόβωι
τοὺς Ἡρακλείους παῖδας ἐξελῶσι γῆς.
οὐ γάρ τι Τραχίς ἐστιν οὐδ᾽ Ἀχαικὸν
πόλισμ᾽ ὅθεν σὺ τούσδε, τῆι δίκηι μὲν οὔ,
τὸ δ᾽ Ἄργος ὀγκῶν, οἱάπερ καὶ νῦν λέγεις,
ἤλαυνες ἱκέτας βωμίους καθημένους. (191–196)

---

Not from Athens at any rate: they shall not banish Heracles' children from their land fearing the Argives! This is not Trachis or some Achaean town, places from which you drove these children unjustly, by praising Argos' importance just as you are doing now, even though they were suppliants, seated at the altar.

The trust he places in the city's freedom translates in positive terms the relationship between Athens and her allies, representing the suppliants in the guise of eager, well-wishing allies. This relationship transforms the bonds of kinship between the families of Heracles and Theseus into bonds of dependency, albeit positively conceived.[27] At the end of his speech, Iolaus supplicates the king and entreats him to "be a kinsman to them, be a friend, a father, brother, master" (γενοῦ δὲ τοῖσδε συγγενής, γενοῦ φίλος/πατὴρ ἀδελφὸς δεσπότης, 229–230). Iolaus acknowledges his subordinate status to Demophon in terms that convey the suppliants' voluntary subjection to the king. The asymmetrical relationship between suppliant and *supplicandus* parallels the unequal relationship between Athens and her subject allies. The parallelism enhances Athens' image as a free city that acquires allies by aiding and abetting the plight of those suffering unjustly.

### FREEDOM FROM TYRANNY

The Spartans sought an advantage in the Peloponnesian War through propaganda that had a clear message: to free the Greeks from Athens' tyranny.[28] At the beginning of the war, when the Corinthians ask the Spartans to free Greece, they refer to Athens as a tyrannical city (Th. 1.122.3, 124.3).[29] The Spartans rallied support to their cause; both those who wanted to be free of Athens' rule[30] and those who feared it,[31] as Thucydides puts it, responded to Sparta's campaign of liberation (Th. 2.8.4).

Unlike the Spartans, who presented themselves as liberators, Athenians during the war found themselves compelled to fight to preserve Athens' rule, as Pericles says (Th. 2.63.1–2). *Children of Heracles*, on the other hand, responds to the charge of tyranny[32] by displacing the negative traits of empire onto Argos[33] and represents Athens as a free city that shelters others from wrongdoing.

The antithesis between Athens and Argos is pivotal for Athens' political self-definition.[34] Argos provides the antithesis of Athens. Argos exemplifies coercion (15–25, 150–155, 191–196),[35] as evinced by the herald's violence against the suppliants and Eurystheus' forced invitations to other cities to extradite them in return for an alliance with Argos. Athens, on the other hand, augments her power by curbing violence, fights against tyranny, and earns allies through her generosity.

### FREEDOM AS SOVEREIGNTY

Athens' motives for going to war to defend suppliants scarcely require elaborate justification in view of the herald's attempt to disrupt the process of supplication. This is why, as Burian notes, the supplication is decided in the first three hundred lines of the play—a short sequence compared, for example, to that of Aeschylus' *Suppliant Women*.[36] The exchange between the suppliants, their adversary, and their soon-to-be protector also contains a rationale of Athens' motives for granting the suppliants asylum. The risk that Athens undertakes by going to war is motivated not only by the desire to remedy the suppliants' unjust suffering but also by the need to safeguard the city's sovereignty. The conflict between Athens and Argos focuses on the defense of Athens' sovereignty and reflects the ongoing struggle for power between Athens and Sparta in this regard as well.

In Euripides' retelling of the myth, the protection of Athens' freedom influences heavily Demophon's decision to offer the suppliants asylum, after the herald threatens that Eurystheus will attack Athens if the Athenian king fails to hand over the suppliants. Similar threats are uttered by the Furies against Athens in Aeschylus' *Eumenides* and by Creon in Sophocles' *Oedipus at Colonus*. The conflicts between Athens and her foes strengthen her hegemonic reputation and underscore her capacity to oppose them. Demophon understands that conceding to Eurystheus' terms and entering in an alliance with Argos (155–161) would be tantamount to surrendering Athens' sovereignty (οὐκ ἐλευθέραν/οἰκεῖν δοκήσω γαῖαν, "it will seem that I am not ruling a free land," 243–245).[37] Dependency on a foreign city would thus amount to loss of freedom. As a result, Demophon proclaims that Athens is a free city and not a client state of Argos (οὐ γὰρ Ἀργείων πόλιν ὑπήκοον τήνδ' ἀλλ' ἐλευθέραν ἔχω, "for the city I govern is not a subject of Argos, but is free," 286–287).[38]

This connection between freedom and sovereignty, as Raaflaub says, points more broadly to the ideological definition of imperial freedom as absolute sovereignty.[39] In the play, Demophon's decision not to compromise the city's sovereignty but to protect it against outside pressure speaks to current concerns over the preservation of the empire, whose sovereignty was now challenged by Sparta. In the play, Athens defends her motives for going to war by emphasizing the threat to her own freedom. The need to protect Athens' freedom from the threat of tyranny also provides ideological justification for her military ventures, since freedom figures as a precondition for the help that Athens is able to offer the refugees.

## THE DEBATE: DEMOCRACY AND THE LAW

The staging of the debate in *Children of Heracles* evokes broadly the setting of the Athenian Assembly where petitions from suppliants and foreigners were regularly heard. Athens' mythical image as protector of the weak and the oppressed is thus aligned with Athenian institutional practices surrounding supplication. In addition, by envisioning the supplication debate as conforming to debates in the Assembly, the play also pays tribute to the city's democratic institutions. Respect for supplication demonstrates the fairness of Athenian democratic institutions and brings it in line with the city's hegemonic image. In this light, the benevolent treatment that the suppliants receive in Athens also showcases the city's opposition to tyrannical domination.

### SUPPLICATION IN THE ASSEMBLY

Supplication at the altar followed by a debate is a common feature in suppliant dramas.[40] In this play, however, the herald's and Iolaus' speeches resemble more closely in form and content the type of debates that took place in the Athenian Assembly. As Michael Lloyd notes, the debate is "more naturalistic, since it is actually portraying a formal debate in which the participants might be expected to make set speeches."[41] The debate (*agon*) itself takes place between the herald and Iolaus and not between the suppliant(s) and the king, as it does in Aeschylus' and Euripides' *Suppliant Women*.[42] The king judges the suppliants' case and reaches his decision after both sides take turns presenting their arguments.[43] The parallel structure of the two speeches underscores the fairness of the Athenian judicial system.[44] Each speech elaborates on the facts of the case by setting forth legal, political, and moral arguments from opposite perspectives. The herald's demand for extradition is judged against Iolaus' plea for asylum; both speakers make speeches of equal length, following the debate rules of the Athenian Assembly. The debate evokes the Assembly in more direct ways as well. In particular, the setting for the debate at the altar of the supplicated god, Zeus Agoraios (70), ties the supplication with Athenian institutions: Zeus Agoraios was associated with the "righteousness of trials"[45] and was the patron of the Athenian Assembly.[46] Suppliants usually supplicated Zeus as *Xenios* ("Protector of Guests"), *Hikesios* ("Protector of Suppliants"), or *Soter* ("Savior").[47] The epithet *Ago-*

*raios* here is not a simple allusion to democratic institutions, fit for a patriotic play,[48] but makes the god an emblem of democratic debate.[49]

As Naiden argues, the Athenian Assembly decided certain petitions from suppliants who supplicated the Assembly formally before their case was heard. Controversial supplications such as this one, which affected the city's interests and security, would fall under the jurisdiction of the Assembly.[50] The evidence for this practice derives from Assembly decrees dating to the fourth and third centuries. The decrees illustrate that the Council and the Assembly had the executive power to decide petitions by suppliants.[51] As Naiden demonstrates, however, tragedy furnishes indirect evidence that this practice may have already been in place earlier. Naiden compares the procedure described in a fourth-century decree in which a metic seeks exemption from his tax contributions by appearing before the Assembly with the assembly of the Argive *demos* that Pelasgus calls to decide the fate of the Danaids in Aeschylus' *Suppliant Women*. As we have seen, in that play, the king's dilemma over whether to accept this band of foreign women in Argos (who were Zeus' suppliants and kinswomen of the Argive Io) and face war with their cousins or to reject them is resolved by coming to a vote before the *demos* (A. *Supp.* 942–943).[52]

The supplication of Heracles' children is treated in a similar manner, even if the matter is not formally brought before the Assembly.[53] The authority of the king in the context of the supplication is analogous to that of the magistrates in the Council.[54] As the chorus point out to Iolaus, only the king has jurisdiction over such matters (111–113).[55] Within this setting, Iolaus' plea before King Demophon on behalf of the suppliants (181–231) exhibits similarities with the procedure described by Aristotle (*Ath.* 43.6), who states that anyone wishing to present a petition before the Assembly went first to the altar, where he placed a suppliant branch. The evocation of this setting is consistent with Athens' panegyric. Heracles' children first take refuge at the altar of Zeus Agoraios at Marathon[56] and seek the city's protection when the herald attempts to drag them away from the altar. After Demophon grants them their request, the chorus emphasize that the king's decision is consistent with Athens' tradition of generosity toward the suppliants (329–332).[57]

SUPPLICATION AND ASYLUM

The second significant element of the ideal image of Athens in *Children of Heracles* is her respect for the Panhellenic custom of supplication. In the experience of the audience, the legitimacy of the suppliant's request was crucial for determining the successful outcome of any supplication.[58] In fifth-century

---

Athens, as Angelos Chaniotis notes, asylum ("immunity from extradition") was granted only if the suppliants could prove before the authorities who were responsible for judging their case that they had been wronged.[59] The legality of the request also plays a crucial role in the dramatic *agon*.

An evaluation of the herald's and Iolaus' arguments in the dramatic debate highlights the priority of legal claims. The herald, who speaks first (134–179),[60] demands the suppliants' extradition by invoking the laws of Argos (134–143). He claims that Heracles' children were condemned to death (140–141) and insists that as Argives they are bound by Argive law (141–143).[61] Though seizure of fugitives could be legally requested for the purpose of punishing offenders who had committed wrongs against the city from which they fled, Heracles' children are innocent. In fact, as Iolaus explains in the prologue (12–17), Eurystheus has condemned them to death[62] to prevent retaliation on their part for the harm he had done to their father (1000–1008).[63] The herald, however, stands by his claims and argues the suppliants have been sentenced to death, following due legal process:

> Ἀργεῖος ὢν γὰρ αὐτὸς Ἀργείους ἄγω
> ἐκ τῆς ἐμαυτοῦ τούσδε δραπέτας ἔχων,
> νόμοισι τοῖς ἐκεῖθεν ἐψηφισμένους
> θανεῖν· (139–142)

> I am an Argive myself, and those I am seeking to take away are Argives who have run away from my country, though they were sentenced to die in accordance with that city's laws.

The participle ἐψηφισμένους ("sentenced"), however, does not refer to a verdict reached by vote: like ψῆφος ("decision, vote"), it can denote the decision of an individual instead of a communal decision. Moreover, this verdict is not the outcome of a democratic process but a tyrant's ruling that distorts the law to serve his own interests. The herald also refers to the suppliants as δραπέτας, "runaway slaves" (140).[64] Slaves were the only group not considered immune from seizure because they were not free.[65] In referring to the suppliants in this manner, the herald undermines his credibility. His overall effort to justify the violation of the suppliants' sanctuary on legal grounds fails to persuade.[66]

In his response, Iolaus counters the herald's specious legal claims. He opens his speech by extolling the virtues of democratic debate and praising Athens:

> ἄναξ, ὑπάρχει γὰρ τόδ' ἐν τῆι σῆι χθονί,
> εἰπεῖν ἀκοῦσαί τ' ἐν μέρει πάρεστί μοι,

κοὐδείς μ’ ἀπώσει πρόσθεν ὥσπερ ἄλλοθεν.
ἡμῖν δὲ καὶ τῶιδ’ οὐδέν ἐστιν ἐν μέσωι·
ἐπεὶ γὰρ Ἄργους οὐ μέτεσθ’ ἡμῖν ἔτι,
ψήφωι δοκήσαν, ἀλλὰ φεύγομεν πάτραν,
πῶς ἂν δικαίως ὡς Μυκηναίους ἄγοι
ὅδ’ ὄντας ἡμᾶς, οὓς ἀπήλασαν χθονός;
ξένοι γάρ ἐσμεν. ἢ τὸν Ἑλλήνων ὅρον
φεύγειν δικαιοῦθ’ ὅστις ἂν τἄργος φύγηι; (181–190)

My lord, since this is the law in your land, I have the right to hear and be heard in turn, and no one shall push me aside before I am done, as they have elsewhere. We have nothing to do with this man. Since we no longer have a share in Argos, and this has been sanctioned by vote, but are exiles from our native land, how can this man justifiably lead us away as Mycenaeans, when they have driven us from the country? We are now foreigners. Or do you think it right that whoever is exiled from Argos should be exiled from the whole Greek world?

Equality of speech (εἰπεῖν ἀκοῦσαί τ’ ἐν μέρει, 182) and the fairness of the political and judicial process evoke the ideal of *isegoria* ("equality of speech"), which constitutes the basis of democratic freedom.[67] By praising the right of equal speech, Iolaus pays tribute to Athens' democracy as well. For among its many meanings, democratic freedom conveyed the sense of "emancipation from prior subordination"[68]—a meaning apposite for describing the suppliants' hope to escape from Eurystheus' tyrannical authority. Iolaus argues before the king and the chorus that Heracles' children have been wronged by Eurystheus, who continues to persecute them, denying them even the option of living as exiles anywhere in Greece (190–191).

In his speech, Iolaus establishes the legitimacy of the suppliants' request for asylum.[69] He refutes the herald's claim that Heracles' children are accountable to the laws of Argos, since they have now fled their home.[70] According to Athenian homicide law, exile was an alternative to death, a choice that Heracles' children make under duress.[71] As Iolaus explains, Heracles' children no longer live in their city (φεύγομεν πάτραν, "we are exiles from our native land," 186). He argues that as exiles, they have forfeited their citizenship (Ἄργους οὐ μέτεσθ’ ἡμῖν ἔτι, "we no longer have a share in Argos," 185) and are no longer subject to the laws of Argos (187–188).[72] Iolaus therefore counters the herald's argument regarding law and justice.[73] Second, he establishes the suppliants' status as refugees, and on these grounds, he rightfully petitions immunity from extradition.

In this debate, the legal arguments of both sides are deployed in a manner that characterizes Demophon's conduct as democratic, while condemning that of Eurystheus as tyrannical. Eurystheus perverts the law, while Demophon respects the "right of the wronged" (*pace* Chaniotis) and remedies the suppliants' unjust exile. Herein lies the civic praise of Athens as protector of the weak. By lending prominence to the democratic elements of the supplication of Heracles' children in Athens, the play construes Athens' imperial image in positive terms. Democracy and empire converge: democracy underpins Athens' openness as a fair and impartial judge of the affairs of others.

The suppliants' recourse to the law in Athens furthermore paints a favorable image of Athenian democracy, which counters the criticism of Athens' rivals. As we saw in Chapter 2, *Children of Heracles* and *Suppliant Women* present Athens as a fair and impartial judge of disputes among other Greeks.[74] Such arguments addressed tensions that inevitably arose from Athens' imperial democracy[75] and sought to justify those benefits that Athenians enjoyed, as they progressively limited the allies' freedom.[76] After all, Pericles himself had stated that Athens' rule was akin to tyranny (Th. 2.63.2).[77] Moreover, in the Mytilenean debate, Cleon too branded the empire a tyranny, as he warned his fellow Athenians against treating their allies as equal partners, reminding them that democracy and empire could not coexist (Th. 3.37.1–3). On the other hand, the allies, for their part, protested their own loss of autonomy and enforced subordination; such complaints are openly expressed in the Mytilenaean debate (Th. 3.10.4).[78] While *Children of Heracles* does not register such complaints openly,[79] the favorable depiction that the play paints of Athens' interaction with the suppliants represents democratic deliberation as the guarantor of others' freedom.[80]

## AN IDEAL ATHENS?

Plays that feature voluntary self-sacrifice such as Euripides' *Iphigenia in Aulis*, *Children of Heracles*, and *Phoenician Women* dramatize a profound impasse, when the community acquiesces to the demand of the god to procure its own safety.[81] In *Children of Heracles*, the demand for a human sacrifice by Kore in return for a fair outcome in the war against Argos also typifies the crisis that regularly arises in the course of the suppliants' acceptance. In other suppliant dramas, this crisis usually precedes the decision to protect the suppliants against the threat of a hostile attack from their pursuers.[82] By coming into play after Demophon has decided to oppose Argos in battle, the emergency of the sacrifice calls attention to the costs and benefits of the suppliants' reception of Athens.

When Kore makes her demand,[83] Demophon withdraws the promise of asylum and emphatically refuses to sacrifice his own daughter or that of any other citizen (410–414). Despite his professed willingness to stand by the suppliants (προθυμίαν, 410),[84] he now enjoins upon Iolaus to seek alternative measures to ensure their safety (420–422). The Athenian king sets clear boundaries between civic safety and that of the suppliants. Setting his duty to his citizenry above his obligation to Heracles' children (415–424), he argues that their protection carries the risk of damaging the city's unity. He paints a picture of the city rent by *stasis* ("strife"). The citizens are divided in two factions: one supporting his decision to help the suppliants and the other opposing it by accusing him of foolishness (415–17). In his view, granting asylum under these circumstances runs the risk of provoking a civil war (419).[85] Mindful of his own reputation, he brands the sacrifice a barbarian custom.[86]

Demophon, with withdrawal of asylum, sets limits to Athens' traditional characterization as a generous city. His current state of indecision contrasts with the chorus' earlier praise of Athens for helping those in need (ἀεί ποθ᾽ ἥδε γαῖα τοῖς ἀμηχάνοις/σὺν τῷ δικαίῳ βούλεται προσωφελεῖν, "this land always wants to help the weak in a just cause," 329–330).[87] Despite his and the chorus' expressions of compassion (410),[88] Demophon finds himself compelled to set the rights of Athenians above those of foreign suppliants.[89]

The crisis of sacrifice therefore marks a turning point not only dramatically but also ideologically. The king initiates a new course of action by enlisting Iolaus' help (συνεξεύρισχ᾽ ὅπως, "join me in finding out," 420).[90] The withdrawal of asylum renders the praise of Athens provisional. When Demophon apprises Iolaus of the situation, the latter does not blame the king but holds the gods responsible for this unexpected trial (437–439). Iolaus expresses his enduring gratitude to the king (εἰ θεοῖσι δὴ δοκεῖ τάδε/πράσσειν ἔμ᾽, οὔτοι σοί γ᾽ ἀπόλλυται χάρις, "since it is the will of the gods that I should do this, my gratitude to you is not lost," 437–438)

On the practical side, Iolaus himself lacks the capacity to negotiate any new deal that would be advantageous for the suppliants.[91] His only attempt to salvage the city's goodwill toward Heracles' children is to offer himself up as a victim for the goddess: a gesture as noble as it is futile (451–457). But his powerful lament for the suppliants' impending extradition must have aroused feelings of pity from the audience:[92]

ὦ παῖδες, ὑμῖν δ᾽ οὐκ ἔχω τί χρήσομαι.
ποῖ τρεψόμεσθα; τίς γὰρ ἄστεπτος θεῶν;
ποῖον δὲ γαίας ἕρκος οὐκ ἀφίγμεθα;
ὀλούμεθ᾽, ὦ τέκν᾽, ἐκδοθησόμεσθα δή.
κἀμοῦ μὲν οὐδὲν εἴ με χρὴ θανεῖν μέλει,
πλὴν εἴ τι τέρψω τοὺς ἐμοὺς ἐχθροὺς θανών·

ὑμᾶς δὲ κλαίω καὶ κατοικτίρω, τέκνα,
καὶ τὴν γεραιὰν μητέρ' Ἀλκμήνην πατρός.
ὢ δυστάλαινα τοῦ μακροῦ βίου σέθεν,
τλήμων δὲ κἀγὼ πολλὰ μοχθήσας μάτην.
χρῆν χρῆν ἄρ' ἡμᾶς ἀνδρὸς εἰς ἐχθροῦ χέρας
πεσόντας αἰσχρῶς καὶ κακῶς λιπεῖν βίον. (439–450)

My children, I do not know what to do for you. Where shall we turn?
Which god have we not garlanded? To what land have we not come for
refuge? We will die, my children, now we shall be given up! I do not care
for myself if I must die, unless by dying I give pleasure to my enemies. It is
for you I weep and have pity, my children, and Alcmene, the aged mother
of your father. How unlucky you are in your long life, and I too am mis-
erable, having toiled so long in vain. It was fated, fated, it seems, that we
must fall into the hands of our enemy and lose our lives shamefully and
wretchedly!

Iolaus' lamentation subtly undermines the praise of Athens' generosity.
The chorus pick up on the emerging tension and respond to it, anxious to
divert criticism away from Athens:

ὢ πρέσβυ, μή νυν τήνδ' ἐπαιτιῶ πόλιν·τάχ' ἂν γὰρ ἡμῖν ψευδὲς ἀλλ' ὅμως κακὸν
γένοιτ' ὄνειδος ὡς ξένους προυδώκαμεν. (461–463)

Old sir, do not accuse this city. For though it may be false, it would still be
an evil reproach, that we betrayed strangers.

The chorus' concern lies with defending the city's reputation, currently at
variance with her treatment of the suppliants. The dissonance becomes clear
in the words of the chorus, who no longer express pity for the refugees.[93]
Iolaus is the only one left to pity Heracles' children as they face the possibility
of renewed exile (442).

It is difficult to determine whether an Athenian audience would have identified with the chorus' point of view. It is likely that many Athenians may not
have expected their civic ideals challenged overtly while their city was at war.
Nonetheless, the religious (the demand for the sacrifice) and political motives
(the threat of war) through which the king justifies the rejection of the suppliants undermine the play's panegyric and highlight the tension between ideal
and pragmatic motivations.

Earlier in the play, the Argive herald had branded Athens' proclivity toward idealism as disadvantageous. In his speech in the debate, the herald rejected the Athenians' tendency to pity the weak as mere folly (147–152) and argued forcefully that the king ought to avoid war with Argos, setting the interests of his city above those of a group of weak suppliants/allies (153–168).[94] Pity (κατοικτιεῖν, 152; οἰκτίσματα, 158) and profit (τί κερδανεῖς, "what will you gain?" 154) serve to characterize Athens and Argos respectively.[95] Pity for the suppliants, as David Konstan has argued, however, does not influence Demophon's initial decision to grant the suppliants asylum; he decides with his city's interest in mind.[96] The new crisis, however, reveals far more clearly the king's pragmatism, as his motives for expelling the suppliants now echo the herald's warnings:

τί δῆτα φήσεις, ποῖα πεδῖ' ἀφαιρεθείς,
τί ῥυσιασθείς, πόλεμον Ἀργείοις ἔχειν;
ποίοις δ' ἀμύνων συμμάχοις, τίνος δ' ὕπερ
θάψεις νεκροὺς πεσόντας; ἢ κακὸν λόγον
κτήσηι πρὸς ἀστῶν, εἰ γέροντος οὕνεκα
τύμβου, τὸ μηδὲν ὄντος, ὡς εἰπεῖν ἔπος,
παίδων <τε> τῶνδ' ἐς ἄντλον ἐμβήσηι πόδα. (162–168)

What will you say then? What lands or booty have you been deprived of that you go to war with Argos? Defending what allies, on whose behalf will you bury the fallen? Your citizens will have nothing good to say of you if you get in difficult waters for an old man, almost a tomb, and for these children.

The cost of accepting this group of suppliants in the city now outweighs any benefits and takes the drama of supplication in a new direction.

### SACRIFICE: ACQUIESCING TO EMPIRE?

The entry of Heracles' daughter is the climactic moment of the play: her sacrifice, an unparalleled act of loyalty to a foreign city, ensures Athens' victory. The maiden's death forges unity among the suppliants and their Athenian protectors, galvanizing the emotions of all participants against Eurystheus, their common enemy, in the impending battle.[97] Her sacrifice also prompts the redefinition of the suppliants' relationship with the city whose plight now evokes more clearly that of Athens' allies. After Heracles' daughter proclaims that she will die to save her family and Athens, Demophon takes up arms against Eurystheus (408–421). Iolaus also joins his hosts, and Hyllus, Heracles' oldest son, arrives on the battlefield with an allied force (660–670).[98]

Euripides' introduction of virgin sacrifice to the political myth of Athens' reception of Heracles' children is an innovation,[99] and it is not taken up by the fourth-century sources. Jennifer Larson comments that the foreign origin of Heracles' daughter can explain why orators omitted mention of her sacrifice in funerary speeches that otherwise commemorated Athenian mythical examples of self-sacrifice, such as those of the daughters of Erechtheus and Leos.[100] By not mentioning her sacrifice, orators could preserve the image of Athens as the savior of all suppliants. By contrast, in Euripides' play, the motif of self-sacrifice reveals the discrepancy between ideal and practice and the limits of Athens' generosity.

The arbitrary divine crisis, itself symbolic of the cost of salvation, helps refashion the earlier image of Athens as helper of the weak.[101] The limits introduced, as we have seen, surface in the other Athenian suppliant plays as well, revealing in each case different dramatic strategies contrived for the purpose of negotiating the admission of foreigners.[102]

The voluntary sacrifice in *Children of Heracles* furnishes a solution to the dilemma that the king faces. The strategy at work here is typical of the operation of ideology at large: the play contrives an illusory, albeit dramatically apt solution — the appearance of a voluntary victim — to resolve the perceived discrepancy between the ideal and the reality.[103]

### SACRIFICE AS IMPERIAL TRIBUTE

At the same time that the sacrifice plays up obstacles that suppliants typically encountered in their reception, the contingencies that arise in this play also appear to address specific concerns that are germane to the empire. In *Children of Heracles*, the sacrifice renders the terms for asylum equivalent to a relationship of dependency with Athens. The suppliants' position and obligation toward Athens now derive from the analogy of foreign suppliant to imperial subject. As soon as Iolaus explains to Heracles' daughter that the only alternative to the sacrifice would be for them to leave the city (494–497), she asks pointedly whether the sacrifice is the only stipulation for their admission (ἐν τῶιδε κἀχόμεσθα σωθῆναι λόγωι; "are we held by this condition for our safety?" 498). When she answers that it is (499), she offers herself willingly to be sacrificed (πρὶν κελευσθῆναι, "before I am ordered," 501).

Her sacrifice in turn secures the kind of military contribution requisite for an Athenian victory. Heracles' daughter and her siblings evoke closely the plight of the allies at this stage of the supplication, since they are compelled to offer military assistance in return for their protection.[104]

Some critics have characterized the shift in the suppliants' roles in positive terms, without addressing its implications.[105] This change, however, needs to be further discussed against the play's historical context. For the Athenians, the mounting costs of war made payment of the tribute an even more pressing matter, while resentment over the tribute on the part of the allies contributed to the growing feelings of hostility and resentment for the empire and its policies.

In the prologue, the herald mocks the suppliant Iolaus for seeking to enlist Athens as an ally (55–56). As William Furley observes, the petition of the suppliant children of Heracles themselves may well have evoked in the mind of the audience the recent embassy the Corcyreans sent to Athens in 432 BC to seek an alliance against Corinth.[106] The dramatic situation, I would suggest, evokes the plight of Athens' imperial subjects more broadly as well. The sacrifice of Heracles' daughter evokes the contributions that the member states of the alliance were required to make to Athens' campaigns in the form of money or ships and manpower for Athens' fleet.[107]

The metaphor of sacrifice as tribute offers a tangible connection with the historical reality of the empire. The king's reluctance to accept the enormous price of the sacrifice offers a window into the Athenians' concern with increases in military expenditure at the beginning of the Archidamian War. At that time, the collection of the tribute was an even more pressing matter than in preceding years.[108]

For the audience, Demophon's decision not to fight against Eurystheus without any support from the suppliants may have also called to mind the tightening of measures to ensure the steady inflow of resources to meet the exigencies of war. Wealth (περιουσία χρημάτων, "abundance of money"), as Pericles argued at the beginning of the war, was essential for winning wars in addition to careful military planning (γνώμη; Th. 2.13.2). Moreover, Athens at the time, he said, enjoyed great wealth thanks to the steady inflow of imperial revenue, calculated at 600 talents annually in addition to the funds stored in Athena's treasury (Th. 2.13.3–5).[109] Already after the first four years of the Peloponnesian War a large part of the city's monetary reserves had been spent, and special measures were undertaken to address the city's diminishing assets. In 428 BC, the Athenians were forced to institute a property tax to finance the ongoing war against Sparta (Th. 3.19). But the pressures were probably already felt as soon as the war broke out. It is likely, for example, that the Athenians began to send out ships to collect money (Th. 2.69, 3.19, 4.50.1) shortly after 431 BC to support their campaigns.[110]

Interpreted in light of the evidence on tribute collection, the sacrifice thus

---

allows us to unravel some of the issues that Athens' mythical war against Argos may have conveyed to the audience when it was first performed. Anxious over the city's and the empire's fortunes, Athenian spectators may have recognized the necessity of pursuing a defensive policy to ensure the city's safety. The sacrificial crisis, however, does not register the anxieties of only the domestic audience. The extreme cost of the suppliants' integration acknowledges the commitment expected on the part of the allies during the war, especially in light of the passing of measures to ensure the timely remittance of the tribute.

The self-sacrifice of Heracles' daughter presents the allies' contributions to the empire as undertaken freely without any coercion on the part of the Athenians. This positive representation evoked the model of the hegemonic alliance and one that evokes perhaps the original compact between Athens and her allies in the Delian League.[111] Athens' treatment of her allies, however, had undergone a significant change: the transfer of the league's treasury from Delos to Athens had a great impact on the empire's relations with its allies. The payment of the tribute designated the allies' financial obligations (φόρου ὑποτελεῖς, "paying tribute," or χρήματα φέροντες, "contributing money") and served as a token of the allies' submission to the imperial city.

The remittance of the tribute in the early days of the alliance did not provoke the same kind of resistance as later (Th. 1.97).[112] Athens' power grew, and as she successively began to enslave her allies, the imposition of the tribute signified the allies' loss of independence (Th. 3.10–11). Thucydides uses different terms to refer to those allies who paid tribute to Athens versus those who did not, designating the former as Athens' subjects (ὑπήκοοι) and the latter as being under Athens' rule (ἀρχόμενοι). Payment of the tribute therefore defined the allies' subject status and was regarded a repressive measure, amounting to enslavement. It was often imposed involuntarily upon those allies who had revolted or upon cities that were brought under Athens' rule through military conquest. The treatment of the Naxians is a case in point: being among Athens' "autonomous allies," they initially did not pay tribute. When they attempted to secede in the 460s, however, the Athenians punished them harshly by pulling down the city's walls, seizing their ships, and imposing tribute payments (Th. 1.97).

Tensions and conflicts inevitably arose, as the tribute was not always paid on time and was on occasion found to be in arrears on account of financial difficulties or due to the growing resistance toward Athens' rule. Though we lack sufficient evidence on the financial resources of the allied cities to determine whether annual payments were affordable or not, the increase of the tribute after the beginning of the Peloponnesian War and Athens' tightening of the collection process in the course of the war (as evinced by Cleinias' decree) suggest that its payment was the chief cause for the allies' growing resentment and hostility toward Athens.[113]

Thus, the play represents the suppliants' adherence to Athenian ideals in more complex fashion than has been previously acknowledged. The voluntary self-sacrifice marks a turning point and brings about a significant change in the characterization of the suppliants. But the subtext of their conversion is shaped by the contemporary historical realities of empire. Heracles' daughter's voluntary sacrifice represents the relationship between the city and the suppliants based on the model of an idealized hegemonic alliance. The priority of the empire's preservation is drawn within the tragic universe: divine agency casts political constraints in terms of ethical imperatives. The Athenian king does not demand compliance with the divine mandate from the suppliants, and yet the sacrifice itself is not entirely unforced, even if Heracles' daughter proclaims that she will die freely (ἐλευθέρως, "freely," 559) and without any compulsion (550–551). Set against the backdrop of the allies' enforced contributions, the dialectic, which underpins the sacrifice, sheds light on the tension between volition and compulsion.

## THE POLITICS OF GENDERED DISCOURSE

By repaying Athens for committing her military resources to ensure the safety of her family, Heracles' daughter can be seen as playing the role of token ally, reciprocating a generous protector. The scenario of her voluntary sacrifice, which seals Athens' victory against Eurystheus, also sets in relief the historical contingencies facing the empire at the beginning of the Peloponnesian War. At this time, Athens relied on the allies' support, and the play pays tribute to their contributions by according prominence to Heracles' daughter. Thus, a more complex image of the empire's relations with its allies emerges in the course of the play. Heracles' daughter plays a crucial role in crafting a portrait of unity between the city and the suppliants. To this end, she presents herself an eager supporter of Athens by embracing the Athenian ideals of male heroism, courage, and self-sacrifice. What is unique about the role, which she undertakes to play as civic savior, unlike other victims of sacrifice in tragedy, is that she dies to save a city other than her own.

Two recent studies have called attention to the dynamic interrelationship between gender and politics in this play. Daniel Mendelsohn has emphasized that Heracles' daughter assumes a male role, as she proclaims her readiness to die "by standing by her sacrifice" (παρίστασθαι σφαγῆι, 502), recalling the vow taken by Athenian ephebes never to abandon their comrade-in-arms (παραστάτης).[114] Through her identification with the ephebe, the ideal citizen-to-be, she offers "a model of correct and appropriate civic boldness" in contrast to the male characters, Demophon and Iolaus, who fall short of resolving the obstacles that surface and fail to discharge their civic obligations correctly.[115]

David Roselli has argued further that female sacrifice constitutes a site for negotiating the disparity of status within the ranks of Athenian citizens:

> The play glorifies a subordinate character whose contradictory social status (both subordinate and elite) embodies the social position of other "marginal" members of Athenian society. The play stages a model for taking political action to transform the social system and for commemorating the tragic costs of such undertakings.[116]

Marginal voices and gendered discourse indeed contribute to the production of Athenian democratic civic ideology in tragedy, as critics have shown.[117] But the identity of Heracles' daughter as a non-Athenian (which neither Mendelsohn nor Roselli examines)[118] looms large, and her agency as a female savior also shapes the play's discourse on hegemony. Through her sacrifice, Heracles' daughter extends the praise normally reserved for Athens to include the contributions made by non-Athenians and claims a similar measure of recognition for those who did not properly belong to the *polis*.

Female sacrifice on behalf of the city constitutes an anomaly: a woman comes forth in public and assumes a role ordinarily assigned to men, thus transgressing female normative duties. Taking the initiative to appear in public, Heracles' daughter first defends her right to speak before her Athenian hosts. She does so by addressing the limits that social norms imposed upon women's participation in the privileged public sphere. Upon emerging from the temple of Zeus, where Alcmene and the other female members of Heracles' family had taken refuge (40–44), she immediately seeks to forestall her hosts' criticism:[119]

προσθῆτε· πρῶτον γὰρ τόδ᾽ ἐξαιτήσομαι·
γυναικὶ γὰρ σιγή τε καὶ τὸ σωφρονεῖν
κάλλιστον εἴσω θ᾽ ἥσυχον μένειν δόμων.
τῶν σῶν δ᾽ ἀκούσας, Ἰόλεως, στεναγμάτων
ἐξῆλθον, οὐ ταχθεῖσα πρεσβεύειν γένους,
ἀλλ᾽, εἰμὶ γάρ πως πρόσφορος, μέλει δέ μοι
μάλιστ᾽ ἀδελφῶν τῶνδε κἀμαυτῆς πέρι,
θέλω πυθέσθαι μὴ ᾽πὶ τοῖς πάλαι κακοῖς
προσκείμενόν τι πῆμα σὴν δάκνει φρένα. (474–483)

Strangers, please do not consider my coming out to be overbold: this is the first indulgence I shall ask. I know that for a woman silence is best, and modest behavior, and staying quietly within doors. But since I heard your anguished words, Iolaus, I have come out. I have not, to be sure, been designated the family's most important member, but since I am in some way fit to hear this and since I care greatly about my brothers and myself, I wish to ask whether some new misfortune on top of our old troubles is vexing your mind.

Heracles' daughter adopts a cautious attitude before her Athenian hosts, wary of offending them by coming forth to speak in the presence of an all-male cast.[120] She acknowledges that her exit violates the norms of silence, self-restraint, and seclusion that women ought to observe (476–477).[121] As Iolaus had mentioned in the prologue, the female members of the group had taken refuge inside the temple of Zeus. Heracles' daughter, however, is able to account for her boldness by stressing her concern for her siblings, arguing that she has come out after hearing Iolaus' cries to find out whether further suffering is in store for Heracles' children.[122] At the same time, she acknowledges that her exit extends the limits of propriety beyond what was deemed socially acceptable.[123]

Her apology serves as preamble (πρῶτον γὰρ τόδ' ἐξαιτήσομαι, "this is what I will ask for first," 475) for the role that she undertakes to play on behalf of her family as she proclaims herself a self-appointed, yet legitimate ambassador (οὐ ταχθεῖσα . . . / . . . εἰμὶ γὰρ πως πρόσφορος, 479–480).[124] Women could not represent themselves or their families in public in an official capacity. Through her speech she lays strong claims to her ability to represent the suppliants before choosing her lot. Her initial transgression of gender boundaries thus paradoxically establishes her authority to speak on the suppliants' behalf.

Her role as female savior becomes progressively fused with her identity as a non-Athenian. Heracles' daughter negotiates her civic marginality by manipulating gender norms. Women offer an apt model for expressing at once civic marginality and belonging, since they themselves possessed an in-between status in Athenian society.[125] Placed in charge of the domestic sphere, they dispensed roles that were hierarchically subordinate to those of Athenian males.[126] Women occupied an intermediate position between the citizen and the foreigner; they were nominally enfranchised but could not participate in political decision-making.[127] Their civic contributions, however, were acknowledged, especially in the religious and ritual spheres.[128] As such, female characters offer an appropriate model for the partial (and symbolic) integration of marginal groups, especially foreigners whose civic standing tragedy articulates in positive terms by highlighting their religious ties with Athens.[129]

Building upon the work of Arlene Saxonhouse (1992), who argues that women in tragedy can offer both positive and negative models of civic action, symbolic of the forces that threaten ("diversity") or alternatively those that support the civic entity ("unity"), the agency of Heracles' daughter as a woman can be seen as forging a path toward mediating and repairing the crisis that has emerged between the city and the suppliants. Her marginality as a woman and as a foreigner redefines the dynamics of the suppliants' relationship with Athens. As such, her apology for transgressing gender norms is rhetorically and politically effective. Assuming the role of spokesperson for the group, she is able to articulate the suppliants' contribution to the city's salvation. She deploys familiar topoi from the funeral oration and represents her sacrifice as an act of civic heroism, akin to those of Athenians who died in battle.

## FEMALE SACRIFICE AND THE ATHENIAN FUNERAL ORATION

Victims of sacrifice in Euripides' plays of voluntary self-sacrifice adopt a heroic stance *de rigueur*, aspiring to obtain a share of men's civic glory. To this end, they routinely renounce marriage, the proper *telos* of a woman's life, in exchange for a glorious death.[130] Iphigenia, who trades a high-status marriage with Achilles for glory: ταῦτα γὰρ μνημεῖά μου/διὰ μακροῦ, καὶ παῖδες οὗτοι καὶ γάμοι καὶ δόξ' ἐμή ("this is my lasting monument and these my children, my marriage and my glory," E. *IA* 1398–1399), is a case in point. As Foley has argued, sacrificial virgins in tragedy do not fully transcend their normative social roles. Their renunciation of marriage does not so much signal their assumption of a male role. Rather, it represents their agency as unusual, since the critical circumstances in which they find themselves compel them to abandon the private sphere of the *oikos* and become actors in the public realm of the *polis*.

In *Children of Heracles*, however, the maiden's self-sacrifice is modeled closely after the standards of male heroism and emulates the patriotic self-sacrifice of the Athenian hoplites. Heracles' daughter declares her willingness to die by casting herself in the role of a male warrior. After exhorting Iolaus not to fear their Argive enemy any longer (μή νυν τρέσηις ἔτ' ἐχθρὸν Ἀργείων δόρυ, "no longer fear the enemy spear of the Argives," 500), she declares herself ready to die and to "stand by her sacrifice," emphasizing her volition through the use of military language (πρὶν κελευσθῆναι ... θνήισκειν ἑτοίμη καὶ παρίστασθαι σφαγῆι, "before I am ordered ... I am ready to die and stand by for sacrifice," 501–502). The use of the verb παρίστασθαι (502) identifies the maiden as a hoplite standing in the line of battle. This figurative representation not only conveys her penchant for male heroism instead of female passivity but also evokes the ideals of hoplitic warfare.

The assimilation of the voluntary sacrifice of Heracles' daughter to the soldiers' willingness to die in the service of the *polis* is inspired by the exemplary deeds of male heroism, amply documented in the funeral speeches. Self-sacrifice in battle stood as the supreme proof of civic duty and furnishes a template for the acts undertaken by Athenian female civic saviors as well, such as the daughters of Leos and Erechtheus. Among the examples of women's patriotic death, we find the most explicit formulation of the idea that female sacrifice could be regarded as equivalent to soldiers' death in battle in Praxithea's speech in Euripides' *Erechtheus* (Kannicht *TrGFF* 360):

τὰς χάριτας ὅστις εὐγενῶς χαρίζεται,
ἥδιον ἐν βροτοῖσιν· οἱ δὲ δρῶσι μέν,
χρόνωι δὲ δρῶσι, δυσγενέστερον <λέγω>.
ἐγὼ δὲ δώσω παῖδα τὴν ἐμὴν κτανεῖν.

. . . . . . . . . . . .

εἰ δ᾽ ἦν ἐν οἴκοις ἀντὶ θηλειῶν στάχυς
ἄρσην, πόλιν δὲ πολεμία κατεῖχε φλόξ,
οὐκ ἄν νιν ἐξέπεμπον εἰς μάχην δορός,
θάνατον προταρβοῦσ᾽; ἀλλ᾽ ἔμοιγ᾽ εἴη τέκνα (25)
ἃ καὶ μάχοιτο καὶ μετ᾽ ἀνδράσιν πρέποι,
μὴ σχήματ᾽ ἄλλως ἐν πόλει πεφυκότα. (1–4, 22–27)

When someone renders favours in the noble way, it is gratifying to others. When they act but to do so slowly <*this is ill*> bred. I, then, shall give my daughter to be killed. . . . If our family included a crop of male children instead of females, and the flame of war was gripping our city, would I be refusing to send them out to battle for fear of their deaths? No, give me sons who would not only fight but stand out amongst the men and not be mere figures raised in the city to use.[131]

In her speech, Praxithea, wife of King Erechtheus, aims to persuade her husband to consent to the sacrifice of their daughter, demanded by Poseidon, if Athens is to win the war against Eumolpus of Eleusis. Praxithea claims, among other reasons, that women could serve their country in the same capacity as men would.[132] She reasons that as a mother, it is her duty to give up her daughter to the city just as she would have done if she had given birth to sons. As things stand, however, the royal *oikos* stands bereft of male progeny, and so she and the king must assent to their daughter's sacrifice. As John Wilkins aptly notes in connection with this passage: "The contribution of each sex is clear: sacrifice is required of all children of suitable age (and a corresponding sacrifice from parents): eligible boys must stand in the battle-line; eligible girls may be called upon for human sacrifice to promote victory."[133]

Female self-sacrifice, as articulated by Praxithea, is modeled after men's death in battle. The assimilation of female into male acts of heroism in *Children of Heracles*, on the other hand, yields a different message: it represents the sacrifice of a foreigner in a similar light with the civic contributions of those who were Athenian born. Heracles' daughter models her sacrifice upon the ideal ethos of the Athenian citizen hoplite and styles herself as Athens' loyal ally, remitting with her death the tribute due the city for protecting the suppliants. The discourse of civic sacrifice, which permeates her speech, alters the dynamics between the city and the suppliants. For in her self-fashioning as a female heroine, she inverts not only the boundaries between male and female acts of heroism but also those between Athenian and non-Athenian and between citizen and non-citizen. Such crossing of boundaries is achieved rhetorically by appropriating the familiar topoi of the funeral oration, which she thereby integrates within her rationale for consenting to die.[134]

Her decision to die voluntarily evokes the gesture of *prohairesis* ("choice"), which is the central praise addressed to Athenian soldiers in the funeral speech. Rather than praising their exploits on the battlefield, Pericles, notably, commends the fallen for their decision to die (Th. 2.39.4).[135] The maiden's choice to die is also modeled after the *prohairesis* of the Athenian hoplites, as she too declares that she will die to save her siblings and the *polis* before she is ordered to do so. The maiden stands firm by her decision and rejects Iolaus' suggestion that the victim instead be chosen among Heracles' female children by lot (549–551).[136]

The maiden's rationale for the sacrifice is modeled upon the civic biography of the Athenian citizens in the orations, whose virtue and excellence were measured against the accomplishments of their ancestors. For just as the orators began their speeches by extolling the ancestors' nobility as a preamble to the praise of the dead (Th. 2.36.1; Lys. 2.3; Pl. *Mx.* 237a; D. 60.4), so the maiden insists that she must live up to her noble lineage by showing herself a worthy daughter of her father (509–510, 537, 539–541, 563, 626–627); in the *stasimon*, following her exit, the chorus too praise her nobility (625–627). Though references to the victim's nobility draw attention to her aristocratic pedigree, they also distinctly evoke the praise of the ancestors in the funeral oration, making her death worthy of praise and emulation.[137]

Like her male counterparts, she firmly rejects *philopsychia* ("love of life") by arguing that a glorious death is the best option available to her (511–526).

As a female victim, she foregoes the prospect of marriage easily, arguing that her prospects of marrying well stood diminished because she was an exile (522–524). To be sure, the funeral oration eclipsed individual contributions and commemorated the soldiers' equal share in the public eulogy of their civic death. But the Maiden's rejection of an inglorious life vies with the "fine death," prized by the orators, making her deserving of the tribute that the city reserved for Athenian soldiers.

The chorus in the second *stasimon* praise her, as she goes offstage, by using the same topoi: they commend her for deciding to die freely (559); they emphasize that she is acting on behalf of the civic good (621–622) and confirm her nobility and courage (625–637). The praise of her sacrifice by the chorus of old men, residents of Marathon, allows her courage and heroism to be envisioned as carrying on Athens' storied victories. The setting of the play at Marathon evoked the famous victory of the Athenians against the Persians; Marathon was also featured in the catalogue of the ancestors' military exploits, typically recounted at the beginning of the orations.

## SACRIFICE AND HEGEMONY

By according equal praise to all Athenian citizens regardless of their rank, orators leveled distinctions of civic standing among the fallen. Praxithea's speech in *Erechtheus* lends support to the idea that civic contributions ought to be appraised on equal terms, regardless of the sex of the participant. If, however, women's civic sacrifice provides the basis for suspending temporarily gender inequality by allocating equal duties to men and women in the military and civic spheres, the same does not apply to distinctions of status, based on civic origin. Foreigners, Praxithea argues, can never contribute in equal measure with citizens, that is, with those who were native born to another city:

... αἱ δ' ἄλλαι πόλεις
πεσσῶν ὁμοίως διαφοραῖς ἐκτισμέναι
ἄλλαι παρ' ἄλλων εἰσὶν εἰσαγώγιμοι.
ὅστις δ' ἀπ' ἄλλης πόλεος οἰκήσῃ πόλιν,
ἁρμὸς πονηρὸς ὥσπερ ἐν ξύλῳ παγείς,
λόγῳ πολίτης ἐστί, τοῖς δ' ἔργοισιν οὔ ... (Kannicht *TrGFF* 360, 8–13)

... other communities, founded as it were through boardgame moves, are imported, different ones from different places. Now someone who settles in one city from another is like a peg ill fitted in a piece of wood—a citizen in name, but not in his actions. ...

Drawing upon a metaphor from woodworking, she argues that just like a peg that fails to provide a good fit for a piece of wood, so the foreigner turns out to be a bad match for the city. Her strong assertion to this effect—a foreigner is a citizen in name only—is offered as proof for her leading claim that Athens is superior to all other cities on account of the autochthonous origins of her people. Praise of autochthony, a recurrent feature of the patriotic rhetoric of the funeral speeches, is fittingly adapted to the rationale that Praxithea provides for the sacrifice of her daughter. Praxithea's logic, which gives preference to Athenians over foreigners, further exposes the bias inherent in this judgment whereby the foreigner in effect serves as foil for the citizen's superior performance. The assertion of homogeneity, implicit in the myth, relies on the normative model of citizenship, which excluded non-Athenians from civic participation. But its specific formulation in this context is consistent with the celebration of Athens' democratic and egalitarian ethos in the funeral speeches, which praised exclusively the *arete* ("valor, excellence") of the Athenian citizen-soldiers.[138]

Not only Praxithea but also the orators differentiated the contributions of foreigners from those of Athenian citizens. For though foreigners, metics, and allies fought in Athens' battles, their participation is scarcely mentioned. Their absence affirms that their contributions were not regarded as being on par with those who were Athenian born. Since the funeral speeches praised first and foremost the city in its democratic guise, their focus on the deeds of the Athenians denies through a process of elimination some share of this honor to those serving the city in a subordinate or auxiliary capacity.[139] Pericles in his funeral oration (Th. 2.39.2–3) commends the Athenians for fighting their battles unaided and highlights their superiority against the Spartans, who, as he claims, mobilized not only their own army but also that of their allies when they went on military campaigns. Lysias (2.23–24) similarly underplays the allies' military participation, arguing that Athenians did not win any battle with the help of the allies that they could not have won on their own.[140]

For the most part, the funeral speeches avoid mention of Athens' rule over other Greeks and praise Athens' hegemony, as Loraux writes, by "transforming it (i.e., the empire) into a manifestation of Athenian excellence."[141] As a result, the speeches for the most part skew the reality of the empire not only by denying foreigners any share in civic commemoration but also by avoiding any mention of their financial contributions. The allies emerge as beneficiaries of the empire, beholden to Athens by gratitude.

The maiden's decision to die for Athens emerges as an anomalous choice against this background. Her appropriation of the traditional topoi through which orators honored the Athenian fallen heroes goes against the customary practice of excluding foreigners from commemoration in the speeches. Through this kind of emulation she strikes a commanding presence, as for a brief while she vies with male Athenian citizens in the sphere of civic engagement. The maiden's decision presents the sacrifice as a supreme act of heroism akin to the self-sacrifice of Athenian soldiers and worthy of the praise accorded to them by the orators. This kind of representation admittedly broadens the scope of civic praise to include a foreigner, but it does not negate the disparity between citizen and foreigner, as defined by the norms of democratic participation. Instead, the inclusion of the foreigners into the Athenian panegyric is emblematic of the hegemonic outlook of the Athenian suppliant plays, which represent the allies' dependency to the empire in positive terms by recognizing the contributions that the suppliants made to Athens. Heracles' daughter becomes an envoy of Athens' hegemony, as she enunciates the stance befitting the ideal ally:

τί φήσομεν γάρ, εἰ πόλις μὲν ἀξιοῖ
κίνδυνον ἡμῶν οὕνεκ' αἴρεσθαι μέγαν,
αὐτοὶ δὲ προστιθέντες ἄλλοισιν πόνους,
παρόν σφε σῶσαι, φευξόμεσθα μὴ θανεῖν;
οὐ δῆτ', ἐπεί τοι καὶ γέλωτος ἄξια,
στένειν μὲν ἱκέτας δαιμόνων καθημένους,
πατρὸς δ' ἐκείνου φύντας οὐ πεφύκαμεν
κακοὺς ὁρᾶσθαι· ποῦ τάδ' ἐν χρηστοῖς πρέπει; (503–510)

For what shall we say if this city is willing to run great risks on our behalf, and yet we, who place toil on others, run away from death when it is possible for us to save them? For it is surely worth of mockery if we sit and groan as suppliants of the gods and yet, though we are descended from such a father as ours, are seen as cowards. How can this be fitting in the eyes of noble men?

She exhorts the suppliants to show themselves worthy of the risk, which Athens is willing to entertain on their behalf. She argues that her sacrifice is the only fitting response to the great risks that Athens is willing to undertake on their behalf. In urging her own sacrifice to support her choice, she affirms the city's willingness to defend Heracles' children. Her exhortation echoes the chorus' earlier words, as they praise their city for undertaking myriad toils on behalf of others (329–331).[142] But Heracles' daughter also underscores suppliants' obligation to contribute to Athens' venture (503–506). Her intervention realigns the course of the plot with the ideal depiction of Athens as a hegemonic city. This is achieved largely through a reciprocal exchange of "toils":

those undertaken by the city and those Athens enjoins upon the suppliants to accept.

The terms of the exchange dictate an active negotiation of consent on the part of the subordinate group. At the same time, the play coopts the voice of the foreigner and thereby suppresses its potential for articulating protest and dissent. The play acknowledges the contributions of the suppliants, effecting thereby a nominal recognition of the participation of foreigners and allies in Athens' imperial enterprise. The emphasis on the suppliants' contribution to their own and their city's salvation is born out of the same historical realities that prompted Pericles to characterize Athens' rule as akin to tyranny (Th. 2.63.2), as he urged his fellow-citizens to go to war against the Spartans. *Children of Heracles* also attempts to come to grips with the problems which imperial domination had already produced. The play sets in relief the unequal distribution of power between Athens and her allies by acknowledging the sacrifices that war required not only of the Athenians, but also of the allies. But on the ideological level, it also dramatizes scenarios in which the allies are offered choices; these choices are not free of constraints. The outcomes, however, are negotiated, not imposed, and though Athens sets the terms of the exchange, such outcomes uphold the promise of Athens' hegemonic ideals.

The battle lends further evidence of the suppliants' military contributions as allies. Significantly, it is their contributions that receive special mention in the messenger's speech. He reports to Alcmene that Hyllus, Heracles' oldest son, led an allied army into battle and that he challenged Eurystheus to single combat (800–818). The Argive king's refusal underscores his cowardice and Hyllus' bravery (815–817). Second, Iolaus too plays a key role in the battle.[143] Praying to Heracles and Hebe to grant him his former strength for one day, riding on Hyllus' chariot, he succeeds in capturing Eurystheus (843–863). Both Hyllus and Iolaus, then, are prominent in the battle, proving themselves to be worthy allies, and set up the trophy at the site of the battle (786–787, 936–937). Their eagerness to avenge themselves against Eurystheus explains the key role they play in this battle, especially in light of the play's final shift to Alcmene's revenge against Eurystheus.[144] But as Athens' mythical foreign allies, they are granted unusual prominence in the battle narrative.[145]

### EURYSTHEUS: SAVIOR AND HERO

The end of the play lends support to Pericles' view that the war against Sparta had to be fought to support the empire and makes a clear statement that Athens was morally superior to her foe by juxtaposing Athens' generosity towards Heracles' children with the later ingratitude of their descendants, the

Spartans; the Spartans, who, as Eurystheus says in his prophecy (1027–1037) before his death,[146] failed to recognize their debt to Athens.[147] Eurystheus' prophecy operates on a number of levels of ideological signification, which tie together the different facets of Athens' image as benevolent *hegemon*, as the play draws to its end:

κτεῖν', οὐ παραιτοῦμαί σε· τήνδε δὲ πτόλιν,
ἐπεί μ' ἀφῆκε καὶ κατῃδέσθη κτανεῖν,
χρησμῶι παλαιῶι Λοξίου δωρήσομαι,
ὃς ὠφελήσει μεῖζον' ἢ δοκεῖ χρόνωι.
θανόντα γάρ με θάψεθ' οὗ τὸ μόρσιμον,
δίας πάροιθε παρθένου Παλληνίδος·
καὶ σοὶ μὲν εὔνους καὶ πόλει σωτήριος
μέτοικος αἰεὶ κείσομαι κατὰ χθονός,
τοῖς τῶνδε δ' ἐκγόνοισι πολεμιώτατος,
ὅταν μόλωσι δεῦρο σὺν πολλῆι χερὶ
χάριν προδόντες τήνδε· τοιούτων ξένων
προύστητε. (1027–1037).

Kill me, I do not beg you not to. But as for this city, since it spared me and refrained from killing me, I shall make a present to it of an ancient oracle of Loxias, an oracle that will in time be a greater benefit than it seems. For you will bury me in the place I was fated to lie, in front of the shrine of the divine maiden, Athena Pallene. I shall lie for all time beneath the earth, a foreign visitor who is kindly to you and a savior of the city but most hostile to the descendants of Heracles' children when they come here with a powerful army, betraying the kindness you showed them. Such are the guests you protected.

His prophecy links the aftermath of the supplication with the return of Heracles' children, which is mentioned twice in the play (310–311, 873–888). Eurystheus invokes the Spartans' ancient debt (1036) to the Athenians to highlight their ingratitude toward the Athenians in the present.

Unlike their rivals, the Athenians come off better in keeping score and reciprocating the favors they have incurred. The telescoping of past and future in Eurystheus' prophecy thus alters the dynamics, which underlie the relationship between Athens and the former suppliants. The change of roles between friend and enemy is conveyed through a concomitant shift in the genealogical register, which defines the Heraclids' ties with Athens as suppliants to those that link them with Sparta by highlighting their Dorian connections. The identification of the Heraclids with the Spartans sets the stage for his change of allegiance, as he pledges his loyalty toward the Athenians in light of their shared enmity toward the Spartans.

His conversion from enemy to hero accords well with the current events at the beginning of the Archidamian War. Eurystheus' paradoxical conversion into friend and ally of Athens sets in relief the constancy of Athens' commitment to her hegemonic ideals. Eurystheus' role as Athens' ally is consistent with his earlier one: as a hero, he will continue to inflict harm upon those who harmed him.[148] His violent death at the hands of Alcmene provides justification for his persistent hostility: his violent death will not be avenged, and he describes himself as "a victim demanding vengeance" (προστρόπαιον, 1015).[149] Eurystheus' transformation from inimical foreigner to savior-hero resembles that of Oedipus and the Furies in *OC* and in *Eumenides*. Like the Furies, who become residents of Athens after accepting Athena's offer of *metoikia* ("residency"), Eurystheus emphasizes his religious and civic status. He will lie under Attic soil as "a foreign visitor," a savior, favorable to Athens (1033). The aetiology thus brings his personal enmity toward Heracles' children in line with Athenian interests. Against the background of the Spartans' ingratitude, Eurystheus' conversion from enemy to hero endorses Athens' perspective, as another foreigner lends his voice to defend her moral standards.

## PUNISHING EVIL: EURIPIDES' *SUPPLIANT WOMEN*

As a coda to the discussion of *Children of Heracles*, I turn next briefly to Euripides' *Suppliant Women* to highlight the play's contribution to an understanding of the development of Athenian hegemonic ideology. In *Children of Heracles* and *Suppliant Women* Athens fights to defend the cause of foreign suppliants, based on a different set of motives. King Demophon in *Children of Heracles* seeks to ascertain the primacy of the city's interests—a position compatible with that of Pericles, who stressed the necessity of war for the survival of the empire (Th. 1.140–144). Theseus, Athens' king in *Suppliant Women*, aligns his role as "chastiser of evils" with Athens' pursuit of just causes (339–349).[150] When Adrastus, king of Argos, first requests Theseus' assistance in the war against Thebes, Theseus refuses on the grounds that Argos' war against Thebes was wrong. Significantly, the play's claim that democracy and the rule of law alone guarantee protection from injustice[151] carries the burden of articulating Athens' moral hegemony, distancing Theseus' city from the palpable distortion of these claims in the 420s.[152] At this time, Cleon's proposals carried the day in the Assembly, advising the Athenians to cast off emotion when making decisions on policy matters and reminding them, as he did in the debate on the fate of Mytilene, that democracy and empire ought to stand firmly apart from each other (Th. 3.37.1–2).

As a key expression of the Athenian panegyric, Euripides' suppliant plays offer critical insights into how the Athenians negotiated their image as benevolent leaders against that of cruel imperialists imputed against them. Euripides' *Children of Heracles* provides a fuller picture of the way in which Athens' hegemonic ideals began to change. His *Suppliant Women*, however, articulates emphatically that democracy as the rule of law underpins the empire. This is paralleled in Sophocles' *Oedipus at Colonus* (and is germane to the characterization of Theseus, the archetypical democratic king). Euripides' *Suppliant Women* thus allows us to trace another stage in the evolution of Athenian hegemony in the 420s BC.

Regardless of what position one takes on how to read the praise of Athens in the play,[153] its negotiation of the motives that prompt Theseus' and Athens' going to war frame this play's stance toward empire. *Suppliant Women* was performed around 424 BC, a few years after the debate at Mytilene in 427 BC. In *Suppliant Women*, the key debate between pity and self-interest forms the subtext of the negotiation surrounding the evaluation of Adrastus' appeal, as Konstan has shown. Theseus, unlike Aethra, Theseus' mother, who both experiences and finds the Argive mothers to be deserving of pity, focuses initially on considerations of right and wrong and rejects Adrastus' request, since his going to war was not justified (155–249). Aethra next approaches the case from a different angle and exhorts her son to undertake the war against Thebes by following a different tactic and urging to pragmatism by exhorting Theseus' reputation and highlighting the benefits that have accrued to Athens as a result of her past military undertakings (338–341). But Aethra qualifies her argument on moral grounds, appealing as she does to the need for morally principled action. To this effect, she insists that Theseus must act to punish evil and choose a just course by insisting on his duty to uphold the customs of all Greeks (301–313).[154]

Theseus follows Aethra's advice and commits to helping Adrastus and the Argive mothers, seeking first to ratify his decision by consultation with the *demos* (E. *Supp.* 354–358). As Rosenbloom puts it: "In Euripides' *Suppliants*, the equivalence of panhellenic laws and democratic decree underwrites institutions of democracy and empire that defined themselves in terms of the rule of law and legal justice. Athens imposed Councils selected by lot on *poleis* and laws and legal jurisdiction on subject cities."[155]

As Rosenbloom shows further in his analysis of this play, Theseus' defense of democracy highlights the privileges that it imparts to all citizens, poor and rich alike. While democracy guarantees freedom (353, 403–405), justice (433–437), equality, and participation in decision-making (352–353, 406–408), tyranny, as Theseus argues, negates freedom and precludes access for all to the law and to right of free speech (438–441). The attack on tyranny not only holds true for the antithesis between Thebes and Athens in Theseus' speech but also emerges in his rationale for rejecting Adrastus' plea, refusing to go to war and ally his city with a cause he deems unjust and insolent and hence not deserving of Athens' support (220–249). But Aethra's arguments, as we have seen, succeed in imposing a different view, when she argues that in helping victims of injustice, Theseus and Athens would uphold the divine imperative of burial, a law common to all Greeks.

The play unites the city's hegemonic mission with its democracy, whose laws aimed to ensure the protection of the weak and the defenseless against those who violate them (511–512, 574–577). Thus, by preventing the Thebans from violating the common laws of Greece, Athens earns in return a glorious reputation and abiding gratitude for her righteous interventions (1165–1179). The play concludes with Athena's appearance as *dea ex machina* ("goddess from the machine") announcing a defensive alliance between Athens and Argos (1183–1200)—and here again we see the consistency with which suppliant plays highlight the exchange of benefits between Athens and the suppliants.[156]

As opposition to the empire continued to mount, the message of Athens' moral hegemony turned more defensive: it sought to highlight morality, not gains, as its primary motive—a message that continued to fluctuate— illuminating the process through which the plays continued to adapt the core message of hegemonic ideology against the changing realities of Athens' rule.

CHAPTER 4

# HEGEMONY IN CRISIS:
## SOPHOCLES' *OEDIPUS AT COLONUS*

Sophocles' *Oedipus at Colonus*, the last of the Athenian suppliant plays, dates to ca. 407/6 BC[1] and dramatizes the reception of the suppliant Oedipus by Theseus shortly before his death and heroization at the end of the play.[2] Composed close to the end of the Peloponnesian War that marked the empire's defeat by Sparta and her allies, the play at once constitutes a panegyric of Athens and raises a host of questions pertaining to the character of this panegyric. At the heart of the play is the treatment of outsiders, a concern directly relevant to the praise of Athens' piety.

As we have seen, the reception of strangers was broadly regarded a measure of individual and collective piety, and the reception of the suppliant Oedipus tackles this issue from a variety of angles.[3] The treatment of suppliants, for example, was relevant to the opening of the hostilities between Athens and Sparta. At the beginning of the Peloponnesian War, both Athens and Sparta used instances of the violation of asylum as negative propaganda to cast aspersions on their opponent's morality and values.[4] Similarly, Athens' compassion toward the suppliant Oedipus furnished a strong argument in support of her conduct during the war and to justify her actions by claiming that Athenians had consistently offered their assistance to those who sought their protection.

Oedipus fits the portrait of the suffering stranger probably more than any other character in tragedy.[5] At the end of the *Oedipus Tyrannus*, following the revelation of his own identity and his crimes against his closest of kin — the murder of his father, Laius and his marriage with his mother, Jocasta — Oedipus blinds himself and decides to leave Thebes an exile. When he arrives at Colonus with Antigone at the beginning of the play, he first presents himself as a wanderer and beggar (1–2) and emphasizes his prolonged suffering. Oedipus, however, is no ordinary beggar and soon his identity begins to be drawn in accordance to the Athenian panegyric.

Significantly, the progress of Oedipus' integration in this play addresses

Athens' reputation as a pious city. Theseus' portrait as a leader affirms the principles that underwrite Athens' hegemony. His eagerness to protect the suppliant from suffering outrage at the hands of the Theban Creon endorses the ideal image of Athens as a city that helps the weak and punishes the insolent.[6]

Oedipus' reception is similar to that of other foreigners in the other suppliant plays we have examined — Orestes, Eurystheus, and the Furies — whom Athens annexed in the capacity of allies, as he too offers the city benefits as a token of his loyalty and gratitude. Nevertheless, the image of the city's openness toward foreigners is challenged in the course of the exile's reception. The *peripeteia* of the suppliant plot, which begins when the chorus bid the exile to leave Colonus, thwarts the progress of asylum. The chorus next initiate a stringent procedure, to evaluate Oedipus' supplication on account of his pollution, which is at odds with the city's reputation for piety. Only after Oedipus reveals to Theseus the future benefits that lie in store for his city does the Athenian king offer Oedipus a home in Athens by making him a citizen. The negotiation of his reception relates his pollution, which hinders his reception and threatens to undermine Athens' praise, to the requirements of admitting foreigners as naturalized citizens.

As in the other suppliant plays, the dramatic crisis mobilizes a dialectic between the ideal of the city's openness and the necessity of inscribing limits to foreigners' reception. The chorus at first are not willing to accept the polluted stranger and instead take steps to guard themselves and the city against his defilement. The emerging crisis articulates from the outset specific limits to Oedipus' integration that impede the enactment of Athens' cherished ideals. The exigencies arising from pollution register a heightened tension between ideal and reality.

The play also affords a closer look at the contradiction that underlies the collocation of democracy and empire in Athenian imperial ideology. As in Euripides' suppliant plays, imperial ideology readily made use of democratic precepts such as justice and the law to justify Athens' power and mitigate its enforcement, enabling in this way what we may call the manufacturing of consent. At the ideological level, the treatment of Oedipus as polluted foreigner points to the implicit contradiction between the two facets of Athens' rule, democratic and imperial, whose system of governance was predicated on the exclusion on non-Athenians and the allies. The confrontation between the city and the foreigner, I suggest, shows signs of a deeper crisis. The constraints imposed upon Athens' ideals in this play point to the decline of Athens' hegemonic ideology at the end of the Peloponnesian War.[7]

We witness a shift from Aeschylus' *Eumenides*, which celebrates the height of Athens' power. Oedipus' reception differs noticeably from that of Orestes and the Furies. The change is palpable if we compare Athena's impassioned plea to the Furies to become her civic partners with Oedipus' elaborate argumentation by means of which he strives to persuade the chorus that he is worthy of admission. In *Oedipus at Colonus*, the resolution contrived to overcome his pollution aligns his reception more closely with the stringent requirements for citizenship and naturalization, prescribed by Athenian law, than do any of the other plays.[8] As such, Oedipus' reception as a foreigner registers far more directly an underlying tension between hegemonic ideology and democratic practice. By this I mean that the foreigner's exclusion is entertained as an alternative, though it conflicts with Athens' image as a city of suppliants. The play reconciles the emergent contrast between hegemonic ideals and democratic norms by treating Oedipus as an exception to the rule. His accession to citizenship is an honor that Theseus grants Oedipus in recognition of his unique contribution. After his reception, Athens' panegyric is far more voluble in the play. But the scrutiny to which Oedipus is made subject undermines confidence in the strength of Athens' ideals.

The play does not succeed in advertising Athens' prestige and power in the same way as, for example, Aeschylus' *Eumenides*. The resistance that Oedipus's reception meets with reflects the progressive weakening of Athenian hegemonic ideology, while Athena's able defense of Orestes reflects the growth of Athens' imperial power. Similarly, Oedipus' standing as a foreigner is far more closely scrutinized, despite the civic benefits that, like Orestes, he promises to confer upon the city. As the Peloponnesian War was coming to an end,[9] the enactment of these ideals falls short of realizing the promise that Athens' leadership had held in the early years of the war.

### EXCLUSION FROM THE GROVE

Like his divine sponsors, the Eumenides of Colonus, who receive their devotee after his death, Oedipus has the ambivalence and marginality that characterize chthonic powers. Oedipus promises Theseus that as a hero he will employ his powers to inflict harm against his own and Athens' enemies. While he is still alive, however, his pollution renders him enormously threatening for the community when he arrives at Colonus. The play articulates the liminality of the hero by characterizing his social marginality as a problem in need of a resolution. Oedipus' standing as a foreigner is far more complex, because his pollution is simultaneously an obstacle to his integration and a mark of his kinship with the goddesses, who inhabit the grove.

The process of Oedipus' integration at Colonus serves as the aetiology for his heroization at the end of the play.[10] The play progressively redefines his marginal standing in a manner beneficial to the city by asserting the priority of his civic integration. To this end, prologue and *parodos* problematize Oedipus' access to the religious space of Colonus and disrupt the process of his religious integration, which Oedipus initiates by supplicating the goddesses.

The opening scenes of the play articulate the problematic contours of Oedipus' status as a foreigner in Athens.[11] Oedipus' reception, staged within a space that was liminal and sacred, aptly expresses the way that the hero's belonging was envisioned. Heroes at large are imagined as being part of the city, yet located in a space apart. The religious cult complex of Colonus Hippius lay at the outskirts of Colonus.[12] The Stranger tells Oedipus that the entire space (χῶρος, 52), including the precinct of the Eumenides, is sacred to Poseidon. Deictic references in the text describe the rest of the stage setting; "this horseman Colonus" (59) and "the name of this man" (61–62) refer to the statue of the founding hero Colonus, which probably stood on the other side of the grove (stage left), closer to the *parodos* that led to Athens.[13] It also contains the brazen-footed Threshold of Athens, an entrance from which Theseus returned from the Underworld (56–57), and the allusion to "this god" probably refers metonymically to the cult complex itself (65, 714–715).[14]

As soon as father and daughter arrive onstage, Antigone describes the place they have come to as a sacred space, brimming with bay, olive, and vines, and a home to sweet-singing nightingales (16–18). No sooner has Oedipus taken a seat to rest after his long journey (11, 21) than a local man (the Stranger), probably a peasant, advises them to leave (36–43), because they have entered a space that is pure, inviolate, and inhabitable (πρὶν νῦν τὰ πλείον' ἱστορεῖν, ἐκ τῆσδ' ἕδρας/ἔξελθ'· ἔχεις γὰρ χῶρον οὐχ ἁγνὸν πατεῖν ... ἄθικτος οὐδ' οἰκητός. αἱ γὰρ ἔμφοβοι/θεαί σφ' ἔχουσι, Γῆς τε καὶ Σκότου κόραι ... Εὐμενίδας, "before you ask me any more questions leave this seat! The ground you occupy cannot be trodden on without pollution ... inviolable ground, which no one can inhabit, sacred to the daughters of Earth and Darkness, ... the Eumenides," 36–37, 39–40, 42).

Though his accidental trespass marks an inauspicious beginning to the suppliant's reception,[15] Oedipus disregards for the moment the Stranger's warning and supplicates the goddesses (84–110). He declares that Apollo had decreed that the grove of the Eumenides would be his refuge and final resting place (89–93).[16] He further stresses the ritual kinship between the goddesses and the suppliant (96–98),[17] noting that he encountered them in a state of sobriety (νήφων) (100).[18] As Albert Henrichs has shown, the Eumenides and the *Semnai Theai* were propitiated in Attica and elsewhere with νηφάλια, "wineless" libations consisting of water mixed with honey.[19] By mirroring winelessness, one of the well-known ritual attributes of the goddesses, Oedipus defines himself as their devotee, seeking to gain their goodwill.[20]

---

Oedipus' supplication is first directed to the goddesses and anticipates his heroization at the end of the play, but this process is temporarily suspended, giving way to the negotiation of his civic reception. As soon as the chorus arrive, his reception takes a different course by concentrating on his "negative" standing as a foreigner: the chorus cast him as a transgressor and an interloper (118–120).[21] They call attention to the fact that he is a foreigner (πλανάτας, "wanderer," 123–124; οὐδ' ἔγχωρος, "an outsider," 124–125; ἀλᾶτα, "vagrant," 165),[22] and though they attribute the defilement he causes to his ignorance of local custom (125–137), they nonetheless regard his behavior as deviant (123–124).[23] They order his departure from the grove out of fear that his defilement may harm the city (152–169).[24]

The first movement of the play therefore disrupts the progress of Oedipus' religious supplication and sets the stage for the negotiation of his civic reception, following the rules of supplication within the secular sphere of the *polis*. As in *Children of Heracles*, the play draws upon contemporary practice[25] — the Stranger tells Oedipus that the local demesmen will decide his petition (τοῖς ἐνθάδ' αὐτοῦ μὴ κατ' ἄστυ δημόταις/λέξω τάδ' ἐλθών. οἵδε γὰρ κρινοῦσί σοι/εἰ χρή σε μίμνειν, ἢ πορεύεσθαι πάλιν, "I will go and speak to the men of the deme here, not to the citizens. They will decide whether you must stay or depart again," 78–80). The chorus whom Oedipus addresses as ἔφοροι χώρας ("guardians of the land," 145) first discharge their duties by guiding Oedipus safely out of the grove, following a path that brings him from the innermost, most sacred part of the grove right to its physical borders.[26]

The careful demarcation of spatial boundaries points up the foreigner's liminality and underscores his "in-between" standing. The chorus designate a new seat for him that lies at the edge of the grove, a place where speech is lawful and no longer sacrilegious (169–170). He is asked to take a seat that is made of natural rock (αὐτοῦ· μηκέτι τοῦδ' αὐτοπέτρου/βήματος ἔξω πόδα κλίνης, "here! do not incline your steps outside this ledge of native rock," 192). This appears to be an in-between zone, in the margins between nature and culture, between the chthonic and earthly realm. The unpolished stone, symbolic of the purity of nature, constitutes the very antithesis of the polished step from which speakers addressed the assembly.[27] Oedipus occupies a position opposite to that of the citizens: he speaks from a marginal location. If we were to block Oedipus' position onstage for a modern production, we could draw a clear line between the grove and the rest of the stage and would define it as an in-between "neutral zone" to demarcate the foreigner's pending status.[28] This first encounter between the chorus and the suppliant anticipates the obstacles surrounding Oedipus' civic reception.

The integration plot reveals a pattern similar to that of other narratives that revolve around the reception and assimilation of foreigners. In many of these, the foreigner figures as a threat and as a source of power. Oedipus fits this pattern clearly: he is at once harmful (pollution) and powerful (savior-hero). As we saw in Chapter 1, the closest example to Oedipus of this pattern is the integration of the Furies in Aeschylus' *Eumenides*, who as outsiders threaten Athens with disease and infertility, but in the end, they accept Athena's honors and become her civic partners, offering many advantages in return. The process of Oedipus' reception also takes stock of the duality that he embodies as threat and boon for the community.

Oedipus' expulsion from the grove and the city distances the drama from the panegyric. At the beginning of the play, Oedipus' dangerous liminality portends harm, not blessings for the city. The full disclosure of his identity (220–225) prompts the chorus to suspend his supplication[29] and to leave the city (233–234), fearing his pollution "lest you fix a greater debt to the city" (235–236).[30] They also reject Antigone's plea (237–253) and refrain from further communication (256–257). Pollution furnished legitimate grounds for denying a foreigner asylum. Oedipus' crimes are extremely polluting: by uniting what must remain separate (incest) and severing ties that must remain intact (parricide), he unleashes danger for the entire community.[31] For the chorus, there is no other alternative for containing Oedipus' pollution than to bar his entry and protect the city against contamination.[32]

Concerns with the suppliants' purity emerge in the other suppliant plays as well. Tragedians depict Athens as the only city able to incorporate polluted suppliants and devise solutions to transcend the risk of contagion[33] and as a haven for those stained by kin murder, which is germane to representing Athens as a city of justice in Aeschylus' *Eumenides*. As Athena's role as judge in that play shows, the city's judicial supremacy was part and parcel of her hegemonic reputation. What is more, in Aeschylus' play, Athens is depicted far more strongly in the role of champion of strangers through the agency of Athena, who founds the lawcourt in response to Orestes' request for asylum. In Sophocles' *Oedipus at Colonus*, Oedipus is not offered the option of a trial; instead, he formulates a defense against his crimes. This plea seeks to establish the legitimacy of his request in the wake of the chorus' rejection of his supplication. There is a subtle but critical shift in the perceptions surrounding Athens' openness toward suppliants. For unlike Athena, who succeeds in thwarting the risk of pollution in *Eumenides*, in this play, the burden of devising a solution lies at first with the suppliant, not with the city.

Oedipus' supplication is not summarily rejected, thanks to the discursive strategy that he chooses.[34] Seeking to temper the chorus' extreme reaction, he defends his "purity" on legal grounds,[35] by arguing against the charge of incest and parricide:

κἄμοιγε ποῦ ταῦτ' ἐστίν, οἵτινες βάθρων
ἐκ τῶνδέ μ' ἐξάραντες εἶτ' ἐλαύνετε,
ὄνομα μόνον δείσαντες; οὐ γὰρ δὴ τό γε
σῶμ' οὐδὲ τἄργα τἄμ'· ἐπεὶ τά γ' ἔργα με
πεπονθότ' ἴσθι μᾶλλον ἢ δεδρακότα,
εἴ σοι τὰ μητρὸς καὶ πατρὸς χρείη λέγειν,
ὧν οὕνεκ' ἐκφοβῇ με· τοῦτ' ἐγὼ καλῶς
ἔξοιδα. καίτοι πῶς ἐγὼ κακὸς φύσιν,
ὅστις παθὼν μὲν ἀντέδρων, ὥστ' εἰ φρονῶν
ἔπρασσον, οὐδ' ἂν ὧδ' ἐγιγνόμην κακός;
νῦν δ' οὐδὲν εἰδὼς ἱκόμην ἵν' ἱκόμην,
ὑφ' ὧν δ' ἔπασχον, εἰδότων ἀπωλλύμην. (263–274)

And where are these things for me, when you made me rise up from this seat of rock you are driving me away, fearing my name alone? For you do not fear my persona nor my person or my actions; since my actions have consisted in suffering rather than doing, if I should mention of the story of my mother and my father, on account of which you are afraid of me. Of this I am certain. Yet in my nature, how am I evil, I who retaliated a wrong against me, so that if I had acted knowingly, not even then would I have been evil? But as it is, I have come to where I came to in all ignorance; but those who wronged me have knowingly ruined me.

His plea stresses his suffering by recounting his problematic past, hoping to gain the chorus' sympathy.[36] But his speech is also tantamount to a legal defense of his crimes. Oedipus sets out to demonstrate that he is a victim rather than an instigator of the crimes (266–267) for which the chorus hold him accountable and does not refrain from naming openly the charges of parricide and incest (268–269).[37]

In his supplication speech, Oedipus emphasizes the paradoxical nature of his predicament and justifies his crimes, as though he were presenting his defense before an Athenian court. The counterfactual condition (εἰ φρονῶν ἔπρασσον, "if I had acted knowingly," 271–272), and the result clause within which it is embedded (ὥστ' . . . οὐδ' ἂν ὧδ' ἐγιγνόμην κακός; "so that . . . not even then would I have been evil?" 271–272), contain two arguments relevant for the refutation of both crimes. Oedipus attempts to undermine the validity of the charges, using his ignorance of his parents' identity as the strongest argument in his favor. He incriminates his mother and father instead for knowingly doing him wrong (ὑφ᾽ ὧν δ᾽ ἔπασχον, εἰδότων ἀπωλλύμην, 274)—an oblique reference to his exposure. Oedipus chooses ignorance of his victims' identity as his main line of defense. Ignorance could serve as grounds for acquittal in an Athenian court, as our sources indicate (e.g., [D.] 59.79–81; D. 23.53; Pl. *Ap.* 25c–26a). Oedipus makes similar claims in the first *stasimon* (οὐδὲν ἴδριν, "ignorant," 525; νόμῳ δὲ καθαρός· ἄιδρις ἐς τόδ᾽ ἦλθον, "I am pure according to the law; I came to this unknowingly," 548) and in the second *epeisodion*, when he defends himself anew against Creon.[38] His plea remains consistent throughout. Provoked later by Creon, he argues that he is guilty of neither incest nor patricide because he did not know who his parents were (ἄκων, "unwittingly," 64; τό γ᾽ ἄκον πρᾶγμ᾽, "unintentionally," 977).

Though Oedipus argues that he is not guilty of parricide, he qualifies the killing of Laius further, claiming that he was retaliating (ἀντέδρων, 271). For an Athenian, Oedipus' description of Laius' murder as retaliation could probably be regarded as an act of self-defense, which MacDowell and Gagarin propose.[39] It could also be placed more broadly within the category of δίκαιος φόνος ("justifiable homicide"). The law, as stated in Demosthenes, applies to a variety of cases (e.g., homicide occurring in athletics, war, self-defense) for which the perpetrator was not subject to punishment and did not incur pollution.[40] Demosthenes' ἐν ὁδῷ καθελών ("killed on the road," 23.53) applies exactly to the circumstances of Laius' murder. In his discussion of the ritual status of the justified killer, Parker characterizes such a person as εὐαγής ("pure") and argues that from a legal point of view, the killer was not considered polluted. When the chorus question Oedipus on his father's murder, he claims that he is pure, according to the law (548).

By rejecting the responsibility for his crimes, Oedipus in effect rejects his guilt. He argues that the chorus' fear of his pollution (269) is based entirely on their belief that he is culpable (κακὸς φύσιν, "evil by nature," 270). The implicit connection between pollution and guilt is a notoriously difficult topic.[41] Plato in the *Laws* (716e–717a), however, relates pollution to morality: ἀκάθαρτος γὰρ τὴν ψυχὴν ὅ γε κακός, καθαρὸς δὲ ὁ ἐναντίος, παρὰ δὲ μιαροῦ δῶρα οὔτε ἄνδρ᾽ ἀγαθὸν οὔτε θεὸν ἔστιν ποτὲ τό γε ὀρθὸν δέχεσθαι. μάτην οὖν περὶ θεοὺς ὁ πολύς ἐστι πόνος τοῖς ἀνοσίοις,/τοῖσιν δὲ ὁσίοις ἐγκαιρότατος ἅπασιν. ("For the evil man is unclean in his soul, while the good man is clean. And it is never proper that any good man or god receive gifts from a polluted person. For the great toil that impious men lavish upon the gods is in vain, though it is most timely for the pious ones.") But, as we have also seen in Chapter 1, penal and ritual restitution did not, for the most part, overlap. Oedipus in his plea defends himself against his guilt to establish the legality of his supplication. To be sure, the source of Oedipus' defilement, incest and parricide, makes his pollution impossible to remove. Even so, like Orestes in Aeschylus' *Eumenides*, Oedipus defends himself on the basis of extenuating circumstances, while ritual restitution for his crimes is not entertained. The purification, which Ismene undertakes soon after (465–509), aims at remedying his unlawful trespass into the grove of the Eumenides, initiating in this way the process of his religious reception, as Walter Burkert has argued.[42]

The next stage of Oedipus' reception is no longer contingent upon the claims of innocence and guilt but is further subject to the norms governing citizenship and naturalization in Athens. The transition from ritual defilement to civic purity enables the process of his reception as a foreigner and a suppliant to move forward.

## A PLEA FOR NATURALIZATION

Oedipus' plea is also relevant to his integration as a foreigner. As in the other Athenian suppliant plays, the crisis of supplication invariably places constraints upon the image of Athens' openness. When the chorus reject Oedipus' supplication, he retorts that their conduct is at variance with Athens' reputation as the most pious city, the one that above all others helps any stranger in distress (258–262).[43] To be sure, the danger of contagion or the threat of war impeded the acceptance of suppliants in real life. The chorus' fear and anxiety make it clear that Oedipus' pollution cannot be disregarded, frustrating as a result an auspicious outcome to his plea for admission. The barrier pollution poses to the suppliant's acceptance, however, also provides the backdrop for exploring the emergent contradiction between Athens' claims to piety and openness against the realities of foreigners' exclusion from civic participation. More specifically, Oedipus next tailors his request for admission by representing himself as a foreigner who brings the city benefits. He thus casts himself as a candidate worthy not only of admission but also of the rare honor of naturalization awarded to Athens' benefactors.

To begin with, Oedipus exhibits an awareness of the limits that his own predicament places upon his reception and at the end of his plea underscores the benefits that will accrue to the city if he is granted asylum. Shifting attention away from his defilement, he describes himself as ἱερὸς, or "partaking in the divine,"[44] εὐσεβής, that is, "reverent toward the gods and the city,"[45] and refers to his civic contribution: ὄνησιν ἀστοῖς τοῖσδ᾽, "an advantage to the citizens here."[46] Sacredness, reverence, and benefits suggest a homology between his religious and civic standing. Oedipus stresses his religious benefaction again in his second appeal to the chorus in the first *epeisodion* (457–460), disclosing its details later when Theseus arrives (551). Only then does Oedipus reveal that he will enlist his supernatural powers against his native Thebes in the service of Athens as a favor to the city, after Theseus' promise to shelter him and oversee his burial (576–628).[47]

The civic significance of his future standing as a hero is especially pronounced in this context because such "benefits" serve as prerequisite for his admission. Viewed within the framework of Athenian institutions, Oedipus fits well the profile of those foreigners whom Athenians naturalized. Benefaction was the only criterion for naturalization in Athenian law. In the fifth century, the law stated that a non-Athenian was eligible for citizenship in return for a singular benefaction: [D.] 59.89: μὴ ἐξεῖναι ποιήσασθαι Ἀθηναίων, ὃν ἂν μὴ δι' ἀνδραγαθίαν εἰς τὸν δῆμον τὸν Ἀθηναῖον ἄξιον ᾖ γενέσθαι πολίτην ("that it not be permitted to grant citizenship to anyone who is not worthy of becoming a citizen on account of some extraordinary act of valor"). Such an honor was as a rule bestowed to those who made significant financial, political, or diplomatic contributions.[48] The military protection that Oedipus offers as a hero can be seen as the equivalent of an ἀνδραγαθία ("an extraordinary act of valor"). Oedipus' reception is tailored to the actual requirements for naturalization in terms that would probably appear as legally binding to an Athenian audience.

## CITIZEN OEDIPUS

The question of Oedipus' accession to citizenship is significant for evaluating the implications of the Athenian panegyric in this play. As in the other suppliant plays, the tensions that emerge between ideology and practice lie at the heart of the negotiation of Athens' hegemonic ideals. In this light, I suggest that Oedipus' adoption as ἔμπολις ("citizen") resolves nominally Athens' ambivalence toward the foreigner by contriving a resolution that attempts to bring into congruence Athens' ideology of openness and generosity toward non-Athenians with the requirements imposed by the Athenian laws of citizenship. The marginality of the foreigner, however, looms large in the background, and the resolution contrived in the end brings into the open the very tension that it seeks to mask.

Theseus' gesture of accepting the suppliant Oedipus as a citizen becomes emblematic of the ideology of Athenian piety, openness, and compassion towards foreigners that the play overtly promotes.[49] Oedipus is the only non-Athenian in tragedy who acquires the status of citizen (ἔμπολις), even though he is an immigrant. One of the heavily debated questions in Sophocles' *Oedi-*

*pus at Colonus*, however, is whether Oedipus becomes a citizen in Athens or not. Admission into citizenship becomes crucial for assessing the relationship between Athens and foreigners, since non-Athenians were rarely naturalized in fifth-century Athens.

Reference to Athenian institutions must be further contextualized within the dramatic and ideological coordinates of the play. Oedipus' standing as a foreigner is not only a matter of civic origin. His indelible pollution makes him an outsider in any community. The Thebans will not allow him to live in the city, even if he were to return (781–790). Oedipus himself denies Theseus' offer to go to Athens as his guest for the same reason (638–641, 643–644). In Athens, the pollution that attaches to Oedipus is rendered relevant to his heroic destiny. As a hero, his association with the Eumenides, the chthonic deities of the grove at Colonus, necessitates his segregation from the civic realm. But his marginality is also negotiated in relation to his standing as a foreigner. Thus, when he pleads for asylum, he pledges such benefits to Athens as would make any foreigner worthy of admission to the city. For this reason, it is possible that Oedipus' new status as ἔμπολις may have been chosen to convey Oedipus' unique standing: a naturalized foreigner who, owing to the special quality that attaches to his destiny through his unintentional pollution, is relegated to a space apart.

When Theseus announces his decision, he gives three reasons for accepting the exile into the city (631–637): the amicable relations between Athens and Thebes ἡ δορύξενος κοινὴ παρ' ἡμῖν αἰέν ἐστιν ἑστία, "the hearth of a spear-ally is always open to him," 632–633),[50] his status as a suppliant (ἔπειταδ' ἱκέτης δαιμόνων ἀφιγμένος, "he has arrived as a suppliant of the gods," 634) and his anticipated contribution to the welfare of Athens (γῇ τῇδε κἀμοὶ δασμὸν οὐ σμικρὸν τίνει, "he is contributing no small gift to this land and to me," 635). Of the three motives, the last one seals the offer of citizenship and, thereupon, Theseus announces Oedipus' reception (636–637): ἀγὼ σέβας θεὶς οὔποτ' ἐκβαλῶ χάριν/τὴν τοῦδε, χώρᾳ δ' ἔμπολιν κατοικιῶ ("for these things I have respect, and I shall never reject his kindness, but I shall settle him in the country as a dweller in the city"). Theseus refers to Oedipus by using the term χάρις, which in this context has religious overtones.[51] Taken together with the verb κατοικίζω ("settle") in the following line, it refers to Oedipus' religious status as a hero and his tomb at Colonus.

The offer of citizenship is the outcome of an ideal exchange, based on reciprocity. Oedipus' religious χάρις ("favor") earns him his reception as ἔμπολις ("dweller, insider"). The term χάρις ("favor") is here used metonymically to refer to Oedipus' religious identity as a hero.[52] His reception is tailored to the actual requirements for naturalization in terms that would probably appear as legally binding to an Athenian audience. His citizenship is nonetheless purely honorary, just as the award of citizenship was for the few illustrious foreigners who were naturalized by the Athenians. His honorary standing, however, does not remedy the exile's marginality but brings it into congruence with the play's panegyric.

I discuss the technical aspects of the rare term ἔμπολις in the Appendix to this chapter. But it is important to note briefly here as well that ἔμπολις denotes primarily physical belonging, not active participation. Outside Sophocles' play, it is attested through Pollux's gloss in a fragment of Eupolis ([fr. 492 PCG 5], Pollux (9.27): τὸν δὲ ἀστὸν Εὔπολις ἔμπολιν εἴρηκεν, οἷον ἐγχώριον, ἐντόπιον ("Eupolis refers to the town-dweller as a city-resident, namely, as though he were one of the local inhabitants"). The equivalence of ἔμπολις with ἀστός, ἐγχώριος, and ἐντόπιος would suggest that Oedipus becomes an "insider," in the sense that he now belongs to the *polis*. In dramatic terms, the status of ἔμπολις (ὁ ἐν πόλει) denotes that Oedipus ceases to be ἄπολις and ἀπόπτολις and that he will be now part of the Athenian community. Given how rare the usage of the word is, it is possible that Sophocles created or selected this word precisely to define Oedipus' status with a term that fused the paradox of his unique standing: his Athenian identity is represented by a term that conveys the honors that Athens is able to bestow upon a foreigner with Oedipus' heroic destiny by remedying his plight as an exile.

The choice of this particular term, however, also fits Oedipus' inherent marginality. To begin with, Oedipus' membership to the city remains nominal; his physical membership, on the other hand, is concretely expressed through his tomb, the site of his cult worship. Since he is relegated into the sacred grove of the Eumenides and occupies a liminal position, the term ἔμπολις aptly defines both facets of his Athenian identity as citizen and hero. The city remedies his permanent exclusion by embracing his marginality and affirming his kinship with the Eumenides. Oedipus is no ordinary foreigner and the dramatist may have chosen this particular term to express his belonging in manner apposite to Oedipus' unique destiny.[53] His reception as citizen sanctions his contributions and affirms Theseus' gesture of accepting one of the most heavily defiled characters in tragedy.

## LIMITS TO ENTRY?

The contours of Oedipus' standing as citizen (foreigner) and hero (ally) define the Athenian identity of this heavily defiled hero. In this play, pollution acquires ideological valence as well, that is, it furnishes a trope for articulating foreigners' secondary standing in Athens. As such, the outbreak of the crisis brings to the fore the limits of Athens' inclusivity and casts doubt upon Athens' professed commitment to remedying the suffering of others.[54] The shortfall between ideology and practice registers a deeper anxiety about Athens' power than do the earlier suppliant plays.

The historical context of the play offers some indication in this regard. It is difficult to identify how specific historical events impinge upon the hegemonic image of Athens in this play, since the precise date of the play's composition is unknown and since the period between that date (probably 407/6 BC) and its first performance in 401 BC, which postdates Sophocles' death, also followed Athens' defeat by Sparta in 404 BC. Even so, the challenge to Athens' piety in the play, which Oedipus addresses to the chorus (258–262), also suggests that Athens was less able to live up to the strength of her ideals.

The ongoing war had tested Athens' financial and military capacity, and in the wake of the disaster at Sicily in 413 BC, Athenians found themselves less eager to support a war for the same reasons, which had prompted them earlier to fight to maintain their rule. Athenian citizens, rich and poor alike, had been eager to continue reaping the wealth and prosperity that had accrued to Athens and its democracy until the 420s BC as a result of the expansion of Athens' rule.[55] Then, a different reality had begun to emerge. The mounting costs of war forced Athenians to exhaust their reserves and compelled them in 411 BC to suspend temporarily full constitutional rights to all Athenians to reduce public payments for office, when other fiscal measures had failed to procure the funds necessary for military expenditures.[56] The oligarchic revolution of 411 restricted Athenian citizens' eligibility for office and suspended public pay.[57]

Though scholars have argued for a more narrow connection between the events of 411 and the play, owing to its setting at Colonus, where the first Assembly met in 411 in the precinct of Colonus Hippius (Th. 8.67.2), their impact on the ideological framing of Athens' praise acquires broader resonance in the play.[58] For in addition to the internal political pressures, the empire also faced an increasingly high rate of desertion on the part of the allies, and at the same time, the Spartans' presence in Decelea had brought the war in close proximity to Athens.[59] Despite the difficulty in identifying correspondences between historical events and Athens' hegemonic image in this play, the contradiction between democracy and empire is more pronounced than in the earlier suppliant plays and is symptomatic of a less robust ideology. Indeed, the emphasis on the suppliant's role in procuring benefits shows indirectly the Athenians' changing stance toward the empire. Though ideology is resistant to change, the enactment of Athens' ideals takes stock of the attenuation of Athens' power (though Athens had gained some victories at the time).[60] The balance sheet of the empire was by now more costly, and the ongoing war had become detrimental to the city and its democracy.

By way of concluding the discussion on Oedipus' standing as a foreigner, I submit that his designation as ἔμπολις ("citizen," "insider") attempts to resolve the emergent tension between foreigners' exclusion from the polity and the demands posed by hegemonic ideology. Even so, the effort expended in defining Oedipus' reception in accordance with the actual norms of naturalization stretches the limits of the ideals that the city purports to uphold. In the end, Oedipus' accession to citizenship reinforces the very limits that Athens' commitment to openness seeks to transcend. The process of his reception underscores the disparity of his standing vis-à-vis his Athenian hosts and defines clear limits to the privileges that foreigners could lay claim to in Athens. The uncertainty surrounding Athens' capacity to lend her support freely and unconditionally begins to reflect a sense of anxiety about the viability of her hegemonic commitments and the status of the empire.

## ATHENS AND THE SUFFERING OF OTHERS

The help that Athens lent Heracles' children and Adrastus and the Argive mothers when they sought it, celebrated by playwrights and orators alike, let Athens advertise its superiority to all other cities by commending her conduct on behalf of the wronged, the destitute, and the oppressed. The enactment of the Athenian panegyric in this play is closely patterned after such celebrated myths; in like fashion, the play's panegyric highlights the city's selfless dedication to remedying the suffering of others, especially when their suffering is the outcome of political hostility and persecution.[61] The story of Oedipus was not part of the regular repertory of the suppliant stories in the funeral speeches (only Demosthenes makes mention of Oedipus' reception [18.186]). In fashioning the story of Oedipus in Athens, Sophocles aligned his earlier treatment of the myth in a manner apposite to Athens' panegyric. The praise of Athens then dictates to a large extent Oedipus' story in Athens. First, Oedipus himself gradually shifts the emphasis away from his pollution and redefines the story of his exile from Thebes as the outcome of an intrafamilial political strife. This sets in motion the familiar enactment of the topos of Athens' praise, as Oedipus and Theseus enact the parts of the weak and outraged suppliant and compassionate, magnanimous king respectively; the latter defends the suppliant against Creon, when he attempts to force Oedipus' return to Thebes against his will.

But the praise accorded the Athenian king for his pity, justice, and flexibility fails to convince. Rather, it reproduces in formulaic fashion the exaggerated praise of Athenian ideals by the orators who praised the city's commitment to moral causes. Unlike the other suppliant plays in which the suppliant's reception is actively negotiated against such ideals and lends a distinctive image of Athens' hegemonic capacities, in this play the panegyric of Athens as a pious city reproduces its contours mechanically.

As the war progressed, the earlier justifications of Athens' power were no longer felt to be necessary. Instead, the praise of Athens' piety may have served to soften the negative impression of her conduct during the war by commending Theseus' city for its steadfast commitment to morally principled action. Respect for suppliants had been, as we have seen, a live concern at the beginning of the war, when both Athens and Sparta claimed the moral high ground by casting aspersions against one another for the treatment of suppliants.

Given that the true objectives of Athens' power were by now clear and unmistaken, however, fulfilling her hegemonic ideals appears more standardized and less open to change and negotiation. Accordingly, the perceived dissonance between Oedipus' threatened expulsion and Athens' praise for his reception is only nominally resolved by paying homage to Athens' hegemonic reputation. To put it another way, the play imposes an encomiastic depiction of Athens, not fully sustained by the dramatic negotiation of Oedipus' reception.

The suppliant plot next highlights Athens' openness by focusing on Theseus' role as a champion of suppliants against the backdrop of Oedipus' exclusion from Thebes.[62] To this end, the play's panegyric relies heavily on the contrast between Athens and Thebes to justify Athens' hegemonic reputation. Attention shifts from Athens to Thebes, when Ismene, Oedipus' daughter, enters onstage. After Ismene announces that the city is on the brink of civil war, and Creon is bound for Athens to force Oedipus' return (361–390), Oedipus responds with anger and indignation. In recounting his past suffering, he now gives a different account of his exile, blaming his sons for casting their father out of the city (427–430, 448–449).[63] He further explains the motives that led his sons to banish him and emphasizes that his banishment was first and foremost political; he further states that the city enforced his banishment violently, long after the perpetration of his crimes: τὸ τηνίκ᾽ ἤδη τοῦτο μὲν πόλις βίᾳ/ἤλαυνέ μ᾽ ἐκ γῆς χρόνιον ("at that time the city drove me out by force, after many years," 440–441).[64]

Ismene's account corroborates Oedipus' version of the motives behind his expulsion by recounting the consequences of the strife between Eteocles and

Polyneices, Oedipus' sons, over the throne (371–373), which now leads yet another family member into exile: Eteocles usurps the throne and casts his older brother out of the city (374–376). Both Oedipus' and Polyneices' exile are represented as the outcome of strife, motivated by the pursuit of κράτος ("power"). It results in the banishment of the weaker party and is destructive both for the individual (Oedipus, Polyneices) and for the community (civil strife).

When Oedipus concludes his reply to Ismene, he declares that he will never become an ally of his sons and that they will never acquire the throne. Moreover, he stresses his determination to resist both Creon and anyone else who attempts to force his return to Thebes (450–456). At the end of his speech, he appeals strongly to the chorus and the goddesses to shelter him from Creon. He now refers more explicitly to his role as savior for the Athenians and as an enemy to the Thebans (457–460) than he had earlier at the end of his first supplication—keeping the full disclosure of his benefaction for Theseus (288–291).

The history of Thebes, past and present, highlights Oedipus' plight as a victim of political strife, deserving of Athens' compassion and generosity. Oedipus' misfortunes, framed against the political context of Theban tyranny, realign the coordinates of his relationship with Athens. It is at this point that the chorus begin to relax their fear and distrust: they express pity for Oedipus (461–464)[65] and take steps to remedy his pollution,[66] cognizant of his heroic capacity (ἐπεὶ δὲ τῆσδε γῆς/σωτῆρα σαυτὸν τῷδ' ἐπεμβάλλεις λόγῳ, "since with your speech you present yourself as a savior of this land," 462–463). By casting his exile as the outcome of Creon's and his sons' political scheming for the throne, Oedipus resembles more closely Iolaus and the children of Heracles, who have fled their native city for political reasons. But as in *Children of Heracles* so in this play, the suppliant's reception remains predicated upon Athens' interests.

PITY IN ACTION

Theseus in this play embodies in ideal fashion pity and generosity, core traits of Athens' image as a hegemonic city, and his handling of the exile's request articulates Oedipus' reception in accordance with the idealized portrait of Athens' exchanges with foreigners in the other suppliant plays. Theseus' paradigmatic display of pity, however, though consistent with his role as helper of exiles and suppliants, contrasts with the more pragmatic negotiation of pity in Athenian politics and with his role in Euripides' *Suppliant Women* and that of his son Demophon in *Children of Heracles*. As Konstan has argued, in these suppliant plays both leaders do not invoke pity as a motive for political action but are guided by pragmatism.[67]

Instead, orators explicitly distance Athens from considerations of self-interest and present her military undertakings as guided by pity for the suffering of others. Theseus' expression of pity toward Oedipus accords with this fixed depiction of Athens' exalted praise in the speeches. Similarly, his offer of benefits to the king and the city, though cast as an act of gratitude, is not the product of the active exchange that takes place between the king and suppliant in the earlier suppliant plays.[68]

When Theseus appears on stage, he immediately reassures Oedipus that he will come to his aid, as he too knows the troubled lot of exiles (562–566). For like Oedipus, Theseus had grown up away from his native city and spent his childhood in Troezen (562). He also shares with him the experience of the perils that accompany life in exile (564), a reference to his Isthmian exploits.[69] Nevertheless, his career as a hero is not an exact parallel for Oedipus' Theban deeds, which cost him the kingship and led to permanent banishment.[70] The depth of understanding that he exhibits towards the suffering of a fellow human being points up his empathy. Theseus experiences pity in its truest form (καί σ' οἰκτίσας, "and feeling compassion for you," 556) because he has experienced similar suffering. Yet the enactment of pity also holds distinctive benefits in store for Athens. Oedipus readily reciprocates Theseus' generosity and compassion when he offers his body as a gift to the city and promises that in time the city will reap profits in return (577–580). He next provides some details of his singular bequest. Asking Theseus to oversee his burial (582), he then reveals the future hostilities between Thebes and Athens, when he tells the king about his enmity with his sons, who are fated to die in Athens (605–628).[71]

The exchange that takes place casts the relationship between the Athenian king and the suppliant as an idealized alliance between the two heroes, based upon consent and reciprocity. As the city representative, Theseus accepts Oedipus formally into Athens by honoring his standing as a suppliant and grants Oedipus honors equivalent to those reserved for distinguished guests by invoking the ties of δορυξενία ("spear-alliance") between the two cities, using the language of diplomacy to honor the new partnership between the hero and the city (631–637).[72] But Theseus goes further: he awards Oedipus not only asylum but also a grant of citizenship by accepting him into the city in recognition of his benefaction (637).

The process of Oedipus' reception brings the ideal in line with the demands of hegemonic ideology by representing the benefits that his annexation brings to the city as the outcome of the king's exemplary treatment of the suppliant. At the same time, the emphasis on pity, a cornerstone of Athenian imperial ideology, precludes a more active negotiation of the nature of such exchanges and suggests more readily the need to defend Athens' ideals on their own right.

## ATHENS AND THEBES

The Athenians had already experienced a long war against Sparta and her allies. The play may not have been completed before the naval battle at Arginusae in 406 BC, which the Athenians won, and it is by no means certain that Athenians had given up hope of winning the war. Yet its emphasis on the city's openness toward foreigners during a war that Athens fought to protect her right to rule over the other Greek cities is consistent with the aims of the Athenian panegyric in the suppliant plays, which aimed to justify her policies before her subjects and enemies alike. Even if the introduction of Oedipus' promise to protect Athens could be associated with a specific historical event—the prophecy he delivered (616–623, 1524–1537) has been said to allude to the defeat of Agis and Boeotian cavalry contingency near Colonus in 407 (Xen. *Hell.* 1.1.33 and D.S. 13.72)—the political message has broader resonance. Lowell Edmunds has argued that the play, composed in the aftermath of the oligarchic coup of 411 BC, whose first Assembly met at Colonus, furnishes an apology for Sophocles' involvement.[73] The resonance of these events, I would suggest, must be construed more broadly and are relevant to the mounting political, military, and financial strictures that Athens faced in the ongoing war.

Athens' rule was no longer financially beneficial for the city and its democracy. Instead, the cost of war continued to foster internal instability and in 411 BC prompted temporarily the suspension of Athens' democratic constitution. In the years following the Sicilian expedition, however, Athens had won significant victories between 411 and 406, and so the play's patriotic tone is not muted by any sense of impending defeat but rather may have imparted hope for Athens' fortunes in the war. In this vein, the play revisits the familiar depiction of foreigners as beneficial allies.

The concern with the city's proper treatment of suppliants, I submit, aimed at highlighting her superiority on moral grounds by setting Athens apart from her foes and Sparta, in particular, who were besetting Attica and Decelea in the last phase of the war (413–404 BC). The strong opposition between Athens and Thebes[74] furnishes a foil for the historical antagonism between Athens and Sparta. The juxtaposition between Theseus and Creon and between their respective offers of integration aims at underscoring Athens' openness toward foreigners and recalls the contrast Pericles draws between

Athens' and Sparta's respective treatment of foreigners (Th. 2.39.1–2). This message would have resonated even more clearly with the audience of the play in 401 BC, who had experienced the harsh rule of Sparta under the reign of the Thirty in 404–403 BC.

At the same time, Oedipus' eagerness to return the favor of his reception by defending Athens against his native Thebes endorses the image of Athens as a city that gained friends through her benefactions. The suppliant's hostility toward his former friends paints a negative image of Theban politics. Oedipus rejects both Creon's and Polyneices' offers to return to Thebes, as each of them seeks to secure political benefits for themselves (761–799); uttering curses against both of his sons, Oedipus cuts off his ties with his sons and Thebes (1370–1396).[75]

Oedipus expresses his goodwill toward Athens by showing himself to be an enemy of Thebes and a friend of Athens.[76] His gradual heroization constitutes a variation on the pattern of the "enemy-hero," whereby following the command of an oracle, an individual inimical to a certain city while alive becomes a protecting figure for that city after his death.[77] The prophecy that Thebes would in time become Athens' enemy (616–623) probably rang true for the contemporary audience, since Thebes and Athens were already on opposite sides during the Peloponnesian War.

The contrast between Athens and Thebes defines Athens' moral and political integrity against that of an inferior and unjust foe. The negative depiction of Thebes as a city characterized by factional strife, tyranny, and injustice serves as the antithesis of Athens' idealized image as a stable and just city. Zeitlin has argued that Thebes is the inverse of Athens, the negative image of the self that is safely displaced upon another city.[78] I argued in my discussion of *Children of Heracles* that this mode of self-definition derives from the attempt to distance Athens' rule from tyranny and injustice by representing the city as a benevolent leader. The antithesis between the two cities frames the dramatic and ideological coordinates of Athens' depiction as a pious city in this play as well. In particular, the play tests Athens' moral superiority by juxtaposing Theseus' superior leadership with that of his morally and politically inferior opponent.

Creon's conduct, the inverse of the model of compassion and piety that Theseus embodies, casts him from the outset as a morally inferior opponent.[79] He first attempts to deceive Oedipus and the chorus by feigning pity and concern for Oedipus' plight, claiming that he has come in the name of the city to bring him back to Thebes (737–738). He gradually reveals his true colors: his kidnapping of Antigone (818–819); the violation of Oedipus' supplication; and his patent disrespect for the gods, justice, and law (922–923) all reflect his duplicitous character. His pity is feigned, his piety is false, and his appeal to Athens' laws deceptive (939–959). Oedipus points up the discrepancy between words and actions (782):[80] his deeds, past and present, reflect that he is guided by political expediency (765–775).

Theseus' portrait as just and compassionate ruler[81] reflects his familiar role in tragedy as protector of refugees and suppliants (e.g., Euripides' *Heracles* and *Suppliant Women*).[82] His confrontation with Creon establishes very clearly the political values of each leader. Theseus' defense of Oedipus is based on justice and law and is contrasted with Creon's undemocratic political tactics, which consist in the pursuit of expediency and violence:

> ὅστις δίκαι' ἀσκοῦσαν εἰσελθὼν πόλιν
> κἄνευ νόμου κραίνουσαν οὐδέν, εἶτ' ἀφεὶς
> τὰ τῆσδε τῆς γῆς κύρι' ὧδ' ἐπεσπεσὼν
> ἄγεις θ' ἃ χρῄζεις καὶ παρίστασαι βίᾳ·
> καί μοι πόλιν κένανδρον ἢ δούλην τινὰ
> ἔδοξας εἶναι, κἄμ' ἴσον τῷ μηδενί. (913–918)

> You came to a city that stands by justice and decides everything according to the law and then scorned this land's authorities when you made this attack to drag away all that you wished and subjugate it by force. You thought my city had no men or was enslaved, and I counted for nothing.[83]

As others too have noted, the portrait of the Athenian leader represents Athens' *polypragmosyne* ("interventionism") in a positive light, but the message of Theseus' piety and compassion differs from that of the earlier panegyrics. At the end of the war, Athens defended her moral ideals to provide justification for her conduct. At that time, Greece had bore witness to the cruelty of the empire and suffered a long and costly war. In highlighting above all Athens' piety (260–262), the panegyric of her commitment to suppliants seeks to defend the city's reputation, as the war was coming to its end. In this light, the protection that Athens offered victims of persecution, a staple of the *encomion*, is developed in its own right, as the second *epeisodion* enacts this theme, emphasizing Theseus' resolve to curb Creon's violence and protect his suppliant.[84]

Oedipus' heroization, set against the exigencies of the war, prompted Athens to defend her superiority by laying claims upon the Theban hero.[85] In this context, the depiction of Athens' true openness emerges as a concern in this play. While mounting anxieties over the preservation of the empire intrude upon the depiction of Athens as an inclusive city, the play in the end delivers the promise that Athens' ideals hold by contrasting Oedipus' inclusion by Athens against his exclusion from Thebes. This positive depiction of

Oedipus' interaction with Athens depends on the dramatic elaboration of the offers of integration from Thebes and Athens.

While Theseus admits Oedipus in the city and thus remedies his exile, Creon invites him to return to Thebes, but he does not allow him access to the city. The offer of repatriation falls short of achieving a full restoration since, as Oedipus says, he will not be allowed ever to return to the city and will live outside the city's boundaries (πάραυλον, "dwelling beside/dwelling on the borders," 785). Thus, if repatriation amounts to complete restoration, and if integration in a foreign community stands for partial integration, the equation here results in a significant chiasmus. Repatriation is partial, and the prospective participation in the welfare of the city is not voluntary (772–775). By contrast, integration in Athens offers complete restoration: Oedipus is admitted to Athens, attains hero status, and provides voluntary service to the community.

As Bernard Knox has emphasized, the play treats the process of Oedipus' growth of prophetic power.[86] This sense of empowerment is presented as the result of his inclusion in Athens. Oedipus' potential return to Thebes would bring no benefits to the hero; on the contrary, Creon and the city intend to exploit Oedipus' power by enlisting him on their side without allowing him ever to live in the city. Ismene says that the Thebans seek his protection for the sake of the city alone: σὲ τοῖς ἐκεῖ ζητητὸν ἀνθρώποις ποτὲ/θανόντ' ἔσεσθαι ζῶντά τ' εὐσοίας χάριν ("that you shall one day be sought by the people there in death and in life for their welfare's sake," 389–390). In this context, εὔσοια refers to the political supremacy of Thebes over Athens: ἐν σοὶ τὰ κείνων φασὶ γίγνεσθαι κράτη ("they say that their power will depend on you," 392). The Thebans plan to exert their dominance over Oedipus as well by stripping him of any power: ὥς σ' ἄγχι γῆς στήσωσι Καδμείας, ὅπως/κρατῶσι μὲν σοῦ, γῆς δὲ μὴ μβαίνῃς ὅρων ... τούτου χάριν τοίνυν σε προσθέσθαι πέλας/χώρας θέλουσι, μηδ' ἵν' ἂν σαυτοῦ κρατοῖς ("so that they can settle you near the Cadmean land, where they can control you while you cannot enter their borders ... then that is why they wish to place you near them, and not where you would be your own master," 399–400, 404–405).[87]

Furthermore, the two cities' attitude towards pollution is instrumental in illustrating the differences in the relationship between exclusion and inclusion in each. Athens is able to overcome Oedipus' pollution because here Oedipus is allowed recourse to justice and law, and Theseus goes beyond the call of duty by inviting Oedipus to join him in his home, a gesture of his friendship, in spite of his defilement. By contrast, Oedipus tells Theseus that his banishment from Thebes is permanent because of his pollution (600–601). He understands well that Creon uses his pollution as a means of perpetuating his exclusion (785–786). Creon confirms his mistrust by bringing the charge of pollution against Oedipus in an attempt to sever his newly formed ties with the city (944–949).[88]

Thus, the confrontation between suppliant, enemy, and savior is deployed to dramatize Athens' hegemonic openness. In this way, the play reminded the audience not only that Athens provided the necessary protection to her subject-allies but also that under Athens' empire, foreigners would always fare better than under the tyrannical and oligarchic climates of some of Athens' opponents.

The difficulties surrounding Oedipus' reception, however, suggest that Athens could no longer lay claim as easily to the influence she wielded in the earlier days of the empire. We have seen in Aeschylus' *Eumenides* that the Furies' integration is the singular achievement of Athena's intervention: a proof of the power that Athens commanded at that time in the eyes of the other Greeks. Instead, this play registers anxieties surrounding the empire, even as Oedipus' adoption as a hero celebrates the same moral standards that Athenians claimed had propelled their rise to power. As Athens was coming to the end of the Peloponnesian War, the play's engagement with the plight of the foreign suppliant indicates that the empire no longer possessed the same power and prestige and could no longer inspire trust in Athens' ideals, as it had done in the past.

# OEDIPUS as ἔμπολις:
# THE CASE for CITIZENSHIP

Ἔμπολιν (637) is Musgrave's emendation of the manuscript reading ἔμπαλιν. The best rendering of ἔμπαλιν in the present context is that of the scholiast who takes the word to mean ἐκ τοῦ ἐναντίου, "on the contrary." Jebb endorses this meaning in his note on this passage and rejects, for example, Ellendt's alternative "in return" or Paley's "once more."[89] Kamerbeek defends the manuscript reading by adducing a parallel usage in S. *Tr.* 358.[90] The expression ἔμπαλιν λέγειν (S. *Tr.* 358), however, is not an exact parallel for S. *OC* 637, χώρᾳ ἔμπαλιν κατοικιῶ. Even though both usages are adverbial, the phrase ἔμπαλιν λέγειν means "to speak in the opposite way" and is not equivalent to the meaning of ἔμπαλιν "on the contrary (I will settle him in the land)" in line 637. The usage of ἔμπαλιν meaning "on the contrary" is unparalleled in extant tragedy. The emendation is not in doubt. Vidal-Naquet and Joseph Wilson, however, have rejected the emendation and argued against the idea that Oedipus becomes a citizen in Athens, but neither presents valid grounds for rejecting ἔμπολιν. Though the emendation is not in doubt, we must take another look at ἔμπολις, since the term specifies Oedipus' civic standing in Athens.

Literally translated, ἔμπολις means "belonging to the city" and constitutes the exact opposite of Oedipus' status, designated by the term ἄπολις or ἀπόπτολις. It is alternatively translated "dweller" (Lloyd-Jones) or as "citizen" (Jebb, Knox, Vidal-Naquet), depending on whether one understands ἔμπολις in the substantive as denoting the city as a physical and geographical entity or more abstractly as a political entity. The word ἔμπολις is used once more in this play (1156) and is also attested through Pollux's gloss on Eupolis' fragment ([*PCG* 5 F 492], Poll. 9.27): τὸν δὲ ἀστὸν Εὔπολις ἔμπολιν εἴρηκεν, οἷον ἐγχώριον, ἐντόπιον ("Eupolis refers to the town-dweller as a city-resident, namely, as though he were one of the local inhabitants").[91] The lexicographer's definition relates ἔμπολις with terms that associate membership with physical belonging. Nevertheless, it also leaves open the possibility that ἔμπολις might also denote the citizen in the political and legal sense, since ἀστός was used for the designation of the citizen as a technical term (see discussion below).

The precise meaning of ἔμπολις also remains elusive in lines 1156–1157: φασίν τιν' ἡμῖν ἄνδρα, σοὶ μὲν ἔμπολιν οὐκ ὄντα, συγγενῆ δέ . . . ("they say that a certain man who does not belong to the same city as you, but is a relative of yours . . ."). Ἔμπολιν clearly refers to the status of residence of Polyneices and does not appear to be used in a technical sense. Those reporting his arrival to Theseus may have told him that Polyneices and Oedipus "are not from the same city," either because Polyneices informed them that he came from Argos instead of Thebes or because he told them that he was an exile from that city. It is also possible, as Jebb suggests, that some trait of his physical presentation betrays his association with Argos. (Otherwise, how could one account for Theseus' suggestion later in line 1167?)

Vidal-Naquet points out that in all of the limited occurrences of this word, "the original meaning was one of locality, rather than of juridical status" (p. 344) and that the word does not carry any of the juridical connotations of the term πολίτης: ". . . nothing that we know of the word, even if we accept Musgrave's emendation justifies any assumption that Oedipus might have become a citizen in the juridical sense of the word."[92] He rejects the emendation on the grounds that Oedipus could never become a citizen in Athens because of his heavy pollution.[93] He concludes that Oedipus' status would be equivalent to that of a privileged metic who was allowed to hold land in Attica (normally not granted to metics).[94] Oedipus' position in that respect, he argues, resembles that of the Athenian metics, who could not participate in political deliberations and remained partially integrated.[95]

Vidal-Naquet derives his interpretation of *empolis* from the verb ἐμπολιτεύειν: he points to two uses of the verb in Thucydides (4.103.4, 4.106.1) and suggests that the verb ἐμπολιτεύω referred to a citizen's involvement in politics.[96] Yet, semantic ambiguity also surrounds the verb ἐμπολιτεύω, which is derived from ἔμπολις. The verb signifies active participation in politics. In the examples from Thucydides, it appears to be used of those residing in a city other than their own (in this case, Athenians residing in Amphipolis), who became citizens there (without necessarily giving up citizenship in their city of origin). It is unclear what the status was of the Athenians who had emigrated to Amphipolis. Any change of residence naturally brings with it questions of status. It remains uncertain whether the verb refers to those who hold citizen rights in their own or in another city. Whatever the case may be, the fact that ἐμπολιτεύω may have denoted citizenship in the legal sense does not suggest that ἔμπολις was used in the same way.

Let us now return to Pollux's gloss.[97] Ἔμπολις and ἀστός are not exact synonyms. Even though ἀστός can be used in reference to political rights (e.g., Ar. *Av.* 33–34, *Ec.* 459–460), the collective ἀστοί could be used to include women, as attested by Pericles' citizenship law, according to the testimony of Arist. *Ath.* 26.3: μὴ μετέχειν τῆς πόλεως . . . ἂν μὴ ἐξ ἀμφοῖν ἀστοῖν γεγονώς ("restricting participation to citizenship to those born of citizens on both sides").[98] This, however, is not the case with the term πολίτης, which in classical usage excluded women.[99] Patterson argues that ἀστός ("insider, dweller") semantically defines and repeatedly occurs in contrast whether explicit or implicit with ξένος ("foreigner, outsider") (e.g., Pi. *O.* 7.89–90; S. *OC* 12–13, 927–928; [D.] 59.16; Pl. *Lg.* 849a–d).

Patterson further distinguishes ἀστός from πολίτης:[100] "In brief, *polites* denoted the member of political community with public and competitive connotations; *astos* derived from the word for town (*asty*), which unlike *polis* remained limited to its physical, concrete meaning, retained a more communal meaning of 'insider'—especially as viewed against the *xenos* or 'outsider' . . . The word has an inclusive and communal, not legal or political, connotation." According to Pollux's definition, all three synonyms through which he glosses ἔμπολις refer to physical rather than political membership, and hence Vidal-Naquet's rationale against the adoption of ἔμπολις is not entirely defensible.

# CONCLUSION

The Athenian suppliant plays, whose production coincides roughly with the rise and the decline of the Athenian empire, promoted an image of the city as open to non-Athenians and as bent on protecting the rights of those wronged. At its core lie quintessentially Athenian traits such as justice, piety, compassion, and generosity. Taken together, these plays trace the beginnings of Athens' preeminence in the distant past and sketch discrete facets of the city's hegemonic history, past and present. Suppliant drama offered an apt template for articulating the mythical history of Athens' ascendancy. Her mythical victories in wars, fought on behalf of others, asserted her military superiority and legitimated her claims to leadership.

Viewed against the backdrop of empire, the suppliant plays afforded an alternative view of Athenian interstate relations. The suppliants' interactions with Athens underwrite an ideal model of leadership, based on consent and reciprocity. The free and unimpeded access that foreigners gain to the city represented Athens as an open and inclusive city, intent on punishing injustice and abetting suffering strangers. Funeral and panegyric speeches of the fifth and fourth centuries also promoted a similar portrait of Athenian hegemony. But the justifications that the suppliant plays offered in support of Athens' leadership were far more complex than those presented by the orators. More specifically, the tragic variety of moral hegemony looked back to Athens' hegemonic alliance in 478/7 BC and instantiated Athens' leadership as deriving from the Athenians' idealized conception of their past and present conduct.

The suppliant plays document the progressive evolution of Athens' hegemonic ideology in the course of the history of the empire. The panegyric of Athens as a city of justice (Aeschylus' *Eumenides*), a free city (Euripides' *Children of Heracles*), and a pious city (Sophocles' *Oedipus at Colonus*) varies the coordinates of the shared pattern in response to key transitions during the history of the empire. More specifically, Athens' claims to sole leadership over Greece and the unrest in Athens following the reforms of Ephialtes underpin the negotiation of her representation as a hegemonic city in Aeschylus' *Eumenides*. In turn, Athens' depiction as a free city in Euripides' *Children of Heracles* defends Athens against the charge of tyranny and offers a response to Sparta's criticism at the beginning of the Peloponnesian War. Sophocles' last play is also the last *encomium* of Athens before the end of the war. *Oedipus at Colonus* underscores Athens' reverent treatment of suppliants as the empire was coming to an end. While its outward aim is to defend Athens' conduct during the war, the manipulation of the play's hegemonic message suggests that this ideology was by then probably on the wane.

Placed against the broader framework of the history of Athenian imperialism, the Athenian suppliant plays also document the progressive evolution of the concept of moral hegemony through which tragedy addresses the evolving realities of Athens' rule. We can sketch the contours of this evolution as well by situating the development of this ideology against the historical circumstances that prompted Athens' rise to power. In this regard, the origins of the empire in the Athenian alliance of 478/7 BC condition the parameters of the dialectic that shapes the suppliant plays, themselves the product of imperialism at a later stage.

The confrontation that takes place between Athens and the suppliants' enemies in the plays provides a foil for the positive character of Athens' interactions with mythical outsiders. The suppliants' recognition of Athens' power and their willingness to reciprocate her generosity in kind idealize Athens' hegemonic leadership and model the partnerships that issue from them upon the principles of a hegemonic alliance. Closely probed, the plays differentiate Athens' hegemonic image from the empire's forceful tactics of domination. The dialectic that the plays mobilize between consent and force is endemic to the process of ideology. The manifestations of Athenian hegemonic ideology are the outcome of a dynamic and open-ended process, conditioned by both external and internal forces. Athenian ideals are defined against the changing historical circumstances of the empire and against other ideologies, which the plays counter, rival, or attempt to align with the message of Athens' moral hegemony.

From Aeschylus' *Eumenides* to Euripides' *Suppliant Women* to Sophocles' *Oedipus at Colonus*, the major changes that the empire underwent under Athens' imperial democracy left their imprint on the plays, which date to the post-Cimonian phase of the empire. By the 450s, the practices of Athenian imperialism had been more fully established, and hence the hegemonic outlook of the plays begins to change, following the consolidation of Athenian democracy—a process that begins with the reforms of Ephialtes and continues under Pericles. While Aeschylus' *Eumenides* bears witness to the vigor of Athens' hegemonic superiority, the tendency, which Euripides' later suppliant plays exhibit, is a shift toward more closely aligning the two facets of Athens' imperial democracy. More to the point, the representation of Athena's hegemonic justice in *Eumenides* presents the Athenian justice system as the source of benefits for foreigners and programmatically unites democracy and empire. The later plays paint a different image of Athens' moral hegemony, better suited to the development of imperialism under Athens' imperial democracy. While the earlier play touts Athens' strength by celebrating Athens' alliance with Argos and the civic partnership between Athena and the Furies, the later plays are more intent on justifying the legitimacy of the benefits that Athens reaps from her ventures on behalf of mythical suppliants.

After Euripides' plays, only Sophocles' *Oedipus at Colonus*, the latest of the plays of this group, returns to the theme of Athens' protection of suppliants (Heracles goes to Athens at Theseus' invitation at the end of Euripides' *Heracles* [416 BC], but the play is not staged in Athens). Similarly, Euripides' *Ion* (ca. 414 BC) is not staged in Athens; the play is significant for its claims of Ionianism and promotes imperialism on the basis of genealogical claims between Athens and Ionia. Like his *Erechtheus* (ca. 422 BC), Euripides' later Athenian plays promote Athens' distinctiveness, based on claims of autochthony. On the other hand, Euripides' plays on the aftermath of the Trojan War (especially *Hecuba* and *Trojan Women*) approach the problem of empire from a different angle. These plays no longer examine pity from a civic perspective but adopt the point of view of the defeated enemy and lend prominence to marginal voices: those of the lamenting, captive women of Troy.

Engagement with the plays, which confront the suffering of war, brings us back to the problem of ideology, that is, the stance, which the plays take on empire and the message, which they impart to Athenians and foreigners in the audience. The plays do not represent a static or unchanging image of Athens' hegemonic ideals. The process of the reception of the suppliants is fraught with obstacles, which raise questions about the moral legitimacy of her power. While the plays support the unequal distribution of power between Athens and her allies, the suppliants' voluntary dependence on Athens promotes and validates the principles that underlie hegemony, not empire. To this end, the inclusion of the voice of suppliants, who at times resist and at others support Athens' enterprise, offers a far more realistic scenario of the process of legitimization. Within these parameters, questioning and contestation are part of the process whereby relations of domination are explored, negotiated, and redefined. In this vein, the Athenian suppliant plays do not subvert the empire; instead, their engagement with morality and power offers a space in which alternatives to force and domination are entertained, probed, and sanctioned. Seen from this angle, the idealized image of Athens offers not only justification but also an alternative to the empire's might.

# NOTES

## INTRODUCTION

1. Tzanetou 2005.

2. Mills 1997, 77–78.

3. For the prevalence of the law of the stronger in human nature, see Th. 1.76.2, 1.77.5, 3.10.3–7, 3.11.1, 4.92.4, 5.89.

4. Mills (1997, 34–42) argues that "the notion that Athens is a civilizing city is of fundamental importance for an understanding of the ideology of the Athenian empire" (p. 34), but she posits that this ideal image predates the Persian Wars. Even so, she admits that it was influenced by and cultivated in the wake of the wars against Persia and especially following the Ionians' appeal for help against the Persians and Pausanias.

5. See, for example, Euben 1986; Goldhill 1987; Connor 1990, 7–32; Winkler and Zeitlin 1990; Pozzi 1991; Gregory 1991; Sommerstein, Halliwell, Henderson, and Zimmermann 1993; Croally 1994, 2005; Goff 1995; Silk 1996; Easterling 1997; Pelling 1997a. For a representative sample of the literature on Athenian democratic institutions, see especially Ober 1989, 1996; Ober and Hedrick 1996. On the predramatic ceremonies, see also P. J. Wilson 2009.

6. Goldhill 1987.

7. Griffin 1998; Rhodes 2003; Carter 2007.

8. On the discrete approaches within the area of Athenian civic ideology and tragedy, see Mastronarde 2010, 15–25.

9. Seaford 1994.

10. Griffith 1995, 1998, 2005.

11. Carter 2011.

12. Carter 2011, 7–16.

13. In this connection, see also Burian (2011), who discusses anew the broad topic of the impact of democratic civic ideology on the plays. He rightly cautions that ideology is not a monolithic framework and that tragedy expresses a wide range of views (p. 117). My own discussion of civic ideology through the framework of empire does not claim to represent the full range of views or reaction by the audience members to the political issues raised in the plays.

14. Dué 2006, 136–150.

15. Hölscher 1998, 183.

16. Mills 1997; Rosenbloom 1995, 2006a; Kowalzig 2006; Dué 2006; Futo-Kennedy 2009.

17. Mills 1997; Futo-Kennedy 2009.

18. Rosenbloom 1995, 2006a. It is Rosenbloom's work that has paved the way for scholars working on tragedy and empire.

19. Gödde 2000; Grethlein 2003.

20. See especially Pelling 1997c.

21. Loraux 1986.

22. E.g., *LIMC* 1.2, s.v. Achilles, 687; *LIMC* 6.2, s.v. Nausicaa, 2; *LIMC* 1.2, s.v. Aias II, 44.

23. *LIMC* 5.1, s.v. *Iphigenia*, 8–9; *LIMC* 4.2. s.v. Herakleidai, 2; *LIMC* 1.2, s.v. Amphitryon 1–2.

24. Cassella 1999, 25–37.

25. Herman 1987, 54–58; Giordano 1999, 12–13; Naiden 2006, 116–117.

26. E.g., Hom. *Il.* 10.454–457, 20.463–469, 21.64–119. See further Giordano 1999, 109–134; Naiden 2006, 34–35.

27. On the theme of the suppliant-exile, see Schlunk 1976.

28. Giordano 1999, 71–103.

29. Gottesman 2006, 32–80.

30. Cassella 1999, 27–37.

31. On supplications at the altars of the gods, see Naiden 2006, 36–41; for this motif in tragedy, see Cassella 1999, 236–246.

32. On the staging of suppliant plays, see Rehm 1988.

33. Chaniotis 1996; Naiden 2006, 171–218.

34. A full list of examples of personal supplication in tragedy is discussed by Mercier (1990, 80–159), who also treats certain supplications (in particular those of Iolaus and the Danaids, which take place within a sanctuary) as personal (pp. 160–166). As I demonstrate below, those supplications replicated Athenian civic procedures of supplication, as discussed by Naiden 2006, 173–194.

35. On the pattern of suppliant drama and its tripartite structure (savior—suppliant—enemy) and its variations, see Kopperschmidt 1967, 46–53; Burian 1971; Mercier 1990, 32–41.

36. Theseus argues that Polyneices' and Adrastus' expedition was fought for the wrong reasons and highlights its harmful consequences for the city (E. *Supp.* 226–236).

37. Pelasgus throughout exhibits strong concern for the welfare of the city: A. *Supp.* 356–357. The Danaids view their supplication in personal terms; when Pelasgus tells them that they are not his suppliants at his own hearth, but suppliants of the city (365–369), they retort that he is the city (σὺ δὲ τὸ δάμιον, 370) and that he alone holds power over the altar (370–375).

38. On the role of supplication and the Assembly, see "Supplication and Democracy (Aeschylus' *Suppliant Women*)," in the Introduction.

39. Lattimore 1958, 46–47. Though Burian (1971, 11–16) and Mercier (1990, 38) disagree that the decision to accept the suppliants is the main determinant of the pattern, Lattimore's structure points in the right direction.

40. Giordano 1999.

41. Divine sanctions for wronging a suppliant in tragedy: A. *Supp.* 347, 381–386, 427–437; E. *Hec.* 798–801, *Heracl.* 101–104, *Supp.* 258–262; S. *OC* 289–297.

42. The following works offer a representative sample of the significant work undertaken to date on the topics of supplication and asylum: Schlesinger 1933; Gottesman 2006; Kopperschmidt 1967; Gould 1973; Mikalson 1991, 69–77; Auffarth 1992; Sinn 1993; Crotty

1994; Chaniotis 1996; Rehm 1988; Gödde 2000; Derlien 2003; Dreher 2003; Grethlein 2003; Naiden 2006.

43. For discussion of the scholarship and the history of ideas on supplication, see Naiden 2006, 8–18.

44. Gould 1973, 78–80.

45. For a full discussion of gestures pertinent to supplication, see Naiden 2006, 43–62.

46. Gould 1973, 77; and see Naiden's comments (2006, 10–11). For the sociobiological basis of the ritualist approach, see Burkert 1996, 85–90.

47. For a critique on the ritualist model, see also Crotty 1994, 89–91; Lynn George 1988, 201. Giordano 1999 and Gödde 2000 underscore the interdependence of ritual and rhetoric.

48. Naiden 2006, 18–25, 30–169.

49. Naiden 2006, 281–295.

50. Naiden 2006, 30–33.

51. Naiden 2006, 173–200.

52. According to Arist. *Ath*. 43.6, the Assembly convened regular meetings to deal with supplications. On the two-step process, see Naiden 2006, 173–177 (and his discussion of Dioscurides' petition as a result of which he received honors from the Assembly [*IG*² 218]).

53. Naiden 2006, 177, with examples of diverse supplications from foreigners, including those by diplomats.

54. On the play's dating, see Garvie 2006, ix–xx; for an earlier date, see Scullion 2002, 7–10.

55. Exceptionally, kings evaluate the petition in tragedy in S. *OT* (1–77); E. *HF* (1–169). See Naiden 2006, 177 with nn. 21, 22. For foreigners' petitions, see also Zelnick-Abramovitz 1998.

56. Kopperschmidt 1967, 46–53; Burian 1971, 26–29.

57. On the dating of Aeschylus' lost dramas, see Hubbard 1992 and Hahneman 1999.

58. Pelasgus emphasizes fear for Zeus' wrath (A. *Supp*. 478–479) as the key factor in his decision.

59. See Friis Johansen and Whittle 1980, II. 204–205 *ad* 255–259. Argos' dominion is coextensive with that of historical Greece (Hdt. 2.56.1).

60. Turner (2001, 40) suggests that Aeschylus' play does not conform to the idealized depiction of Athenian/Greek values in the manner of the other suppliant plays.

61. Turner (2001, 42) argues that Argos serves in this regard as metonymy for Athens, but his later statement that the blurring between Greek and barbarian in the play probably stems from Argos' medizing during the Persian Wars (p. 47) seems to run counter to this argument.

62. Sommerstein 1997, 148. Friis Johansen and Whittle (1980, 1.48, 50) maintains that Danaus succeeds Pelasgus as king. On the reconstruction of the other two plays in the trilogy, see Garvie's (2006, 163–233) detailed treatment and Sommerstein 2010, 100–108.

63. Though critics have emphasized his strong characterization as a democratic king: Garvie 2006, 150–153; Burian 1974a; Podlecki 1966, 82–85.

64. See further, Chapter 1, "An Athenian Hero."

65. On the historical association between Argos and Athens, see more recently Sommerstein 1997; Gottesman 2006, 101–113.

66. Zeitlin 1990.

67. Bakewell 1997.

68. On tragedy, democratic institutions, and Athenian civic ideology, see especially Goldhill 1987, 2000; Goff 1995; Pelling 1997; Sourvinou-Inwood 2003, 15–140. For the controversy that has arisen from Griffin's 1998 and Rhodes' critique of Goldhill 2000, see Carter 2007, 35–43.

69. Grethlein 2003. He nonetheless misses an opportunity by not exploring how the dynamics of supplication further shape the exchanges between Athenians and foreigners, so critical for understanding Athenian civic identity in the theater.

70. On Athens' panegyric in tragedy, see further Schröder 1914; van Hook 1934; Butts 1947; Mills 1997; Tzanetou 2005. On morality and politics, see Herman 2006.

71. On the question of the "popularity" of the empire, see especially, de Ste. Croix 1954–1955; Bradeen 1960; Quinn 1964; Fornara 1977. On the allies' hatred, see especially Th. 1.75–78, 3.36–48, 5.84–116, 6.76–80; Xen. [*Ath.*] 1. 14–18. On the benefits that the empire reaped from the allies' contributions, see Arist. *Ath.* 24.1–2; Plut. *Per.* 12–17. Isocrates balances his critique of Athenian imperialism with the benefits the empire conferred not only on Athenians but also on the allies (4.103–109).

72. For a comprehensive treatment of the history and development of the Athenian empire, see Meiggs 1972; Rhodes 1985; *CAH*, vol. 5 1992. On imperialism, see also Balot 2006, 138–176.

73. This definition was developed by Antonio Gramsci (1971) and has gained wide acceptance; see Fontana 2000. See below, "Hegemony and Ideology."

74. For these and other constraints, which reflect the practice of supplication and could lead to the rejection of the suppliant, see Naiden 2006, 129–165.

75. Auffarth 1992.

76. See further Gomme 1945, 93–94, and Hornblower 1991, 12–14 *ad* Th. 1.2.5–6.

77. Even so, as Lape 2010 argues, the passage of Pericles' citizenship law prompted the Athenians to define their superiority by developing their own sense of their ethnic and national heritage (especially as expressed in myths of autochthony).

78. See Cohen (2000, 11–78), who argues that the number of foreigners and the degree of their integration makes Athens an anomalous or unique case. Whitehead (1977), on the other hand, offers a less positive account of the realities of the lives of metics in Athens. On Athens' hospitality toward strangers, see also Isoc. 4.41.

79. See also Th. 1.144.2; Ar. *Av.* 1012–1013; Xen. *Lac.* 14.4; Pl. *Prt.* 342a–d. Gauthier (1988, 24) argues that the practice of expelling foreigners was less frequent in reality than Pericles claims.

80. Cleon comments on the negative aspects of such openness, claiming that the Athenians extend their habits of daily interaction (absence of fear and intrigues) to their dealings with foreigners (Th. 3.37.2).

81. As Hornblower (1991, 303–304) suggests *ad* Th. 2.39, Athenian military training was more significant than Pericles would have us believe. Pericles, for that matter, had said of naval training that it required substantial preparation and dedication (Th. 1.142.9). For a clear synoptic treatment of the rivalry between Athens and Sparta, see Fornara and Samons 1991, 114–147.

82. Arist. *NE* 9.7 (1167b15–20) notes that the benefactor feels more affection than the beneficiary. Low 2007, 246–247, rightly points out that the passage links generosity with the tactics of the empire, noting that the generosity of *charis* does not altogether succeed in masking the enforced inferiority of the allies. On the concept of intervention as an ideal in Greek diplomatic relations, see Low 2007, 175–211. For a positive account of Athens' interventions, see Isocrates' *Plataicus*. The speech, written (but most likely never

delivered) for the purpose of a diplomatic mission (the speaker is Plataean ambassador before the Athenian Assembly), contains distinctive elements of the Athenian panegyric of the funeral orations and tragedy. The Plataean envoy, who seeks the help of the Athenians against the Thebans who in 373 BC destroyed Plataea, makes numerous references to Athens' reputation for aiding the weak (e.g., 14.1–2, 6), to the help that she had lent Adrastus against the Thebans (14.53–54), and to the services the Plataeans had rendered to their city in the course of the Persian Wars (14.57).

83. Gomme 1956, *ad* Th. 2.41.4 argues that this idealized depiction of Athenian *polypragmosyne* ("meddlesomeness") is consistent with that furnished by the examples of Athens' interventions on behalf of suppliants in tragedy. Pericles, however, paints an entirely different picture on the eve of the war, stressing as its motives, fear, honor, and self-interest (Th. 1.76.2–3). Euphemus makes a similar point in his speech to the Camarinians (Th. 6.85.3). On Athenian *polypragmosyne*, see further Ehrenberg 1947.

84. On the features of Greek hegemonic alliances, see Ehrenberg 1969, 111–116. See also Hammond 1969. For the variety of relationships that issue from supplication, see Naiden 2006, 116–122. These include truces and grants of citizenship for individuals and groups (118–119).

85. See also Arist. *Ath.* 23.5; D.S. 11.46.6–47; Plut. *Arist.* 23–25 and *Cim.* 6.2–3. On the character of the Delian League, see further Larsen 1940; Sealey 1966, 233–255; Hammond 1967; Popp 1968; Meiggs 1972, 458–64; Rawlings 1977; Robertson 1980; Smarczyk 2007.

86. Herodotus claims that the Athenians used Pausanias' *hybris* ("insolence") as a pretext for wresting the hegemony away from the Spartans (8.3.2), while Thucydides argues that punishing the Persians was the alleged, not the real, motive (1.96.1) for their leadership of the league. See further Rawlings 1977.

87. For the established view that the empire developed gradually after the "Peace of Callias" (dated either to 450/49 or to 449/8 BC), see Meiggs 1972, 152–174. For the contrary view, see Fornara and Samons (1991, 76–104), who also demonstrate that the repressive and coercive measures Athens undertook had already been in place by the 460s. There is general agreement, however, that the move of the treasury from Delos to Athens ushered in the final phase of Athenian imperialism in the early to the mid 450s. The dating of the Assembly decrees, which offer information on the bureaucracy of Athenian imperialism, has similarly been the subject of intense controversy. The orthodox view (Meiggs 1972), which dates these decrees to the 440s based largely on the shape of the letters inscribed, has been challenged by Mattingly (1996), who dates most of the decrees to the 420s. Samons (1998, 121), who follows Mattingly's dating, argues that the bureaucracy of the empire should not be confused with the exercise of force that was already present soon after the formation of the Delian League. On the character of Athens' rule, see further, Chapter 2 and the essays in Low 2008 and Ma, Papazarkadas, and Parker 2009.

88. On the problems regarding the dating of the events of the Pentacontaetia (479–432 BC), see Meiggs 1972, 42–204; Badian 1993, 73–107.

89. Tribute denoted subordination (Hdt. 1.6.2–3) and was a form of penalty. When the Delian League was formed, tribute collection was assigned to ten Hellenotamiai. By 454 BC the treasury was moved to Athens and one-sixtieth of the tribute was dedicated to Athena. Most cities paid tribute, and only a few (probably Samos, Chios, Lesbos, Naxos, Thasos) gave ships, though Thucydides suggests that some of them chose to pay tribute instead, thereby weakening their own power (1.99). See further Pritchett 1969. On the finances of the empire, see Samons 2000; on the bureaucracy of the empire, see Sickinger 2007.

90. Though see the commemoration of the Athenians' victory at Eion (*FGE* XL): the

epigram links the Athenians' exploits with those of the Athenian hero Menestheus. The Athenians, however, had nearly brought the inhabitants of Eion to starvation and then sold its population into slavery (Th. 1.98.1). See further Rosenbloom 2006a, 28–33.

91. For the celebration of the Panhellenic victory against the Persians, see Simonides' epigram on Plataea (on which see Boedeker and Sider 2001).

92. For a discussion of the problems surrounding its dating and the principal ancient testimonies (D.S. 11.33.3; D.H. 5.17.4; Plut. *Publ.* 9.7; *Thuc.* 2.35.1), see Ziolkowski 1981, 13–21. Most scholars rightly reject the idea that the funeral oration originated in the time of Solon. Jacoby (1944) dates the origins of the practice later in 465 BC after the battle at Drabescus. Kierdorf (1966) places the beginnings of the Athenian funeral oration in 478/7 BC by adjusting the testimony of Diodorus Siculus, who states that it was established after the battle at Plataea. See further Loraux 1986, 58–61.

93. In addition to Pericles' speech in Thucydides, Gorgias' was probably composed in the course of the Peloponnesian War.

94. Ziolkowski 1981, 100–137; Loraux 1986, 305–330.

95. I agree with Kierdorf (1966, 89–95), who argues that the catalogue of the ancestors' exploits in the funeral speeches contain traces of the nascent hegemonic ideology (the myths of the supplications of Adrastus and Heracles' children) and of the idea of Panhellenism (the mythical victories against Eumolpus and the Amazons).

96. Mills 1997, 58–73.

97. On the concept of hegemony in Greek political thought, see Fontana 2000. Aristotle (*Pol.* 1333a–1334a5) uses the same conceptual contrast between hegemony and domination to discuss the difference between despotic and constitutional forms of rule. Isocrates also posits a similar antithesis between hegemonic and despotic rule in his *Panegyricus* by praising Athens for her hegemonic leadership and contrasting it with Sparta's (e.g., Isoc. 4.80: ἐπιθυμοῦντες ἡγεμόνες ἢ δεσπόται προσαγορεύεσθαι καὶ σωτῆρες ἀλλὰ μὴ λυμεῶνες ἀποκαλεῖσθαι, "wishing to be addressed as leaders or masters and saviors, but not to be called destroyers"). In both the *Panegyricus* and *On Peace*, Isocrates develops the pivotal antithesis between hegemony over domination, praising Athens' hegemonic past but also offering criticism of her conduct toward the allies (e.g., 8.80–90).

98. See Fornara and Samons (1991, 76–113), whose chapter on Athenian imperialism offers a comprehensive discussion of the development of the empire and the restrictions imposed upon the allies over time (e.g., the imposition of democracies in allied states, the establishment of cleruchies, the adjudication of legal disputes in Athens, and the imposition of coinage).

99. For the contrast between Athens' encomiastic depiction in the funeral speeches and Thucydides' speeches and history, see especially Strassburger 1958. See also Loraux 1986, 360–70; Mills 1997, 79–86.

100. Mills 1997, 80.

101. Other plays register the changing nature of Athenian imperialism in the post-Periclean phase of the war. Outside the panegyric context of the Athenian suppliant plays, scholars demonstrate that tragedy offers a complex view of empire. See, for example, Rosenbloom 1995, 2006a; Futo-Kennedy 2006, 2009; Dué 2006. Comedy, on the other hand, offered bold criticism against Athenian imperialism from the earliest plays, such as Aristophanes' *Babylonians* (426 BC), which voices the criticism of the tribute-bearing allies, to later plays, notably, Aristophanes' *Birds* (414 BC), which offers contrasting views on Athenian imperialism in the wake of the Melian revolt and the Sicilian expedition and especially in his war plays (*Acharnians, Peace, Lysistrata*).

102. Loraux 1986, 123.

103. Loraux 1986, 125–126. The primary justification for hegemony is naturally securing the freedom of others and defending the city from the charge of tyranny and domination. The orators too stress that the relations between Athens and her allies were voluntary, as does Pericles in his funeral oration in Thucydides, though, unlike the orators, Pericles' speech does not define Athenian identity on the basis of descent but on national character. It is possible that definition of Athenian identity was a gesture toward Athens' metics who served in Athens' wars. In this connection, this speech contrasts with the more chauvinistic speech of Plato's *Menexenus*.

104. This began in 426/5 after the decree of Cleonymus, which tightened the existing regulations on tribute collection (*ML* 68).

105. Goldhill 1987 sees these ceremonies as integral to the democratic character of the festival and the plays. For the scholarly debate on this issue, see Carter (2004); P. J. Wilson 2011. On the financing of theatrical productions, see P. J. Wilson 2000. For an account of the relationship between cultural production and democracy and empire in fifth-century Athens, see Kallet 1998, 43–58.

106. At the Panathenaea, the allies brought a cow and a panoply to Athena (Cleinias decree [*ML* 46]; see further Smarczyk 1990, 549–592). On religion and empire, see Barron 1964; Smarczyk 1990; Parker 2008.

107. Carter 2007, 41–43. On the audience, see further Goldhill 1997.

108. As we have seen, the only play that does not conform to this pattern is Aeschylus' *Suppliant Women*, staged in Argos. The keen interest in democratic institutions is largely owed to the fact that Argos was a democracy at the time and enjoying favorable relations with Athens; see Podlecki 1966, 50; Sommerstein 1997; Grethlein 2003, 97–107. By contrast, references to democracy and its institutions appear in some of the Athenian suppliant plays, where they serve to highlight Athens' imperial democracy and promote her portrait as a hegemonic city. On the impact of Athenian democracy as a shaping force in the Athenian suppliant plays, see Grethlein 2003. Athenian democratic institutions and discourse shaped Athens' image as a hegemonic city and contributed to the examination of Athens' imperial democracy. The bibliography on this issue is extensive. See, for example, Fornara and Samons 1991; Boedeker and Raaflaub 1998; Rhodes 2007, 24–45; Forsdyke 2007. See further Rosenbloom 2006a; Futo-Kennedy 2009.

109. On the theme of Athens' protection of outsiders in Euripides' *Medea*, see further Sfyroeras 1994. On Euripides' *Heracles*, see Tarkow 1977.

110. For a discussion of techniques of closure in Euripidean aetiologies, see Dunn 1996.

111. See Goff (1999), who relates the aetiologies historically to the anxious mood of the Athenians during the years of the Sicilian expedition.

112. Naiden 2006, 160–162. Athens in a number of plays takes the lead in remedying the plight of severely defiled murderers. The city acquires the reputation of offering a safe haven for the polluted by accepting Orestes, Oedipus, Heracles, and Medea, all heavily stained by kindred blood (Seaford 1994, 132–139). From the vantage point of ideology, the severe pollution of kin-killers offered an additional strategy for legitimizing Athenian claims to superiority. Athens earns her reputation for inclusiveness by entertaining requests from suppliants whom every other city would justifiably have shunned. The narratives of the annexation of heavily defiled murderers helped construct the mythical image of Athens as a stable center and used it to justify the city's primacy.

113. Euripides' *Suppliant Women* is discussed in Chapter 3 ("Punishing Evil: Euripides' *Suppliant Women*").

---

114. Kowalzig 2006.

115. See Rosenbloom (2011), who relates the ideology of Panhellenism to the development of Athenian imperialism.

116. See further Mills 1997, 229–234.

117. On hegemony in *Eumenides*, see further Rosenbloom 1995; Futo-Kennedy 2006, 2009; and below, Chapter 1.

118. Gramsci 1971.

119. Fiske 1992, 291.

120. R. Williams 1977, 113.

121. Eagleton 1986.


## CHAPTER 1

1. Quincey 1964, 190.

2. Th. 1.102. See further de Ste. Croix (1972, 181–183), who argues that fear of the Spartans after Cimon's ostracism was an operative motive behind the conclusion of the alliance.

3. Ar. *Lys.* 1137–1144 parodies Pericleidas' supplication. The terms helots and *perioikoi* (or *perioeci*, "dwellers around") refer to Sparta's slaves and resident population respectively. The latter did not have citizenship rights.

4. Th. 1.102; D.S. 11.63; Plut. *Cim.* 16.8. See further Fornara and Samons (1991, 127–129), who emphasize that the Spartans' refusal to accept the Athenian force reflects concern with the revolution in Athens.

5. On the ostracism of Cimon, see Arist. *Ath.* 27.4; Plut. *Cim.* 14.3–5. See further Forsdyke (2005, 167–170), who notes that the political divisions that led to Cimon's ostracism, were profound and that political unrest persisted for a few years after the murder of Ephialtes (Antiph. 5.68; Plut. *Per.* 10.7–8; D.S. 11.77.6) and is evinced within the play, when the chorus, following Athena's speech, pray for the absence of civic discord (976–986). Incidentally, she also notes a minor plot to overthrow the democracy in 457 BC (Th. 1.107.4).

6. On the opposition between Cimon and Themistocles, see further Fornara and Samons 1991, 125–126.

7. Podlecki 1989, 19.

8. Dover (1957, 235) notes that the triple reference to the alliance deviates from the practice of introducing explanations for contemporary institutions and cults at the end of the play. The seeming incongruity may be explained in part by the bipartite division of the plot into Orestes' trial and the Furies' conflict and reconciliation with Athena. As in *Eumenides*, so in Euripides' *IT* the mythical aetiology for the feast of the *Choes* (*IT* 943–960) precedes the aetiologies of the double cults of Iphigeneia at Brauron and Orestes at Halai Araphenides (*IT* 1435–1474). On the play's mirroring of the historical alliance, see further L. A. Jones 1987, 70–71; Podlecki 1966, 88–94; Sommerstein 1989, 30. Thus, in his introduction to his commentary, Alan Sommerstein comments that the fictionalized account served to present the recently concluded alliance with Argos as "a great and unmixed blessing for Athens; a proposition with which not all Athenians would necessarily have agreed."

9. Both Dodds (1973, 23) and Macleod (1982, 132) also interpret the Argive alliance and the political reforms of the Areopagus more broadly.

10. After concluding two alliances at once in 462/1 BC—one with the Argives and a

second one with the Thessalians (Th. 1.102.4) — they soon accepted the Megarians as their allies and entered into war against Sparta's allies, Corinth, Aegina and Epidaurus (Th. 1.105–106). See further Fornara and Samons 1991, 129–131.

11. Costa 1962, 24–31 and esp. 27–28; Lardinois 1992, 321–322.

12. The rules and procedures governing the judgment of supplication varied in actuality. In the Athenian suppliant plays, suppliant and enemy consistently debate their claims before the civic authorities, usually the king, who decides whether to accept the suppliant(s), if he proves worthy of assistance. On both institutional and dramatic practices, see Naiden 2006, 106–116.

13. Sommerstein 1989, 165–166 (ad 469) points out that Athena's dilemma echoes Orestes' dilemma in Ch. 924–925.

14. I follow Lobel's transposition of line 475 after 482 and emendation ἀμόμφους ὄντας ("being blameless," referring to members of the Areopagus) of the manuscripts' reading δ' ἄμομφον ὄντα σ', which could refer only to Orestes. Sommerstein 1989, 169 ad 475 notes that "the phrase is admirably suited to the members of the Areopagus council, for the most stringent precautions were taken to preserve the integrity and irreproachability of this body. All members of it had passed a severe scrutiny (δοκιμασία) of their public and personal lives before taking office as archons (cf. Lys. 26. 11–12; Arist. Ath. 55.2–5) and another a year later before "going up to the Areopagus" (cf. D. 24.22; Arist. Ath. 60.3).

15. Naiden 2006, 173–183.

16. Despite the play's overt political allusions to the politics of the day, the debate on the relationship of the foundation of the mythical court of Areopagus (681–710) and the reforms of Ephialtes has been one of the most controversial aspects of the interpretation of the political message of Eumenides. For a detailed exposition of the history of the scholarship on this problem, see Braun 1998, 105–133. Braun's discussion of the historical reforms surrounding the Areopagus leads him to see Aeschylus as a democrat who supported the Solonian constitution but not the radical democracy. I concur with the opinion of Jacoby 1954 and Dover 1957, that the depiction of the mythical court reflects broadly the reforms of 462/1. On the interpretation of specific allusions relevant to the interpretation of the court's functions, see also Dodds 1960; Macleod 1982; L. A. Jones 1987; Meier 1990 and 1993, 132–137. On the question of Aeschylus' political sympathies, scholarly opinion is similarly divided. In support of Aeschylus' conservative views, see Calder 1981; Rhodes 1981, 261–263; Conacher 1987, 195–206. I have cited above representatives of the opposite view. Others such as Macleod (1982), Goldhill (1992, 89–92) Meier (1993), Griffith (1995), and Pelling (2000, 167–177) like to see Aeschylus as rising above partisan lines by celebrating the ideals that united all Athenians; by helping to overcome the civic conflict, which the reforms had brought about; or by specifically attempting to reconcile democrats with aristocrats by praising the democracy for its institutions by preserving all the while the power that the aristocrats traditionally held. On the dramatic mirroring of these issues, see further Grethlein 2003, 210–247. See also Bowie 1993 for the relevance of Athenian rituals in this play.

17. Macleod 1982, 128–129; Sommerstein 1989, 13–17, 25–29. For the historical background of the development of the functions of the Areopagus Council, see Wallace 1989 and de Bruyn 1995.

18. Apart from Homer (Od. 3. 307), who mentions that Orestes returns to Argos from Athens, Orestes is represented as arriving in Athens as a polluted exile in the aetiological myth for the feast of the Choes at the festival of the Anthesteria, attested in E. IT 947–960 (cf. also Phanodemus FGrH 325 F 11; Scholiast Ar. Ach. 961; Scholiast Ar. Eq. 95) and in

the mythical tradition of his trial by a jury of gods (E. *Or.* 1650–1652; D. 23.66; Apollod. 6.25). For fuller testimonia and discussion of Aeschylus' innovations concerning the trial, see Sommerstein 1989, 3–6, and Grethlein 2003, 200–204—both of which agree that Aeschylus was probably innovating by replacing a preexisting tradition of a divine tribunal with a jury of mortals. On the dramatic and ethical issues raised by the mythological trial, see Mitchell-Boyask 2009.

19. In this respect, my argument parts way with Futo-Kennedy (2006), who also views the Argive alliance as typifying the ideal model of an alliance between Athens and her allies. Her reading is that the play is proimperialist and attempts to tie Orestes' trial to historical evidence on Athens' judicial authority over allied trials, which were later judged in Athens, by dating this practice as early as the Phaselis decree in the 460s BC. To this end, she emphasizes Athena's role in imperial administration. Against this view, see Rosenbloom 1995.

20. Text from Page 1973 and translations from Sommerstein 2009.

21. On the political implications of Apollo's support of Athena here, as interpreted by their relationship as patrons of the empire—the treasury of the league was still on Delos before its transfer to Athens in 454 BC—see Shapiro (1996), who argues this point based on one group of vase paintings representing Athena and Apollo with Orestes and a second group of vases representing Athena and Apollo receiving joint sacrifices.

22. Pollution posed a significant obstacle to entry (cf. Oedipus in S. *OC* 229–236), and thus most suppliants are concerned with dispelling their hosts' suspicion that they are seeking asylum on account of defilement (cf. A. *Supp.* 5–7 [and 366–367, 375, where the Danaids' threat of suicide compels Pelasgus to bring their case before the Argive Assembly]; E. *Med.* 846–850). Orestes had already addressed his ritual status (235–243) by claiming that he is no longer a suppliant, seeking purification (οὐ προστρόπαιον οὐδ' ἀφοίβαντον χέρα, "not one seeking purification nor with an impure hand," 236–237); though note Apollo's preceding statement that he will protect the suppliant to avoid incurring the wrath of the "one seeking purification" (δεινὴ γὰρ ἐν βροτοῖσι κἀν θεοῖς πέλει/ τοῦ προστροπαίου μῆνις, εἰ προδῶ σφ' ἑκών, "for the wrath of the one seeking purification is terrible among mortals and gods, if I intentionally betray him," 233–234)—a statement that acknowledges that the issue of bloodguilt remains unresolved by Apollo's attempt to purify him at Delphi. On the meaning of προστρόπαιος, see Sommerstein 1989, 124 (*ad* 237); Parker 1983, 108. In Orestes' prayer to Athena, he provides a detailed explanation of his purification, mentioning both his purification by Apollo through the customary sacrifice of a pig and the purificatory effect of his subsequent wanderings (276–285). On the vexed question of Orestes' pollution and purification, see Neitzel 1991, 69–89; Sidwell 1996; and my discussion of his purification in this chapter.

23. Athena's role as ἀρωγός ("advocate," 289), taken together with Apollo's earlier instructions to Orestes, refers to her role as judicial rather than as military advocate. Dover 1957, 237, makes this point, arguing against the military connotations of φίλοις ἀρήγουσ' ("helping friends," 295). Futo-Kennedy 2006, 56 with n. 69 and 70, takes ἀρωγός in a military sense, offering as the only parallel for this usage Hom. *Il.* 8.205 (its other occurrences in the *Iliad*: 4.235, 408, 18.502, 21.360, 428, 23.574 are, as she admits, ambiguous). The mixture of the military and the judicial flavor of the term are evident in *Agamemnon* (47). Its use in the present context does not preclude that both meanings are applicable, as Orestes invokes Athena in her guise as a military leader in this passage (292–298).

24. My argument here relies on Dover 1957 and Futo-Kennedy 2006.

25. The Egyptian campaign (460/59 to 454 BC) marked a great defeat for the Delian

League. The Athenians initially sent their fleet from Cyprus to Egypt to help Inarus, who had persuaded the Egyptians to revolt against the Persians; and though they were successful at first, by 454 BC after six years of operations in Egypt they were forced out of Memphis by Megabyzus, the Persian commander. On the failure of the Egyptian campaign, see further Meiggs 1972, 103–108, 473–476; Fornara and Samons 1991, 88 n. 32, with the relevant sources and bibliography.

26. This precise linking of these geographical references with historical events has not always met with acceptance. Dover (1957, 237) has argued against both identifying the Athenian campaign in Egypt and inferring that there was trouble in Potidaea, a Corinthian colony. But see Podlecki 1989, 133; Sommerstein 1989, 133 *ad* 292–296. Futo-Kennedy (2006, 43–47) argues that the reference to the Phlegrean plain may allude more broadly to the sphere of operations of the empire in Chalcidice and Thrace, citing Herodotus (7.123) as evidence for Phlegra as an ancient name for Pallene in Thrace. As she notes, the Athenians had already successfully pursued their strategic interests in the area of the Strymon and Thrace (p. 47). In her response to Dover's arguments against the Egyptian campaign, she cites Herodotus' testimony (2.15–17) on the relationship between Egypt, Libya, and the Nile Delta.

27. Athens had undertaken operations in the Aegean and northeast in the 460s BC, including the capture of Eion (Th. 1.98.1), the subjection of Thasos and the attempt to colonize Ennea Hodoi at the Strymon (Th. 1.100.2–3), the capture of Scyros (Th. 1.98.2), and the campaign in Chersonese. The campaigns against Cyprus and Egypt date to the 450s BC. See further Meiggs 1972, 68–108. For Futo-Kennedy 2006, 47–48, the inclusion of the mention of these locations, which include specific regions of activity associated with the empire, also "supply a mythological precedent or charter for Athenian presence in those regions . . . and link it explicitly to an expansionist agenda" (p. 48). Her argument on geography and empire is a refutation of Dover 1957.

28. Futo-Kennedy 2006, 56–57: "ταγοῦχος is a hapax . . . and in addition to the technical term *summachos*, places the geography and also the court proceedings squarely in the realm of military (and allied) action." In addition, Athena's appearance from the area of the Troad (397–402) reinforces this interpretation. Athena's presence in the vicinity of the river Scamander similarly evokes the league's early military operations in the area to free Greek lands that had been conquered by the Persians. The suggestion that Sigeum furnishes the most historically apt allusion to Athena's presence in the area of the Troad must be taken as referring to the annexation of Sigeum to the Delian League rather than to the sixth-century conflict between Athens and Mytilene over Sigeum, as Futo-Kennedy suggests (p. 42). Though see Macleod (1982, 125), who posits that in the sixth century the Athenians had invented a myth that Theseus' sons bequeathed to Athena territory in the Troad to justify their claims on Sigeum against Mytilene.

29. The role of Athena has been seen as analogous to that of the king in other suppliant plays. See Mills 1997, 56. Futo-Kennedy 2006 has argued that Athena in *Eumenides* represents the Athenian empire and its interests: the role she played historically after 454 BC, when Athens was made the seat of the empire with the transfer of the allied treasury from Delos to Athens.

30. The semantic implications of "without a spear" are not to be taken as literally, as Quincey (1964, 191–193) suggests, when he points out that the alliance will require that Athens will intervene militarily on behalf of Argos in the future. For δορυξενία ("spear-alliance") as defining the character of the alliance between Athena and Orestes, see Griffith 1995, 100.

31. Futo-Kennedy 2006, 54–55, suggests that the expression "without spear" readily refers instead to the reality of imperial domination. She cites the examples of Carystos, Naxos, and Thasos as evidence of cities that had been brought into the empire through the use of force already by 458 BC. But Orestes' representation as Athens' ally deploys Athens' and Argos' shared antagonism against Sparta to solidify Athenian hegemony.

32. Pericles' account of Athenian altruism and the political exchanges, which it helped to foster, is at odds with the realities of imperial expansion and the allies' plight as subjects. Denying that self-interest played a role, he attributes instead the empire's growth to the Athenians' confidence, inspired in them by freedom (Th. 2.40.5). See further, Low 2007, 246–247, on the relationship between Athenian altruism and imperial acquisitiveness. On reciprocity, see further Herman 1987, 116–142; Konstan 1998; Missiou 1998.

33. The only other source where Zeus, Apollo and Athena appear together is Homer (*Il.* 8.540, 13.827, 16.97). Harrison (1927, 501–502) points out that the alliance between the three gods whom she identifies with the *tripatores* in *Eumenides* reinforces the claims of patriarchy. On Zeus as Savior and Fulfiller, see Burian 1986. It is important to note that Apollo claims that he is carrying out the will of Zeus (616–618). On the ambiguities surrounding Apollo's role, see Roberts 1984 and Bierl 1994.

34. His return restores the disruption in the line of succession, caused by Clytemnestra's usurpation of the throne. Not surprisingly, as Griffith (1995, 79 n. 66) notes, Clytemnestra and Aegisthus are mostly referred to as tyrants, not kings. Clytemnestra's power is recognized during Agamemnon's absence (A. *A.* 258–260); see further Denniston and Page 1957 *ad* 259–260. On Clytemnestra's political aspirations and the complexities inherent therein, see Thomson 1941; Jones 1962; Betensky 1978; Zeitlin 1978; Winnington-Ingram 1983, 101–131.

35. On the form of the oath that Orestes swears, see Quincey 1964, 199–200: "Oaths taken by states and individuals were commonly reinforced with an imprecation by which the contracting party invoked a dire penalty, normally ἐξώλεια ("destruction"), upon himself in the event of any transgression." Among the parallels that he cites, note especially the oath prescribed by the Athenians upon Colophon, dated to 447/6 BC, which includes similar language regarding the infringement of the oath, also brought against the Colophonian's family as well as the mention of blessings. In pronouncing the oath, Orestes also takes on the role normally assigned to a god in other plays, which end with aetiologies of hero-cult, as do also Oedipus in S. *OC* and Eurystheus in E. *Heracl*. On this type of oath, see also E. *Supp.* 1183–1196. On the role of gods in bringing about closure in Euripidean aetiologies, see Dunn 1996, 26–44.

36. Quincey (1964, 202) suggests that the aetiology refers to Orestes' Spartan cult, a view with which I disagree; see further the following section: "Relocating Orestes from Sparta to Argos." Though there was no known cult of Orestes in Argos at the time, the aetiology relates Orestes' Argive cult with the recently concluded alliance and more broadly with Athens' change of foreign policy toward Sparta. On this count, the dramatic fiction of his burial in Argos counters the established tradition of Orestes' Spartan cult, explaining the new ties between Argos and Athens by locating his tomb in Argos.

37. Kowalzig (2006) also situates the adoption of non-Athenian heroes within the specific historical background of the plays she discusses and more broadly within the context of Athens' imperial democracy.

38. J. M. Hall 1999; McCauley 1999.

39. The introduction of new hero-cults could also be prompted by political realign-

ments in the sphere of interstate relations. Blomart (2004) offers representative examples of the different types of the transfer of the hero, which served military and political purposes. I mention two of the examples: the transfer of Theseus' relics from Scyros to Athens, which enabled Cimon to annex the island to the Athenian empire (Paus. 1.17.6, 3.3.7), and Cleisthenes' introduction of the Theban Melanippus (to Sicyon) whose worship was intended to supersede the existing cult of the Argive Adrastus (Hdt. 5.67) (the Argives at the same time probably established a memorial in honor of the seven Argive leaders to enhance their military power) (p. 84). J. M. Hall (1999, 49–59 provides the best account of the phenomenon of "multilocal" heroes, that is, heroes who were worshiped in diverse locales. He argues that while in some cases an army could appropriate a hero to win the military advantage over another city by transferring his cult into their own, the founding of hero cults also articulated new ties with another city, as the cults of the Argive Seven and those of Agamemnon in the Argolid in the archaic period evince. On the distinction between hero-cult and tomb-cult, see Antonaccio 1993: "Hero-cult is distinct from tomb-cult. . . . It finds formal expression in scheduled ritual action at specific locations, including processions, sacrifice, and games and is often emphasized by the construction of a monument such as a naiskos and/or an altar" (p. 52). Orestes' burial in Argos corresponds more readily to a tomb cult, though in this discussion I use the term "hero-cult" as well to draw connections with other types of heroes with whom he shares typological similarities.

40. For a typology of the transfer of heroes, see Blomart 2004, 92–93. Kowalzig (2006) considers an even broader spectrum of non-Athenian heroes who receive burial and heroic honors in Athens in tragedy. Among these, she includes the appropriation of the Salaminian Ajax, whose heroization, she argues, reflects the degree to which his Athenian identity was contested, even though Athens' possession of Salamis was not. On Sophocles' *Ajax* and the much-discussed problem of his prospective hero-cult, see, for example, Burian 1972; Henrichs 1993.

41. Festugière 1973; Kearns 1990; Visser 1982; Seaford 1994, 126–139.

42. Like Oedipus and Eurystheus, Orestes' future worship centers on his tomb (αὐτοὶ γὰρ ἡμεῖς ὄντες ἐν τάφοις τότε, "when I am in my tomb," 767), but he does not die at the end of the play, as do Oedipus (S. *OC* 1657–1666) and most probably Eurystheus (E. *Heracl.* 1026–1037; the text is lacunose after 1052).

43. Dunn 1996, 45–63.

44. On the talismanic power of heroes, see Brelich 1958.

45. By this I mean that that most savior heroes in tragedy are noteworthy non-Athenians, while the funeral orations do not specifically commemorate the contributions of non-Athenians (metics or the allies). On the representation of the Athenian dead in the funeral orations, see Parker 1996, 135–140.

46. Kowalzig 2006. Seaford (1994) has argued that the social power of hero-cult in tragedy resides in transforming reciprocal violence and rendering it beneficial for the entire city, often at the expense of another city.

47. On savior heroes in Athens, see Kearns 1989. For a typology of patriotic heroes, see Kron 1999. On hero worship, see, in general, Burkert 1985a, 203–215.

48. Kearns (1990) emphasizes the vital role played by figures normally relegated to the periphery of the city. She singles out civic marginality as the identifying mark of those who performed saving acts on behalf of the city such as foreign heroes and women.

49. Bolmarcich 2003 cites Th. 3.70.6, 3.75.1, 7.33.5; Xen. *Hell.* 2.2.20, 5.3.26;

Aeschin. 3.100; Plut. *Pel.* 27. See Griffith (1995, 104), who views Orestes' promise of the alliance as the equivalent of an aristocratic alliance, brought about through elite networks of exchange, but depicted as a benefit for all Athenians regardless of rank and standing.

50. Athenian rituals, in particular, furnish a framework for exploring the manner in which tragedy defined the empire against the legacy of Panhellenism. See further Saïd 2002; Kowalzig 2006, 79–86; Rosenbloom 2006a,Rosenbloom 2011. On Panhellenism in the fifth century, see Georges 1994; Green 1996; Flower 2000; E. Hall 1989; J. M. Hall 2002; Mitchell 2007.

51. Snodgrass 1971; Nagy 1999; Hall 1997, 2002; Morris 2000.

52. Lardinois 1992. On hero cult and the Homeric epics, see Farnell 1921, 280–322, and Coldstream 1976. On the emergence of hero cult and its antecedents, see Bérard 1982, 89–105; Morris 1988; Snodgrass 1987, 159–164; Antonaccio 1994; Whitley 1988.

53. de Polignac 1984; Snodgrass 2000.

54. Malkin (1994, 28) aptly remarks that there is no contradiction between myths that relate Sparta to legendary "Achaean" figures such as Menelaus and Agamemnon in the eighth century BC and those of the return of the Heraclidae to the Peloponnese, which established the Spartans' identity and claims as Dorians (earliest literary attestation in Tyrtaeus fr. 12 Gentili/Prato). As he notes: "The Achaean connections that seem to have become prominent in Sparta after the mid-sixth century were not an alternative to any of its constitutive historicizing self-images. Sparta's past was enriched and pan-Hellenized but underwent no fundamental metamorphosis. . . . Now other princes of the land from the Achaean past, especially Agamemnon, Odysseus, Orestes, and Teisamenus, now found new emphases and articulations in *ad hoc* political contexts in response to external challenges."

55. On the uses of Spartan genealogies, see Calame 1987, esp. 176–177, on the role of Achaean genealogies in consolidating Spartan hegemony from the middle of the sixth to the fifth century.

56. Blomart 2004, 81–94. Capturing the goodwill of the hero did not always involve transfer, as evinced by the example of Solon, who offered sacrifices to the heroes of Salamis (Plut. *Sol.* 9.1–2).

57. Podlecki 1966, 141–142; Malkin 1987, 81–84.

58. Leahy 1955. Tisamenus' transfer takes place soon after that of Orestes, but he was not as prominent as Orestes; the tomb of the latter was located in the *Agora* according to Pausanias (3.11.10).

59. Argos' power in the Peloponnese had increased significantly under the tyrant Pheidon, who unified the Argolid in the seventh century BC, following his important victory on the plain of Thyrea in 545 BC (Hdt. 1.82). By the sixth century BC, however, Sparta had already displaced Argos; Cleomenes weakened Argos' power further (Hdt. 6.76–82), and the Argives later refused to join the Hellenic League (Hdt. 7.148–152). See Stadter 2006, 250. On the history of Argos in the archaic period, see T. Kelly 2009, esp. 73–144. On Sparta's relations with Argos, see *CAH* 4, 363–364; and on Argos and the Peloponnesian League, see *CAH* 4, 353–358.

60. Tegea was probably the first in a series of alliances that Sparta entered into with other cities in the Peloponnese and eventually grew into what is commonly referred to as the "Peloponnesian League," a modern name for what the ancient sources more accurately refer to as "the Lacaedemonians and their allies." After the conclusion of the treaty with Tegea (Plut. *Mor.* 292b), Sparta was able to settle her claims over Thyreatis and Cynouria and defeat Argos in 546 BC. On Sparta's alliances in the archaic period, see *CAH* 3, 351–359,

4, 350–353, and Yates 2005, 65–76, with ample testimonia and bibliography. Cawkwell (1993) and T. Braun (1994, 44) have argued against the mid sixth-century date.

61. Dickins 1912, 21–24; Leahy 1958; Cartledge 1979, 138–139; Huxley 1979; Forrest 1980, 73–83; Malkin 1987, 26–33.

62. Boedeker (1993, 165–167) disagrees with this view and doubts that the Tegeans would have accepted Sparta's attempt to legitimize her hegemony in this way.

63. Spartan kings claimed their descent from Achaean heroes: Hdt. 6.53; Malkin 1994, 19. Through Orestes, the Spartans traced their ties back to Pelops via Atreus' lineage.

64. J. M. Hall 1997, 91–93.

65. Hdt. 6.61.19–20; Paus. 3.19.9. See Cartledge 1987, 339; Antonaccio 1993, 57.

66. Argos in Homer designates the territory that Diomedes ruled as king (*Il.* 2.559–568; *Od.* 3.180–181) and is also used more broadly in reference to the regions over which Agamemnon held sway (*Il.* 1.30, 4.171, 6.456, 9.22).

67. Stesichorus fr. 39 *PMG*; also Simonides, scholiast E. *Or.* 46. Athenaeus (513 A) says that Xanthus was Stesichorus' source, though Garvie (1986, xvii) says that no evidence supports Xanthus' existence as a poet. On the political alignment of Stesichorus' *Oresteia* with the Pelopids' presence with Sparta, see Bowra 1961, 107–119; though see further Garvie (1986, xviii with n. 29) who suggests instead that the genealogy Stesichorus follows is older and derives from Hesiod, *Catalogue* fr. 194, where Agamemnon is the son of Pleisthenes, son of Atreus.

68. Pi. *P.* 11.31–37; *N.* 11.34. Antonaccio (1993, 54) argues that the cult site at Sclavohori near Amyclae appears to have been active already in the Iron Age and that votive offerings increased significantly in the sixth century. Cassandra and Agamemnon were worshiped at Amyclae in Pausanias' time.

69. See Fraenkel (1962, 209–210 *ad* 400 with n. 2), who argues that a motive for the change of setting was to strengthen the case against Paris by representing both brothers as plaintiffs of Priam (ἐπεὶ Πριάμου/μέγας ἀντίδικος/Μενέλαος ἄναξ ἠδ' Ἀγαμέμνων, "when Menelaus, Priam's great adversary and lord Agamemnon," *A.* 40–42).

70. Costa 1962, 24–31 and esp. 27–28; Lardinois 1992, 322; Braun 1998, 102–104.

71. J. R. Cole 1977 elaborates on the connections between Agamemnon and Cimon in an effort to argue that the play supports Cimon's early recall from ostracism. See further Rosenbloom (1995 and 2011, 364–366), who argues that the *Oresteia* represents a transitional moment between Cimon's and Pericles' policies on the empire.

72. On the use of genealogical claims in Athenian imperial ideology, see Bremmer 1997 and Zacharia 2003.

73. Orestes' sojourn in Athens, whence he departs to return to Argos to murder Aegisthus, is attested in Homer's *Odyssey* (3.306–307).

74. Meier (1990, 251 n. 49) argues against Dodds 1986 that the ambivalent outcome of Orestes' purification is integral to representing the "factional conflict" between Athena and the Furies. On the ambiguities surrounding purification, see discussion below.

75. Orestes himself announces at the end of *Choephori* that he will go to Delphi to be purified by Apollo (1034–1039).

76. Pollution, however, is suppressed in the *Agamemnon*. The killings within Atreus' family are described as singular departures from the norms that underwrite the proper performance of sacrificial rituals. See especially Zeitlin 1965 and 1966.

77. The possibility of exile is raised by the chorus, who state that Clytemnestra should be banished from the land for Agamemnon's murder (A. *A.* 1410–1411). She retorts (1412–1420) that no such punishment was imposed on Agamemnon for his pollution (χρῆν σ'

NOTES *to* PAGES 43–45

147

ἀνδρηλατεῖν/μιασμάτων ἄποιν', "you ought to have banished him as punishment for his pollution," 1419–1420). Toward the end of the play, the chorus call Clytemnestra the "pollution of the land and of its gods" (1645), and accuse Aegisthus of "polluting Justice" (1669). These references characterize the "corrupt" new order. Occurring as they do late in the play, they set the stage for the emergence of pollution in *Choephori* where, not incidentally, the chorus also make reference to Clytemnestra's and Aegisthus' pollution (944). Alternatively, the coexistence of reciprocal violence and exile is not incompatible, since homicide between two kinship groups could be settled by exile or compensation; the two alternatives coexist in Homer's epics: see especially Westbrook 1992; Cantarella 2001. Dramatically, however, such measures are not imposed against those who perpetrate crimes against their own kin. Inbred violence (i.e., violence among members of the same kinship group) is dramatically treated in *Agamemnon* as coextensive with the earlier regime of self-help, which the advent of the *polis* and its institutions had abolished. The persistence of Atreus' family vendetta then is represented as a manifestation of this earlier law of vengeance whose poetic conception is attributed to the curse of the house, its avenging spirit (ἀλάστωρ, 1500–1502) or alternatively the child-avenging Fury, who works through human agents (1433). It is difficult to pin down more precisely the correspondence between the historical and dramatic reality; the mixing of mythical and historical elements from different periods was a feature of anachronism in tragedy, where references to practices and institutions belonging to different times existed alongside each other. See further Easterling 1997.

78. Garvie 1986, 314–316 (*ad* 966–68) discusses some of the textual uncertainties in these lines. Garvie follows Page's text and translates: "when all pollution has been driven from the hearth by rites of purification." The chorus then for their part suggest that ritual cleansing may be sufficient, though the killings that Orestes is about to perpetrate will require his removal from the house and the city. Garvie also cites numerous parallels from tragedy on the purification of the house from pollution (e.g., A. *Eu.* 63; S. *El.* 69–70, *OT* 1228; E. *IT* 1216).

79. See chorus' words at A. *A.* 1217–1222, 1242–1244); Zeitlin 1965.

80. As Parker (1983, 133–143) has shown, there is no secure date for the emergence of pollution historically. See below, "Why does Purification Fail?"

81. I am not seeking to revive Thomson's theory (1941, 1966) that the *Oresteia* depicted an evolution of social organization from tribal society (Furies) to aristocracy and purification (Apollo) to democracy and the lawcourt (Athena).

82. On the transition from *oikos* to *polis* and its relevance for the evolution of justice in the trilogy, see Conacher 1987, 5; Meier 1993, 123–137 and 1990, 69–119; Seaford 92–105.

83. Orestes wraps Clytemnestra's and Aegisthus' bodies in the blood-stained garment in which Clytemnestra had ensnared Agamemnon, so that his vengeance mirrors that of the perpetrators (A. *Ch.* 1010–1015). In *Choephori* 577–578, Aegisthus' murder is specifically conceived as part of the chain of kin-murders to be traced back to the quarrel between Atreus and Thyestes. Thus, the "third drink" suggests either that Aegisthus is third after Thyestes' children and Agamemnon or, as Garvie 1986, 199–200 notes *ad loc.*, that the number 3 is meant to evoke more generally the "blood" drink of the Furies with corrupt performance of the third libation to Zeus Soter.

84. Both the images of a storm and of wounding are conveyed hereby; see Garvie 1986, 112 *ad* 271–272. See also *Ch.* 291–294; Orestes' projected trials are similar to the treatment of the polluted killer; see Garvie 1986, 118 *ad* 291–296.

85. I agree for the most part with Delcourt 1959; for other interpretations on Apollo's

oracle, see Garvie (1986, III *ad* 269–296), who argues that there is no specific Delphic doctrine here but that the punishments Apollo mentions are associated with the chthonic realm. The Furies as chthonic deities and protectors of the rights of dead kin inflict the same kind of punishment upon the perpetrators as upon the relatives of the deceased who neglected their duty toward his kin.

86. The worldview of *Choephori* is permeated by blood vengeance; both the Furies and the laws of vengeance structure the mental attitude of the participants toward the crimes, emphasizing all the while the perpetuation of violence within the family (A. *Ch.* 287–290, 398–404, 471–475, 575–578, 648–651). See further Lebeck 1971, 80–91.

87. To be sure, Clytemnestra not only undertakes responsibility for Agamemnon's murder but also engages in an exploration of the motives, alternating between viewing herself as bringing justice against Agamemnon (A. *A.* 1431–1433, 1551–1559) or as the avenging spirit that perpetuates the killing of children (A. *A.* 1475–1480, 1497–1504).

88. On Orestes' dilemma, see Garvie 1986, 293 *ad* 899, with the relevant bibliography.

89. When he claims responsibility for his action, Orestes addresses Clytemnestra as a "father-slaughtering pollution, hated by the gods" (πατροκτόνον μίασμα καὶ θεῶν στύγος, 1028), calling attention again to the pollution that attached to her heinous and impious action.

90. As Parker (1983, 108–109 with n. 13) points out, προστρόπαιος refers to the supplication of Orestes *qua* killer (cf. also 234), though it is also used of suppliants at large (A. *A.* 1587; S. *Aj.* 1173, *Phil.* 930, *OC* 1309). More broadly, προστρόπαιος can designate the pollution of the killer, that of his victim, and that of the avenging spirits.

91. Taplin 1977, 381–384; Brown 1982; 1983, 30–32; Parker 1983, 386–388; Neitzel 1991; Sidwell 1996.

92. See Dyer (1969), who remarks that "these oracular instructions [Dyer is referring to lines 74–84] are fulfilled by Orestes (235–243) and lead to his trial and acquittal on the Areopagus. No words in the text indicate that any purification ritual takes place at Delphi, and it would be natural to assume that, when Apollo later claims to be καθάρσιος ("purifier," 578) of this murder, he only claims responsibility for giving Orestes an oracle that leads to purification (in the same way that he admits responsibility for Orestes' crime [579–580, cf. 84] on the grounds that his oracle suggested the deed), and does not refer to an actual purification" (p. 39).

93. Taplin 1977, 382. On the timing of the purification, see Dyer (1969, 39 n. 5), who divides the various solutions into three groups: (1) Orestes is already purified, when the Pythia enters; (2) Orestes is in the process of being purified, when the Pythia first enters, but she does not or cannot see Apollo; (3) Apollo purifies Orestes after the Pythia leaves and is in the process of purifying him when he first enters onstage; (4) Apollo purifies Orestes onstage, that is, after his entrance in line 64. Alternatively, Sommerstein 1989, 124 *ad* 237 suggests that Orestes was purified some time after he left Delphi and before reaching Athens, as he is described as προστρόπαιος at 234, but claims that he is no longer polluted (237, 445).

94. Brown 1982, 26–30; Sommerstein 1989, 92–93 *ad* 64–93; Sidwell 1996, 53.

95. Taplin 1977, 365–374. Sommerstein (1989, 93) notes that Orestes is sitting close to the altar and that there are at least three chairs in front of him on which the Furies are sleeping (cf. 140).

96. See A.R. 4.685–717 for a description of Medea's and Jason's purification: their silence serves to indicate their standing as polluted murderers awaiting purification. To be sure there are instances when polluted killers converse with other characters onstage. But

the danger of contagion is noted, as it is by Heracles, for example, who fears that his pollution will affect Theseus S. *OC* 94. Similarly, Oedipus shows similar concern, when Theseus invites him to come to Athens with him E. *HF* 1200–1202. This is where I part ways with Sidwell (1996, 52–56), who argues that the scene the Pythia describes—the bloodstained Orestes, seated at the altar, surrounded by the sleeping Furies inside the temple—already represents the aftermath of purification. He argues further that Apollo appears in the guise of purifier, holding a sacrificial piglet and a branch of laurel (as he is in South Apulian vase paintings [p. 53 n. 46]), an indication that the ritual had already been performed.

97. They are agents of Clytemnestra's vengeance; Clytemnestra offers them libations in contravention of ritual custom (106–109)—the Furies never received libations qua Erinyes, but only in their positive guise as Eumenides.

98. Seaford 1994, 102–105.

99. A.R. 4.712–717: ἡ δ' εἴσω πελανοὺς μειλικτρά τε νηφαλίῃσιν/καῖεν ἐπ' εὐχωλῇσι παρέστιος, ὄφρα χόλοιο/σμερδαλέας παύσειεν Ἐρινύας ἠδὲ καὶ αὐτός/εὐμειδής τε πέλοιτο καὶ ἤπιος ἀμφοτέροισιν,/εἴτ' οὖν ὀθνείῳ μεμιασμένοι αἵματι χεῖρας/εἴτε καὶ ἐμφύλῳ προσκηδέες ἀντιόῳεν. "And she (i.e., Circe) was burning cakes of appeasement without wine by the hearth that she might check the terrible Furies from their wrath, and that Zeus himself might be propitious and gentle to them both, whether they should happen to supplicate him with hands polluted by the blood of a stranger or by the blood of a kinsman."

100. Parker 1983, 370–374.

101. Parker 1983, 387. On vengeance and honor, see Visser 1984.

102. Such offerings were made in cult to the Eumenides, who represented the Furies' benign attributes, as Henrichs 1983 and 1991 has shown.

103. MacDowell (1963, 33–84) discusses the different types of courts: the Areopagus was assigned cases of intentional homicide; the Palladion, cases of unpremeditated murder; and the Delphinion, justifiable homicide. The court of the Phreatto tried cases of unintentional homicide for persons who had gone into exile but were not yet pardoned by the family of their victim, while the Prytaneion charged unknown murderers as well as animals or inanimate objects cf. Arist. *Pol.* 1300 b24–30.

104. Parker 1983, 113–115 with nn. 42, 387.

105. Parker (1983, 114) notes that only in cases of justified homicide was the killer considered pure in the eyes of the law. As Visser (1984, 196 with n. 6) points out, the trial itself did not obliterate defilement. As a result, trials at the Areopagus, for example, were held in open air to guard against pollution, and the city had to close down for three days during the trial.

106. Parker 1983, 387–388.

107. For a comprehensive discussion of examples of exile and purification of the killer in Greek myth, see Parker 1983, 374–392.

108. As Parker (1983, 125) notes, the doctrine of pollution may have emerged even earlier, as it is suited to a society without recourse to a developed legal system. Dramatically, the regime of exile and purification similarly suggests a stage before the development of judicial institutions. See further Moulinier 1975; Blickman 1986.

109. The development of homicide laws did not erase pollution: in Draco's law, the relatives of the victim are ordered to make a proclamation for excluding the killer from public participation (*IG* I² 115, lines 20–21; thus Blickman 1986, 201 with n. 32; *contra*, see Gagarin 1981, 165–167); it was also made by the *basileus* before whom the relatives brought the charge against the accused (D. 20.158). See also MacDowell 1963, 25–26, 139–140.

110. Orestes states that he has already been cleansed by Apollo and then again later in the course of his wanderings. Further weakened by the long interval of exile, he is no longer defiled and can thus reassure his Athenian hosts that no harm will befall them by coming into contact with him (235–242).

111. See Samons 1998–1999; Seaford 1994, 92–105.

112. Sommerstein 1989, 11. For a fuller discussion, see Brown (1984), who does not accept the identification of the Erinyes with the Eumenides. But see Henrichs 1991.

113. On the interplay between the animal sacrifice and *xenia*, see Bacon 2001.

114. On the gender dynamics, see especially Zeitlin 1978. As she argues, the association of the Furies with the past and regressive models of administering justice presages their defeat, as their time-honored rights are rendered obsolete by the new male Olympian order.

115. For the transformation of enemy to hero, see Visser 1982. This pattern refers to mortal heroes such as Eurystheus and Oedipus, but it also applies to the Furies' dramatic conversion. On the gradual change of the Furies throughout the trilogy, see Lebeck 1971, 145–149.

116. The Erinyes in Homer punish a variety of offenses against family members (e.g., *Il.* 9.447–457); they can be seen as the embodiment of the curse of the parent (e.g., *Il.* 9.454; *Od.* 2.134–136); they punish oath breaking (e.g., *Il.* 19.259–260) and are purveyors of justice and order (e.g., *Il.* 19.418). For a fuller discussion, see Harrison 1903, 203–256; Rohde 1925, 178–182; Solmsen 1949, 178–224; Wüst RE Suppl. 8.82–166; Zeitlin 1978, 163–165; Brown 1983, 1984; Henrichs 1984; Garvie 1986, 344–348; Sansone 1988; Podlecki 1989, 1–9; Sommerstein 1989, 6–12; Lloyd-Jones 1990, 204–205; Padel 1992, 172–181 and 1995, 79–80; Johnston 1999, 139–142, 251–258.

117. Lloyd-Jones 1990, 205. On their association with Zeus' justice, see Solmsen 1949, 189, 197; Winnington-Ingram 1954, 21; Brown 1983, 27–28.

118. See *A.* 147–55, where the connection between the cyclical repetition of sacrificial violence and vengeance is rendered explicit and attributed to the "child-avenging Anger." *Menis*, the personification of wrath, is closely associated with the role, which the Furies embody as avengers of kin-killing. Sommerstein (1989, 7 with n. 25) notes that the name Erinyes as an abstract noun means "Wraths."

119. Cassandra describes them as drunk with blood in *A.* 1188–1190; Orestes refers to the "third drink" of the Furies (*Ch.* 577–578) in reference to his impending murder of Aegisthus. Their participation in corrupting hospitality and the ritualized conviviality of the symposium occurs at the point, when they prepare to punish Agamemnon for the sacrifice of Iphigeneia, since the chorus make mention of her participation in her father's sympotic gatherings in their account of her sacrifice in the *parodos* (*A.* 243–247).

120. See also *A.* 1431–1433, where Clytemnestra also justifies Agamemnon's murder by swearing to the trinity of Justice, Ruins and the Erinys of (her) daughter." Clytemnestra also describes herself as the instrument or personification of the "savage avenging spirit of Atreus" (1500–1504).

121. See especially, *A. Ch.* 646–650. The Erinys, an instrument of justice, will punish the blood pollution for the murder of Agamemnon, perpetrated long ago.

122. See Lloyd-Jones 1990, 205: "Since Clytemnestra has no heirs to avenge her, they must appear in person; thus Aeschylus takes the momentous step of departing from the general rule that Greek gods work not directly, but through human actions to accomplish their purposes on earth."

123. See further Brown 1983, 13–22.

124. Their close association with the dead victim may suggest that their origin as per-

sonifications of the souls of the dead, as Rohde 1925, 146–279, first proposed. Lloyd-Jones 1990, 204–206, suggests that the Aeschylean conception of the Furies as closely identified with their dead victims is closer to their earlier, pre-Homeric function (though he notes that the Furies do not figure in the *kommos* in *Choephori*, where the participants instead invoke Agamemnon's ghost). On the Erinyes as souls, see discussion of the Derveni papyrus in Henrichs 1984; Johnston 1999, 127–160, 273–279.

125. On the impasse that intrafamilial violence in the *Oresteia*, see especially Seaford 1994, 103–105.

126. In Hesiod's *Theogony* (180–187) they are children of the Earth, born of the castrated genitals of Uranus.

127. On the Keres and their association with the Erinyes, see Harrison 1903, 163–172, 213–232; Sommerstein 1989, 8.

128. As Brown 1983, 14, notes, the idea of the blood-drinking Furies, which is emphasized at the beginning of *Eumenides* as a source of concern, arises earlier in the trilogy and may be an Aeschylean invention. In addition, Brown suggests that Aeschylus may also be basing his depiction on the Hesiodic Keres (Hes. [*Sc.*] 248–257).

129. On their association with the dead, see Henrichs 1994, 54–58; Johnston 1999, 273–279. On artistic representations of the Furies, see Prag 1985, 48–51; Lissarague 2006.

130. Henrichs 1991 has demonstrated that the dramatic conception of the Aeschylean Furies is based on their nature of chthonic goddesses. Thus, the positive powers that they acquire in Athens are not the result of a transformation, as has previously been assumed, but a manifestation of the benign side of their religious character. For a review of earlier views on the topic, see pp. 164–166 (and esp. 165 n. 10, where he refutes the views of Reinhardt 1949; Meier 1990 and Herington 1986).

131. Henrichs (1994, 38) states emphatically that "the Erinyes *qua* Erinyes" never received cult (with the exception of the special cases of Demeter Erinys at Arcadia and that of the Erinyes of Laius and Oedipus at Sparta and on Thera). On the euphemistic appellations of these chthonic divinities, see Henrichs 1991, 169–179. On their designation as "anonymous goddesses," see Henrichs 1991, 174–179, and 1994.

132. On the duality of the Furies' dramatic character, see Winnington-Ingram 1954, 18–22; Lloyd-Jones 1983, 244; Visser 1984, 202.

133. The name Eumenides appears only in the title of the play, in the Hypothesis, in a scholium on line 761 and in the list of dramatis personae. See further Brown 1984, 267–276; Sommerstein 1989, 280–282 *ad* 1027, on the likelihood that Aeschylus named the Erinyes Eumenides (*contra* Brown 1984) or *Semnai* in the course of Athena's speech. Brown 1983 and 1984 has argued against the identification between Erinyes, and Eumenides/*Semnai Theai*. But as Henrichs 1991 has argued the eventual identification of the mythical Erinyes with the Eumenides/*Semnai Theai* stems from the polarity that is characteristic of chthonic deities at large. For full literary references, see Brown 1984, 260–265 and Henrichs 1991, 170 with n. 18; e.g., Eumenides: E. *Or.* 38, 321, 836, 1650; S. *OC* 42, 486; and D. 23.66 refer to the Erinyes as Eumenides. *Semnai Theai*: Ar. *Eq.* 1312, *Th.* 224–225; S. *OC* 89–110, 458; Th. 1.126. 11; Din. 1.47. In *Eu.* 383, 1006, and 1041, the Furies appear to be identified with the *Semnai Theai* of the Areopagus. "Anonymous goddesses": E. *IT* 944.

134. For sources and discussion, see Henrichs 1983, 97–99. For the offerings to the *Semnai Theai* in Athens, see *Eu.* 834–836 (first-offerings), 107 (libations), 108–109 (burnt offerings), 1006 (animals). In S. *OC* 100, 469–481, wineless libations are also mentioned (though without sacrifices); Aeschin. 1.188 (prayers); Callim. fr. 681 Pfeiffer suggests that

---

the female members of the *genos* of the *Hesychidae* in charge of the cult of the *Semnai Theai*/Eumenides in Athens poured wineless libations over sacrificial cakes. On the cults of the Eumenides and the *Semnai Theai*, see Brown 1984, 260–263.

135. Henrichs 1991, 166.

136. Henrichs 1991, 164–169.

137. Though no such sacrifices were attested for the Furies, Pausanias (2.11.4) mentions the sacrifice of a pregnant sheep to the Eumenides of Sicyon—indicating their association with fertility. On Demeter Erinys, see Johnston 1999, 260–264. As she notes: "Erinys' interest in the parent-child relationship, particularly the mother-child relationship, would make it especially easy for her to be identified with Demeter in the context of a story where Demeter's actions are motivated by the loss of a child. . . . But the similarity between the two goddesses that allowed them to be combined in these myths goes beyond this into a broader context for fecundity, particularly human fecundity" (p. 261). Beyond the association of chthonic divinities with fertility, it must be noted that the association of the Furies in Athens with marriage and thank-offerings for successful births are in line with the restoration of the sacrificial murders of children as well as offer a counterpart to the ill-omened union of Paris and Helen (*A. A.* 699–749). See further, Lebeck 1971, 48.

138. In terms of gender dynamics, this shift emphasizes the progressive relegation of the female to the power of the male that Athena champions through her close association with Zeus A. *Eu.* 736–738.

139. Sommerstein 1989, 10 n. 35: Paus. 1.28.6; E. *El.* 1270–1272; *IT* 968–969; Th. 1.126.11; Paus. 7.25.2.

140. Ar. *Eq.* 1312, *Th.* 224; Th. 1.126.10–11; Plut. *Sol.* 12.1; Paus. 7.25.1.

141. Historically, the Areopagus' authority in deciding asylum must have been significant before the court was assigned homicide trials. In fact, not only the Areopagus, but other courts as well were located close to sacred sites, since those escaping murder may have sought protection there first. Orestes in *Eumenides* supplicates Athena before his trial (cf. also Paus. 1.28.6).

142. D. 23.67; Wallace 1989, 123.

143. The Furies attempt to persuade Orestes to swear an oath (429). See further Lardinois 1992, 319. On curses in Greek poetry, see further Watson 1991.

144. As Visser (1984, 198) aptly notes: "Areopagite procedure, too, undoubtedly incorporated pollution symbolism and avoidances."

145. On the reforms of the Areopagus and the new functions of the tribunal, see Wallace 1989, 94–127.

146. As Visser (1984, 194) points out, there are vestiges of the family's right to avenge their kinsman in contemporary Athenian legal practice: only family members could prosecute on behalf of their dead relatives; in addition, before the formal initiation of the proceedings, relatives of the victim would place spears on his tomb (Din. 1.46–47).

147. Hdt. 1.68.6: πολλῷ κατυπέρτεροι τῷ πολέμῳ ἐγίνοντο οἱ Λακεδαιμόνιοι· ἤδη δὲ σφι καὶ ἡ πολλὴ τῆς Πελοποννήσου ἦν κατεστραμμένη, "since then the Spartans were far superior (to the Tegeans) in battle; and they had already by them subjected most of the Peloponnese."

148. Sommerstein 1989, 263 *ad* 919–921 demonstrates that the Athenians presented themselves as avenging the Persians' widespread acts of sacrilege in Ionia and Greece (Hdt. 6.19.3, 6.96, 8.143.2, 8.144.2) that were discussed at a congress that took place in Athens at the instigation of Pericles (Plut. *Per.* 17). Rosenbloom (1995, 105–111) contrasts the positive image of the empire with its negative instantiation, embodied by Agamemnon who sacked the altars of the gods at Troy (*A.* 338–342, 527–528). On the cautionary attitudes toward

empire, contained in *Persians*, see further Rosenbloom 2006a; on history and drama in this play, see further Pelling 1997a, 1–15. On similar negative resonances of the Athenian empire in *Agamemnon*, see also Bakewell 2007.

149. 807: ὑπ' ἀστῶν τῶνδε τιμαλφουμένας, "honored by my citizens here"; 833: ὡς σεμνότιμος καὶ ξυνοικήτωρ ἐμοί, "since you will receive honors and live with me"; 854–855: καὶ σὺ τιμίαν/ἕδραν ἔχουσα πρὸς δόμοις Ἐρεχθέως, "and you will have an honored seat near the house of Erectheus"; 868–869: εὖ δρῶσαν, εὖ πάσχουσαν, εὖ τιμωμένην/χώρας μετασχεῖν τῆσδε θεοφιλεστάτης, "giving and receiving benefits, honored, you will share in this land, most dear to the gods"; 890–891: ἔξεστι γάρ σοι τῆσδε γαμόρωι χθονὸς/εἶναι δικαίως ἐς τὸ πᾶν τιμωμένηι, "it is possible for you to have a share of this land, honored justly for all time"; 992–995: τάσδε γὰρ εὔφρονας εὔφρονες ἀεί/μέγα τιμῶντες καὶ γῆν καὶ πόλιν/ὀρθοδίκαιον/πρέψετε πάντως διάγοντες, "for, if you always greatly honor with kindness the kindly ones as well as your land and city, you will be renowned, keeping a straight path of justice."

150. Headlam 1906, 272–274 points out that red robes were worn by the metics at the Panathenaic procession. The term metic (1011), however, is not used in a technical sense, but served to denote the Furies' change of standing from outsiders to honorary foreign residents in Athens and is initially described by Athena as ξυνοικία ("living together," 916). On processions in tragedy, see Kavoulaki 1999.

151. Rabinowitz 1981.

152. In this vein, the generational conflict between old and new gods has been seen as recasting the partisan struggle by representing the Furies as proponents of oligarchic interests and Athena as the spokesperson for radical democracy. For a detailed review on the scholarship concerning this issue, see Braun 1998, 150–203.


CHAPTER 2

1. The anti-Persian objective is also present in Herodotus' narrative of 470–489 BC (Hdt. 8.3.2, 108.4, 9.90.2, 106.2).

2. Raaflaub 2004, 84–89, 118–122, 126–128; Samons 2004, 106–108.

3. Meiggs 1972, 47. See also, Th. 3.10.3, 6.76.3.

4. Rawlings 1977.

5. Meiggs 1972, 68–91; Sealey 1976, 248–253; Samons 2004, 107–111.

6. For detailed treatment on this question, see Meiggs 1972, 42–305; Sealey 1976, 238–323; Rhodes 1985; Fornara and Samons 1991; Samons 2004, 76–146.

7. First mentioned in the fourth century (I. 4.120). On the historicity of the Peace of Callias, see Meiggs 1972, 129–151; Sealey 1976, 278–282; Fornara and Samons 1991, 96–99 and 171–175.

8. Meiggs 1972, 220–233.

9. Hornblower 1991a, 15–17.

10. Aegina and Thasos were among the highest paying members, each paying 30 talents a year.

11. On the dating of the decrees, I follow the orthodox view, proposed by the editors of *ATL*, that the form of the change in the form of the letters around the middle of the century can be used to date texts, which do not otherwise contain information on their date. See further Rhodes 1985, 1–3. For the opposite view, which favors dates in the 420s BC, see Mattingly 1996. Mattingly's dating suggests that the decrees furnish evidence pertaining to the bureaucratic administration of the empire, which emerged in the later years of

Pericles and was implemented under Cleon. However, if the specific measures date earlier, as is generally accepted, their evidence provides firm insights into the institutionalization of the allies' subjection.

12. Meiggs 1972, 234–238.

13. *ATL.*

14. Meiggs 1972, 238–254; Sealey 1976, 273–278.

15. D.S. 11.47.1; Meiggs 1972, 46–49.

16. I have benefited from the discussion of tragic Panhellenism in Rosenbloom 2011, 353–381.

17. For example, when Theseus decides to accept the suppliants, following Aethra's advice, he is careful to distinguish between persuasion and force—and argues that he will go to war only if he fails to persuade the Thebans to give back the bodies for burial (E. *Supp.* 346–348). But he also specifically presents himself as κολαστὴς τῶν κακῶν ("chastiser of evils," E. *Supp.* 341; cf. also Adrastus' similar characterization of Theseus in lines 253–256).

## CHAPTER 3

1. Text from Diggle 1984 and translation adapted from Kovacs 1995. On the myths regarding the children of Heracles, see Nilsson 1951, 68–73; on the cults of the Heraclidae in Athens, see Wilkins 1990a.

2. Marathon and the Tetrapolis (32, 80–81) is the setting of Euripides' play, primarily because of its association with Heracles and the Heraclidae. See further, Wilkins 1993: xxvii. Athens is the location in Paus. 1.32.6 and Apollod. 2.8.1 and in the oratorical tradition (Lys. 2.11–16; Isoc. 4.54–60, 5.33–34, 10.31; D. 60.8–9).

3. Williams 1993, xiv–xv. Hecataeus of Miletus (*FGrH* 1 F 30) mentions the persecution of Heracles' children by Eurystheus, Pherecydes (*FGrH* 3 F 84) their arrival in Attica; Herodotus (9.25–28) is the first to mention the protection that Athens grants them as suppliants. For the protection of Heracles' children, a topos in fourth-century oratory, see Lys. 2.11–16; D. 60.8–9; Isoc. 4.54–60, 5.33–34, 10.31, 12.194. The few fragments that survive from Aeschylus' *Heraclidae* are insufficient for a reconstruction of the lost play. See further Allan 2001, 25–27.

4. On the principle of reciprocity on interstate affairs, see Missiou 1998; Low 2007.

5. Visser 1982; Kearns 1990.

6. Adrastus also expresses explicit criticism toward Sparta (E. *Suppl.* 187–189, cf. 210–213 *Tr.* 208). See further, Stevens 1971, 148 *ad And.* 445–53; Collard 1971, 157 *ad Suppl.* 187–8a.

7. U. Wilamowitz-Moellendorff 1882, 343; Pearson 1907, xxv; Grube 1941, 166; Rivier 1944, 169; Fitton 1961, 460; J. Jones 1962, 266; Burnett 1976, 4.

8. Pohlenz 1930, 371–379; Grube 1941, 240; Butts 1947, 105–106.

9. Zuntz 1955, 27. Textual critics starting with Hermann in 1824 also argued that the text was mutilated. Kirchoff in 1867 speculated that the original text contained a speech describing Heracles' daughter's sacrifice, followed by a scene of lamentation. U. Wilamowitz-Moellendorff (1882) next argued that the text had been revised in the fourth century. Zuntz 1947 challenged Wilamowitz's point of view. Zuntz's arguments were refuted by Lesky (1977) and Lesky's by Cropp (1980). For a complete history of the debate, see Wilkins 1993: xxvii–xxxi and Mendelsohn 2002, 6 n. 8 with full bibliography.

10. Spranger 1925; Delebecque 1951, 74–94; Goossens 1962, 188–230.

11. See Conacher (1967, 109–124), who focuses on *charis* as a unifying theme. Zuntz (1955, 32–54) thinks the play's coherence rests in the depiction of the ideal Athens, despite the Athenian chorus' acquiescence toward Alcmene's murder of Eurystheus. Avery (1971) sees the parts that different characters play as descendants or opponents of Heracles as invested with moral/spiritual consequences. Stoessl (1956) identifies a pattern of "tragic reversal," as Heracles' children move away from their position of weakness and prevail over Eurystheus. Burian (1977) examines the dissonance between the final scene of Eurystheus' conversion and the idealism that pervades the rest of the play.

12. Mendelsohn (2002, 13) seeks to provide "an interpretative strategy that aims to integrate fully both the feminine *and* the political." Grethlein's discussion (2003, 381–428) shows that the play undermines Athens' ideal image through the handling of the sacrifice. Gödde (2000, 131–142) discusses the interplay between ritual and rhetorical features.

13. Acamas appears in the play but remains silent throughout. It is Demophon who acts in the capacity of king. Paus. 1.32.6 features Theseus as king of Athens.

14. For the idea that other mythical cities in tragedy represent the antithesis of Athens, see Zeitlin 1990 and Saïd 1993. I argue that the antithesis between democracy and tyranny characterizes favorably Athens' imperial democracy. On democracy and empire, see Boedeker and Raaflaub 1998; Rhodes 2007.

15. Goossens (1962, 187–230) places the events of the play loosely within the context of empire; but he dates the play later than most, placing its performance in 426/5, that is, after the capture of Plataea and the destruction of the Marathonian Tetrapolis.

16. Many scholars also emphasize that the ideal Athens is undermined through the treatment of Eurystheus as prisoner of war in the play. See, for example, Guerrini 1972; Burian 1977, 16–19; Allan 2001, 43; Grethlein 2003, 419–424. For the opposite view, see Mendelsohn 2002, 123.

17. On the role of tyranny in Athenian political thought, see Raaflaub 2003, esp. pp. 77–81, in connection with empire; Henderson 2003.

18. For the antithesis between Athens' freedom and Persian despotism, see Aeschylus' *Persians* 402–405; Rosenbloom 2006a, 68–72.

19. In Euripides' *Suppliant Women* (467–477), the Theban herald demands that the suppliants be extradited under threat of war. As Collard 1975a, 236 *ad* 476–478 notes ὡς δὴ ἐλευθέραν πόλιν ἔχων ("claiming that you have a free city," 477) is heavily ironic and hearkens back to Theseus' defense of Athenian freedom (ἀλλ' ἐλευθέρα πόλις, 405).

20. Contrast Lysias' account where pity figures more prominently as the primary motive for the Athenians' help to Heracles' children, while freedom, justice and bravery figure prominently among Athenian values: τοσοῦτον κίνδυνον ὑπὲρ αὐτῶν ἤραντο, τοὺς μὲν ἀδικουμένους ἐλεοῦντες, τοὺς δ' ὑβρίζοντας μισοῦντες . . . ἡγούμενοι ἐλευθερίας μὲν σημεῖον εἶναι μηδὲν ποιεῖν ἄκοντας, δικαιοσύνης δὲ τοῖς ἀδικουμένοις βοηθεῖν, εὐψυχίας δ' ὑπὲρ τούτων ἀμφοτέρων, εἰ δέοι, μαχομένους ἀποθνῄσκειν ("they made this perilous venture on behalf of those children, pitying the wronged ones and hating the oppressors . . . conceiving it a sign of freedom to do nothing against one's will, of justice to help the wronged, and of courage to die, if need be, in fighting for those two things at once," 2.14).

21. On the combination of religious and political motives surrounding the reception of suppliants in tragedy, see Gould 1973, 90; Mikalson 1991, 70–72.

22. Raaflaub notes briefly that freedom is primarily associated with sovereignty in *Children of Heracles*; see further Raaflaub 2004, 166–193.

23. Raaflaub 2004, 187–190.

24. Loraux 1986, 81, notes that the term "subject" (ὑπήκοος) was not used in funeral orations and that the term "ally" (σύμμαχος) was also used infrequently.

25. Strassburger 1958; de Romilly 1963, 13–104; Mills 1997, 79–86.

26. Hdt. 8.3.2. For a more detailed account of Athens' challenge to Sparta and her claims to political leadership, see Raaflaub 2004, 169–172.

27. On the language kinship diplomacy, see C. P. Jones 1999. Alcmene serves as the link between the Heraclidae and the Pelopidae. She is the first cousin of Aethra, Theseus' mother. See further Allan 2001, 149 *ad* 207–209.

28. Raaflaub 2004, 195. On the Spartans' use of freedom as motto, see Th. 2.72.1, 3.13.1, 3.59.4, 4.85.1, 4.85.5, 4.86.1, 4.86.4–5, 4.87.2–6, 4.108.2, 4.114.3–4.

29. On its negative associations, see further Raaflaub 2003, 77–81.

30. On Athenian suppression of other Greeks' freedom, see Th. 3.10–11, 4.60.1–2, 4.64.4–5, 5.86, 5.91–93, 5.99–100, 6.20.2, 6.69.3, 6.77.1, 6.88.1, 6.66.2, 6.68.2.

31. Fear: Th. 1.75, 5.91, 5.95; tyranny: 2.63.2.

32. Raaflaub (2004, 141–143) argues that the idea of Athens as a *polis tyrannos* arose not only by the use of force in response to individual rebellions but also through the gradual restriction of the allies' equality and independence compared to the initial stipulations regarding treaties and institutions.

33. References to violence, especially in connection to the violent disruption of supplication abound in the play: 47, 59–60, 64, 79, 96–97, 102–103, 105–106, 112, 127–128, 221–222, 225, 243, 249, 254, 365.

34. Zeitlin 1990; Saïd 1993.

35. Demophon comes close to using violence against the herald (271–273). On this point, see Allan 2001, 153. See also E. *Supp.* 347, 560, 749. Moreover, the Athenians' acquiescence to Alcmene's violence against Eurystheus compromises Athens' virtuous character.

36. Burian 1977, 4.

37. Both Wilkins (1993, 82 *ad* 243) and Allan (2001, 152 *ad* 244–246) briefly note that freedom here refers to the protection of Athens' external and not internal freedom. Euripides' *Suppliant Women* also presents the conflict between Athens and Thebes in similar terms and stresses the danger to Athens' sovereignty (518–520). Freedom, however, as Theseus uses it, refers to the democratic freedom of the citizens (see 404–405, with the herald's rebuttal in lines 476–478).

38. See further Raaflaub 2004, 129–130.

39. Raaflaub (2004, 181–184) relates the defense of Athens' sovereignty in Euripides' suppliant plays to Pericles' admonition that Athenians not yield to outside pressures in connection with the Megarian decree (Th. 1.140).

40. Strohm 1957, 17–28.

41. Lloyd 1992, 73.

42. The chorus do not vote, as does the *demos* in Aeschylus' *Suppliant Women*. Burian (1977, 6) does not attribute the difference in the way that each poet handles the supplication to politics, but to the dramatic situation, arguing that in *Children of Heracles* the situation is so "clear-cut" that no vote is necessary to decide the fate of the suppliants.

43. Fitton (1961, 451–452) compares this relatively simple *agon* with the more complex *agon* in *Suppliant Women*. Dubischar (2001, 74) classifies the *agon* in *Children of Heracles* as a simple form of a supplication debate that takes place between suppliant and enemy before the savior.

44. Lloyd 1982, 72.

45. Farnell 1896–1909, vol. 1, 112.

46. There is no evidence for Zeus Agoraios in Marathon; but since the altar of Zeus Agoraios was in the *Agora* in Athens, it was possible to imagine it as being similarly located in the *Agora* and, as Allan (2001, 135 *ad* 32, 138 *ad* 70) remarks, this was part of the blending of Athens with Marathon in the play. As Wilkins (1993, 59–60 *ad* 70) and Wiles (1997, 195 with n. 23) both note, later sources mention the Altar of Pity as the site of Heracles' children supplication (e.g., Apollod. 2.8.1; Zen. 2.61). Wilkins (1993, xix) maintains that Euripides did not link the two traditions. Zeus Agoraios is mentioned also in A. *Eu.* 973–975; see Sommerstein 1989, 269 *ad* 973.

47. Allan 2003, 48.

48. Wilkins 1993, 60; Allan 2001, 48–49.

49. Rosivach 1978 argues unconvincingly that Euripides is intentionally blending the altar of Zeus Agoraios in Marathon with that of Zeus Eleutherios in the Athenian *Agora*.

50. Naiden (2006, 173–191) argues that such requests were judged by the Council and the Assembly.

51. Naiden 2000, 14 n. 34. The relevant inscriptions mention honors to foreigners: the three fourth-century inscriptions come from Attica (*IG* II² 218, 276, 337) and one, dating to the third century, comes from Samos (Michel 371= *LSGG* 123). Naiden offers an extensive comparison of *IG* II² 218, the supplication of the metic Dioscurides, with the supplication of the Danaids in Aeschylus' *Suppliant Women*.

52. See further the Introduction ("Supplication and Democracy [Aeschylus' *Suppliant Women*]").

53. The king usually decides the outcome of any supplication in tragedy, with the exception of Aeschylus' *Suppliant Women*, where the *demos* votes in the Assembly, and Aeschylus' *Eumenides*, where Orestes is judged by a jury of citizens (though here too Athena casts the deciding vote).

54. Naiden (2000, 15) notes that the stages of supplication are the same whether the petition was heard first by the Council or by the Assembly.

55. On anachronism in Greek tragedy, see Easterling 1985. On figures of political authority, see further Griffith 1995 and 2005.

56. Foreign diplomats also supplicated at the altar of the Twelve Gods (Hdt. 6.108.4).

57. To be sure, the play does not engage specifically with contemporary issues in Athenian democracy, but instead evokes democratic institutions broadly. As Mills (1997, 102) notes, Demophon appears to rule democratically, even though he does not explicitly state that Athens is a democracy, as Theseus does in E. *Supp.* 404–405.

58. Naiden 2000, 11–37. Naiden's thesis is that supplication was a *nomos*, a procedure that was in part legal and in part customary. A suppliant could make a legitimate or illegitimate supplication (ἔννομος versus παράνομος) and his/her supplication would be granted, if s/he "were found to have made a legitimate request" (ἔννομα ἱκετεύειν ἔδοξεν p. 18, cf. *IG* II² 218).

59. Chaniotis 1996.

60. The herald's speech, which follows historical examples of extradition and combines legal with political arguments, culminates in a threat of war against Athens. For discussion of actual cases of extradition, see Lonis 1987. Among these, only the extradition of Pactyes is executed (Hdt. 1.154–161). If the extradition was not successful, the receiving cities either entered into war, as is reported regarding the refugees from Sybaris in 511 (D.S. 12.9.4), or the refugee fled elsewhere, as, for example, Themistocles did (Th. 1.136; D.S.

---

11.56.1–3; Plut. *Them.* 24.2). Athens refuses to extradite Harpalos, but in the end he flees (Plut. *Phoc.* 21.2, *Dem.* 25; D.S. 17.108.7).

61. ἄγω is the technical term for extradition (64, 68, 135, 139–140). Wilkins (1993, 69 *ad* 142 ff.) argues that the matter lacked clear definition and that this kind of ambiguity motivates similar conflicts in other suppliant plays, precisely because the city that demands the extradition calls into question the sovereignty of the receiving city.

62. Lonis 1987, 75.

63. The expulsion of a legitimate heir because he threatens those who have usurped his position and the revenge which he exacts upon return is familiar in tragedy: A. *A.* 879–885, *Ch.* 915–917; S. *El.* 11–14; E. *El.* 15–18. In the case of Heracles' children, once their enemy is defeated, their *nostos*, as Alcmene envisions it, will amount to full reintegration (873–878). On revenge in tragedy, see Burnett 1998; Belfiore 1998.

64. He also did so earlier, when he referred to them as his master's possessions, mere slaves who are to be "dragged away" (τούσδε . . . ἄξω, 67–68). See Wilkins 1993, 58–59 *ad* on 68 and Friis Johansen and Whittle 1980, vol. 2, 499 *ad* 612, vol. 3, 234 *ad*/237 *ad* 918, 924.

65. For slaves as σῦλα ("property"), see Bravo 1980, and Chaniotis 1996, 79–83, on legal procedures against suppliant slaves.

66. Fitton 1961, 451: "But of course the legal plea is a thin disguise for a crude argument from strength."

67. Lloyd 1992, 75: "The proem to Iolaus' speech (181–183) serves not only to draw attention to the balance of speeches which is a feature of the Euripidean *agon*, but also makes it clear that the opportunity for speeches on both sides is characteristic of Athenian democracy." See Raaflaub 2004, 221–225, for the close association of *isegoria* with democracy. As Raaflaub remarks: "*Isegoria* was thus the quality best describing the condition—achieved by emancipation from prior subordination—of assimilation with a socially or politically higher class in society; for slaves with the free, for metics with the citizens and for the lower-class citizens, who hitherto lacked full rights, with those citizens that had enjoyed them before" (pp. 222–223).

68. Raaflaub 2004, 222.

69. Chaniotis 1996, 83: "The idea that asylia should not be provided anymore *unconditionally* and *automatically* to anyone who had reached a sacred precinct is expressed indirectly also in Attic drama, which often presents suppliants explaining why they are seeking asylum and underlining the fact that they have been wronged." On the notion of ἀδικεῖσθαι ("being wronged"), see also Bravo 1980, 719.

70. In Aeschylus' *Suppliant Women*, the Danaids beg not to be extradited (A. *Supp.* 341, 418–432, 608–614). Medea also anticipates the possibility of extradition and seeks asylum from Aegeus (E. *Med.* 749–751).

71. Exile may have been considered as an alternative punishment to death in trials of homicide. MacDowell (1963, 114–117) presents evidence from the fourth century for the choice between exile and death for those accused of homicide. The legal evidence is not sufficiently clear. In Antiphon 2b.9 the accused was granted the option of going into exile after the first set of speeches. The situation in *Children of Heracles* probably parallels more closely the conversation between Socrates and Crito (Pl. *Cr.* 44c–45b). Crito's attempt to persuade Socrates to flee suggests that this option may have been available to those convicted to death.

72. On exile as loss of civic rights (*atimia*), see Hansen 1976, 55–82; Grasmück 1978, 16–20.

---

73. Lloyd (1992, 75) notes that Demophon does not explicitly state that he decides in favor of the suppliants because they have won the case legally.

74. The tribute paid to Athens' democracy in this suppliant play is even more expressly formulated in Euripides' *Suppliant Women* and has been broadly connected with Pericles' ideas and vision of the empire. For a discussion of democracy in Euripides' *Suppliant Women*, see Carter 2007, 115–130. But see Mills (1997, 87–128, esp. pp. 89–91), who argues that some traits of the play's *encomion* may undercut values associated with imperial Athens. See further Collard 1975, 29–30; Storey 2008, 45–61. Rosenbloom 2011, 367, argues that the depiction of Athens as defender of Panhellenic laws is connected with democratic ideals of the Periclean phase of the empire.

75. On the contradictions inherent in Athens' imperial democracy, see Fornara and Samons 1991, 76–113. On the question of the "popularity" of the empire, see de Ste. Croix 1954–1955; Bradeen 1960; Fornara 1977.

76. Finley 1978. On the allies' dissent, see Xen. [*Ath.*] 2.3 and Th. 1.75–78, 3.46–49, 6.76–83. On the benefits the empire derived from the allies' contributions, see Arist. *Ath.* 24.1; Plut. *Per.* 12–17.

77. For a discussion of Periclean policy, as viewed against his ideal vision of the city, presented in the funeral speech in Thucydides, see Palmer 1992, 15–42. On Pericles and the empire, see Samons 2004, 117–142. On the causes of the Peloponnesian War, see Kagan 1989, 345–374; Pelling 2000, 82–111.

78. Similarly the Athenian ambassadors in Sparta argue that the unpopularity of the empire stems from the allies' resentment toward Athens with whom they had formerly been accustomed to dealing as equals (Th. 1.77.1–4). See also Th. 1.99.2. Dissident voices were heard from members of other allied cities as well, expressing collective resentment over the loss of equality and autonomy as members of the alliance, one of the founding principles of the alliance (Th. 1.97.1). On the topic of autonomy, see further Smarczyk 1986.

79. See, for example, Th. 1.68.2, 1.121.5, 1.122.2, 1.124.3, 3.10, 3.31.1, 3.63.3, 3.64.3, 3.70.3, 3.71.1, 4.92.4.

80. The allies had access to institutions such as the lawcourts, the Council, or the Assembly; such access, though, was not always regarded as a benefit by the allies in whose eyes Athens interfered and controlled their affairs. On courts and imperial administration, see Meiggs 1972, 220–233; Schuller 1974, 211–217; Koch 1991; Forsdyke 2005, 205–239.

81. Nancy 1983; Foley 1985, 59–64.

82. Burian 1977, 8.

83. On demands for human sacrifice, see Henrichs 1981; O'Connor-Visser 1987, 211–232. On Kore's demand, see Larson 1995, 107; Allan 2001, 166 *ad* 408–409. See further below, "Sacrifice: Acquiescing to Empire."

84. See also E. *Ph.* 588–589.

85. That internal *stasis* could lead to tyranny and the overthrow of the democracy constituted a standard feature of Athenian political discourse (A. *Eu.* 976–987; Th. 3.70–81, 3.82–85.1). On *stasis*, see Price 2001; Loraux 2002. See also Chapter 1 ("Hegemony Revealed").

86. Cf. E. *IT* 30–41.

87. The state of ἀμηχανία ("indecision") is repeatedly emphasized: 464, 472, 487, 492, 495. Oedipus similarly criticizes Athens for failing to live up to her reputation for piety, S. *OC* 258–265. The chorus' traditional praise of Athenian compassion and generosity is

echoed in funerary and encomiastic speeches; similar sentiments are echoed in the Plataeans' address (Isoc. 14. 1–2).

88. Yet both are also intent upon defending the grounds for such rejection: for the king, it is a matter of avoiding conflict with his citizens (μὴ διαβληθήσομαι, 422); the chorus focus on divine compulsion (οὐκ ἐᾷ θεὸς ξένοις ἀρήγειν τήνδε χρῄζουσιν πόλιν; "does the god indeed forbid this city to help the strangers in need of help, though it is eager to do so?" 425).

89. Isocrates in his *Panegyricus* (4.63) captures precisely this point: "it is not ancestral custom for foreigners to place themselves over those born of this land . . . nor those who are refugees over those who received them."

90. Among the encomiastic critics, Zuntz (1955, 27, 32–33) does not find Demophon's change of mind problematic; instead, he emphasizes the suppliants' duty toward their protectors. Burian (1977, 7) notes that the concern for the city's salvation justifies the king's decision to reject the suppliants. On this point, see section on "Sacrifice as Tribute."

91. Pearson 1907 interprets Iolaus' words at 435–438 as attaching blame to the city. Not so Allan 2001, 168 *ad loc.* The chorus' response at 461 anticipates criticism on the part of the suppliants. For parents' willingness to die in the place of their offspring, see E. *Hec.* 382–400, *Ph.* 962–969.

92. On laments performed by male protagonists in Euripides, see Schauer 2002, 283. On laments over exile, see Schauer 2002, 271, 276. On the subversive power of lament in tragedy, especially when performed by women, see Foley 2001, 19–56.

93. On pity in tragedy, see Konstan 2001, 2005; Tzanetou 2005; Johnson and Clapp 2005; Visvardi 2011.

94. It is clear nonetheless that his position aims to serve Argive interests by cementing an alliance between Athens and Argos under terms which would render Athens a subject of Argos (155–157).

95. In spite of the herald's criticism, pity in that context is marked positively, since Athens herself came to be known as φιλοικτίρμων, "prone to pity," Pl. *Mx.* 244e1–3). In effect, the herald's speech successfully sets the ideal Athens apart from Argos and reinforces belief in the civic myth of Athenian pity and compassion.

96. Konstan 2005, 62–64. Theseus also in E. *Supp.* 246–249 weighs what is advantageous for his city and refuses Adrastus' plea before Aethra's intervention. Cleon (Th. 3.37.2) similarly warns the Athenians not to give in to the allies, persuaded by their arguments (λόγους) or out of pity (οἴκτῳ).

97. Allan 2001, 34. On the sexual connotations of virgin sacrifice before battle, see Burkert 1979, 74–75.

98. Not so in Lys. 2.15: παραταξάμενοι δ' ἰδίᾳ δυνάμει τὴν ἐξ ἁπάσης Πελοποννήσου στρατιὰν ἐλθοῦσαν ἐνίκων μαχόμενοι, καὶ τῶν Ἡρακλέους παίδων τὰ μὲν σώματα εἰς ἄδειαν κατέστησαν, ἀπαλλάξαντες δὲ τοῦ δέους καὶ τὰς ψυχὰς ἠλευθέρωσαν ("having arrayed their own sole force against the host assembled from the whole Peloponnese, they conquered them in battle, rescued the sons of Heracles from bodily peril, liberating also their souls by ridding them of fear"). But Euripides follows Herodotus who makes Heracles' children participants in their salvation by fighting in the battle: Ἡρακλείδας . . . πρότερον ἐξελαυνομένους ὑπὸ πάντων Ἑλλήνων ἐς τοὺς ἀπικοίατο φεύγοντες δουλοσύνην πρὸς Μυκηναίων, μοῦνοι ὑποδεξάμενοι τὴν Εὐρυσθέος ὕβριν κατείλομεν, σὺν ἐκείνοισι μάχῃ νικήσαντες τοὺς τότε ἔχοντας Πελοπόννησον ("When the Heraclidae had formerly been rejected by every Greek people, to whom they resorted to escape the tyranny of the Mycenaeans, we alone re-

ceived them. With them we vanquished those, who then inhabited the Peloponnese, and we broke the pride of Eurystheus," 9.27.2).

99. U. Wilamowitz-Moellendorff 1882, iii–x; O'Connor-Visser 1987, 37–38; Wilkins 1993, xix. Zuntz 1955, 11–13, and Larson 1995, 107–109, argue in favor of a preexisting tradition. Heracles' anonymous daughter is named Macaria in the hypothesis of the play; see O'Connor-Visser 1987, 37–38. The name survives in post-Euripidean sources: Strabo (8.4.6) mentions that Macaria gave her name to a spring at Tricorynthus; Pausanias (1.32.6) explains that the spring was named Macaria after the girl died by committing suicide.

100. For Erechtheus' daughters, see Lyc. *Leoc.* 98–101; for Leos' daughters, see [D.] 60.29.

101. For the theory that there was a lacuna at line 629, see Kirchoff 1867. U. Wilamowitz-Moellendorff (1882) further conjectured that the present text is abbreviated and revised by a fourth-century director. Their arguments have since been challenged by McLean 1934 and Zuntz 1947. See further O'Connor-Visser 1987, 32–43; Allan 2001, 35–37 and n. 9.

102. Vellacott 1975, 182–192; Nancy 1983; Bonnechere 1994, 268–269; Galeotti Papi 1995.

103. Eagleton 1981.

104. Demands for human victims as pre-battle sacrifices to guarantee salvation figure in Euripides' plays of voluntary self-sacrifice (*Hecuba, Erechtheus, IA, Phoenician Women*), though not in connection with supplication.

105. Avery (1971), for example, sees Demophon, Iolaus, and Heracles' daughter as united because they conform to the moral values that Heracles is said to represent in the play.

106. Furley 1995.

107. Th. 1.96: this money was initially collected by the Hellenotamiai to protect the allies against the Persians. Th. 2.9.5: all allies except Chios, Lesbos, and Corcyra paid tribute by 431. Th. 1.99.3: some of the allies had exchanged their participation in military campaigns with money which they paid in tribute in the amount that they would have invested in ships.

108. See Kallet 1993; Samons 2004, 72–99. For the figures of the tribute assessment between 454–31 BC, see Meiggs 1972, 524–529, Appendix 12.

109. The tribute, however, could not have exceeded 400 talents. Meiggs (1972, 253–254) argues that Pericles' figure, as reported by Thucydides, does not match the figure for the tribute in 432, assessed at 388 talents; this is verified by calculation of the tribute in the *aparchai*, which gives a total of 376 talents.

110. See Hornblower 1996, 93–97, 206; Meiggs 1972, 254.

111. Meiggs 1972, 42–49.

112. On the progressive limitations of the allies' freedoms and the loss of autonomy, see Chapter 2 ("Democracy and Empire"). See further Meiggs 1972, 234–254.

113. Meiggs 1972, 265. Cleinias' decree was formerly dated to 447 BC, and now dated ca. 424 BC (*IG*³ I, 34).

114. Mendelsohn 2002, 97.

115. Mendelsohn 2002, 89–101.

116. Roselli 2007, 81.

117. Roselli 2007 follows Loraux (1986), arguing that the maiden styles her civic agency

in ideal and egalitarian terms by reproducing closely important topoi of the *epitaphios logos*.

118. Both critics are interested in demonstrating how the prominent role assigned a marginal (female) character contributes to the production of a discourse of civic participation which either privileges democratic egalitarianism (Mendelsohn) or succeeds in negotiating tensions issuing from inequities of civic standing in Athenian society (Roselli).

119. No source before Euripides mentions Heracles' female children (41–44, 544), as Allan (2001, 32) notes in his introduction.

120. For female characters' inversion of social roles in relation to *oikos* and *polis* as spatial categories, see Shaw 1975, with Foley's 1982 critique of his thesis. Contra Shaw, see Easterling 1987. See also O'Connor-Visser 1987, 27; Seidensticker 1995; McClure 1999, 25.

121. Pericles articulates the ideal of silence and women's exclusion in his funeral oration, see Th. 2.45. For the restrictions governing women's speech and lament, as reflecting the curtailment of women's laments in the context of the funeral oration, see Loraux 1986, 45–49; in the context of tragedy, see Foley 2001, 19–55.

122. Compare Medea's address to the chorus of Corinthian women (E. *Med.* 214–218) when she first appears onstage before the chorus of Athenian women. On her exit, see Reckford 1968. Zeitlin (1990, 85) rightly notes that women who speak on behalf of their family or represent the community are not considered dangerous. McClure (1999, 25) adds that marital status is also a consideration by arguing that the agency of maidens is considered benign, as opposed to that of married women. Aethra, however, is an exception. Aethra, like the maiden, breaks with custom not only by appropriating the right to speak in public (E. *Supp.* 297–300), but also by advising her son Theseus to assist Adrastus and the Argive mothers, by adducing arguments in favor of Athens' intervention. Her position can be summed up as follows: it is Athens' duty to ensure the right of burial for the Argive dead by leading a campaign against Thebes; military intervention is desirable and advantageous, because it reinforces the city's hegemony (E. *Supp.* 306–325, esp. 321–323. For parallels between the Maiden's and Aethra's agency, see Mendelsohn 2002, 164–170).

123. For the appearance of *parthenoi* in public: S. *Ant.* 579, *El.* 518; E. *Andr.* 877–879, *Hec.* 975, *Ph.* 88–95 and 1276–1283, *Or.* 1276. In *IA* 821–834, 1028–1032, Clytemnestra's remarks give evidence for women's speech toward men as inappropriate. On women's blame for speaking in public, see Euripides' and *Supp.* 297–300. Many of these parallels, also collected by Stevens 1971, 199 on *And.* 877.

124. Roselli (2007, 134) notes that the maiden hereby acknowledges her marginality.

125. On women's ritual agency in tragedy, see Goff 2004; Kearns 1990, 337, discusses women's in-between status in relation to their roles as saviors in literary sources.

126. For the gendered division of social roles in Athenian society, see Just 1989, 13–75; for the economic contributions, Schaps 1979; for their legal position, see Sealey 1990. On women's speech in drama, see McClure 1999 and, more generally, the essays in Lardinois and McClure 2001.

127. Pericles' citizenship law defined status distinctions between citizens and foreigners by making Athenian birth the sole criterion for citizenship and by acknowledging women's citizenship only in the sphere of reproduction. For a discussion of Pericles' citizenship law, see Boegehold 1994; Patterson 1981; on women's citizenship in the context of the law, see also Patterson 1987, 2009.

128. Foley 2001; Dillon 2002; O'Higgins 2003; Rehm 1994; S. G. Cole 2004; Goff 2004; Ebbott 2005.

129. For the laws and decrees of naturalization, see Osborne 1981. Tragedy, however, commemorated foreigners' contributions through the institution of cult, as I argue in connection with the heroization of Oedipus in *OC* and Eurystheus' transformation into a savior-hero in this chapter.

130. Wilkins 1990, 182–184, provides a very useful overview of the common ritual and rhetorical elements in Euripides' plays of voluntary sacrifice.

131. Translation from Collard, Cropp, and Lee 1995.

132. The fragment that contains her speech was preserved by the orator Lycurgus, in his speech *Against Leocrates* 100, who argues against draft-dodging and holds up the sacrifice of Erechtheus' daughter as a model for male emulation, exhorting the Athenians to live up to her courage and inviting them to prove their love for their country to be superior to women's bravery. For testimonia and discussion of Euripides' *Erechtheus*, see Collard et al. 1995, 148–155.

133. Wilkins 1990, 180.

134. For a list of the topoi, see Ziolkowski 1981, 74–99. On the question of originality in the manipulation of the topoi, see Loraux 1986, 305–330. On the adaptation of motifs and themes from the funeral oration in *Children of Heracles*, see especially Galeotti Papi 1995.

135. Th. 2.42.2–4; Gorgias DK B6; Pl. *Mx.* 246d1–248d6; Lys. 2.24–26; D. 60.27–31.

136. On the rejection of "lottery," see further Roselli 2007, 128.

137. In the funeral oration, the individual *arete* of the fallen had become and aristocratic values had been redefined by the egalitarian ethos of the democratic *polis*. See further Loraux 1986, 73–94. The idea of a noble death is found in other examples of female self-sacrifice: E. *Hec.* 378, *IA* 1385.

138. As Loraux (1990 and 1993) has shown, autochthony operates on the principle of exclusion based on gender and civic origin. Autochthony defines citizenship through sameness, according at the same time a privileged position to Athenians against all other Greeks.

139. On the inclusion of foreigners, either as allies or metics, in the Athenian casualty lists, see Loraux 1986, 30–37. See further Bradeen (1969, 149–152), who argues that the *xenoi* of the lists were metics not allies, because the casualties of the latter with one exception (*IG* I² 928) were recorded on a separate list. He notes that it is unlikely that *xenoi* could refer to allies, since the *xenoi* mentioned in the casualty lists are not designated by ethnics. For *xenoi* as designating allies, see Gauthier 1971.

140. Lys. 2.23.

141. Loraux 1986, 88.

142. Cf. also E. *Supp.* 577.

143. On Iolaus' arming for battle and the comic elements of that scene, see Mendelsohn 2001, 109–112; Burian 1977: 11.

144. Alcmene's intended revenge is problematic, because he is a war prisoner and it goes against Athenian law (961–974), as Allan (2001: 46) notes.

145. In this respect, it is worth noting Theseus' command to Adrastus not to join him in the expedition against Thebes (588–593). Adrastus has already been defeated by the Thebans and Theseus deems his cause unworthy and had previously condemned his undertaking (219–237). What is more, in that play, the messenger, an Argive captive, gives an account of the battle narrative that explicitly extols Theseus' bravery (707–718), moral rectitude (723–730) and compassion toward the dead (764–767). In Euripides' *Suppliant Women*, then, the foreigners' contributions to the military effort Athens expends on their

behalf is suitably minimized in favor of highlighting the justness of Athens' undertaking of the war.

146. As Wilkins 1993, xvii, notes, Euripides is probably following Pi. *P.* 9.78–83. See also Apollod. 2.8.1; Str. 8.6.19. There is a lacuna in the text, so we do not know whether Alcmene carries out her plan at the end of the play. See further, see Wilkins 1993, 193 *ad* on n. 1052.

147. Wilkins 1993, xxxiii–xxxv, reviews the scholarship on the dating of the play. I agree with Zuntz 1955 who argues that the play was produced in 430, that is, before Archidamus' main attack against Attica.

148. Admittedly, the Athenians' acquiescence to Alcmene's violence against Eurystheus casts doubt on Athens' virtuous character (962–982); Falkner 1989. On the treatment of war captives, see Ducrey 1968.

149. On the pattern of the enemy-hero, see Visser 1982 and my discussion in Chapter 4. As I argue there, the blending of Oedipus' religious with civic standing downplays their secondary status as foreigners. Bakewell 1999, by contrast, argues that in Eurystheus' case his designation as *metoikos* refers to his standing as a resident alien in Athens. It is possible that for the contemporary audience Eurystheus may have represented a high-standing metic in positive terms. If this is the primary meaning of the term here, it undercuts Eurystheus' new role in cult by calling attention to his legal status as a foreigner. The end of the play instead underscores his permanent reception on the basis of the benefits that he offers Athens. For this reason it may be appropriate to define the term *metoikos* literally (and not legally) to designate Eurystheus' change of residence from Argos to Athens.

150. On the connections between pity, justice and self-interest, see Konstan 2005. Konstan rightly argues that considerations of self-interest underlie both Demophon's and Theseus' decision. The difference between the two plays concerns the variation in the way self-interest is expressed. Thus, Aethra's argument with which Theseus later agrees is based on Athens' interest (337–341), but it is aligned with the claims of justice, as expressed through the necessity of upholding divinely sanctioned custom (301–313). This is different from the course that Demophon follows, as he reneges on his offer to accept the suppliants, until they themselves fulfill the conditions necessary for their own and an Athenian victory.

151. E. *Supp.* 404–408 and 429–441.

152. I have drawn upon the major recent interpretations of the play and used them to highlight its place in the evolution of Athenian hegemony. On the historical background of the play, as it relates also to the theme of Athens' panegyric, see Mills 1997, 87–128 who denies the limits of the Athenian panegyric (e.g., by reference to the Argive mother's mourning, Athena's endorsement of the war with the Epigonoi and Adrastus' funeral speech). The relevance of Athens' praise for an understanding of the play has been treated from a variety of perspectives. In addition to Mills (1997), Storey (2008 [esp. 11–44, 90–104]), has discussed the play's historical background and includes an overview of major interpretations. There are several excellent recent treatments of this play (Foley 2001, 36–44 [lamentation]; Goff 1995a [ritual]; Bowie 1997, 39–56 [religious elements]; Pelling, 1997, 230–235 [ideology]; Mendelsohn 2002, 135–223 [gender and politics]. Among these, Mills, Bowie and Grethlein 2003, 109–99 have focused more closely on supplication, democracy and Athenian ideals. Pelling 1997c articulates most clearly the debate surrounding ideology and the pro- versus anti-Athenian orientation of the play. My own remarks in this chapter further the line of argument developed by Pelling (1997c) and rely especially on the analyses by Konstan (2005) and Rosenbloom (2011).

---

153. Both Bowie (1997, 47–56) who reads the play against the historical battle of Delium which the Athenians fought against Boeotia in 424 BC and Pelling (1997c, 229–235) who concentrates on the critique of democracy and the funeral speech, contained in the play, offer balanced treatments of the positive and negative evaluation of the play's mythical image of Athens.

154. This is different from the course, which Demophon follows in *Children of Heracles*, as he reneges on his offer to accept the suppliants, until they themselves fulfill the conditions necessary for their own and an Athenian victory.

155. Rosenbloom 2011, 367.

156. Collard (1975, 10–11): "Such an alliance was contracted (Elis and Mantinea being co-signatories) in 420, and renewed in 416. The similarity in language between the actual treaty and Athena's prescription in the play is attributable to the terminology conventional in diplomacy and familiar from public inscriptions to all Athenians, not least the poet; it does not indicate that Euripides 'copies' the terms of an existing treaty any more than it shows that he was recommending those of a future one. . . . Euripides may perhaps be suggesting wishfully an Athens-Argos alliance, but the terms of Athena's treaty exclude his *post factum* endorsement of the historical one."


CHAPTER 4

1. Text from Lloyd-Jones and Wilson 1990 and translations adapted from Lloyd-Jones 1994. The date of composition is uncertain; Sophocles died in 406 BC, and the play was produced posthumously in 401 BC. The year 405 BC, the same year of the performance of Aristophanes' *Frogs*, provides a terminus ante quem for the poet's death. See further Jebb 1928, xliii; Nemeth 1983. Tanner 1966 argues for a revision of the play after Arginusae.

2. On the religious significance of the play, see Méautis 1942, 139–171; Linforth 1951. Hester 1977, provides a full bibliography of earlier works in this category. Recent political interpretations argue against the "moral rehabilitation" of the hero; Vidal-Naquet 1990; Slatkin 1986; Blundell 1993; Edmunds 1996; Mills 1997; Markantonatos 2007, 167–193.

3. Auffarth 1992.

4. Mikalson 1991, 69–70.

5. Oedipus' new fate, his death and heroization in Athens, naturally led critics to focus on his characterization in the play. See, for example. U. von Wilamowitz-Moellendorff 1917, 313–376; Rosenmeyer 1952; Easterling 1967.

6. On the opposition between Athens and Thebes, see Segal 1981, 362; Vidal-Naquet 1990, 335–339; Zeitlin 1990, 155–167.

7. Edmunds 1996 interprets the play as a plea for the reenfranchisement of Athenian citizens after the restoration of the democracy in 411 BC. Against the view that the play offers an apology for the events of 411 BC and for Sophocles' own involvement, see Markantonatos 2007, 35–39, with the relevant bibliography on this question. See also Calder 1985.

8. On foreigners, see more recently Baslez 1984; Lonis 1987. On foreigners in tragedy, see Vidal-Naquet 1997; Gibert 2011.

9. Knox 1964, 154–156 argues that the Athenians already knew that they would lose the war. Hence, the praise of Athens becomes the poet's swan song for Athens.

10. On the traditions of Oedipus' death and burial before Sophocles, see Edmunds 1996, 95–100; Mills 1997, 161–162. On locality in *Oedipus at Colonus*, see J. Jones 1962,

222–235, and on the vocabulary associated with it, see Winnington-Ingram 1980, 339–340, Appendix E. On the topography of Colonus in this play and the location of the grove, see Jebb 1928, xxix–xxxviii; Kearns 1989, 208–209, Appendix 2. For Oedipus' myth, in general, see Robert 1915, 59–118. For its treatment in epic and tragedy, see Markantonatos 2007, 41–70.

11. On the setting, see Allison 1984; Krummen 1993; Edmunds 1996; J. P. Wilson 1997.

12. On the differences between Athens from Colonus, see Kirkwood (1986), who also treats the theme of empire.

13. On the setting, see Wiles 1997, 146–153; Markantonatos 2002, 167–197; A. Kelly 2009, 98–106.

14. Though the stage setting probably does not reproduce the actual cult complex in detail, we know from Pausanias (1.30.4) that there was a shrine of Colonus Hippius here, dedicated to both Poseidon and Athena Hippia and that there were also hero shrines of Oedipus, Peirithous, Theseus, and Adrastus and a shrine to the *Semnai*, who are similar to the Eumenides. See also Apollo. *FGrH* 244F 147.

15. But note that Oedipus instructs Antigone to choose carefully where she will seat him, whether it will be in secular or sacred space (10). He recognizes that their position as foreigners is secondary to that of the citizens (μανθάνειν γὰρ ἥκομεν/ξένοι πρὸς ἀστῶν, ἂν δ' ἀκούσωμεν τελεῖν, "we have come to learn from the citizens and to do what we hear," 12–13). See also A. *Supp.* 196–203; E. *Med.* 223–224.

16. The sanctuary of the Semnai at the Areopagus was a place of refuge, and the audience was wont to relate the two in some measure (see Chapter 1). The text, however, provides virtually no information regarding the specific attributes of the cult of the Eumenides at Colonus. On the cult names of the Erinyes in Athens and elsewhere, see Jebb 1928, 18 *ad* 43 and 25 *ad* 84; Henrichs 1994. On the relationship between Oedipus and the Erinyes, see Winnington-Ingram 1980, 264–273. On sanctuaries as a place of refuge, see Sinn 1993.

17. On the cults of Oedipus, see Edmunds 1981.

18. The similarity between Oedipus' and the Eumenides' characters as avengers/ ἀλάστορες is evoked through the reference to Oedipus' ἀλάστωρ, his avenging spirit that dwells in Thebes and that could bring harm to the city in the event of Oedipus' forced return (787–790). Polyneices refers to their father's Erinys as the cause of the strife between the brothers (1299). Oedipus calls upon the Eumenides at the moment when he curses his sons, in Polyneices' presence, to die by killing each other (1390–1392). His association with the Eumenides as punishers of injury inflicted by blood kin explains why Oedipus takes refuge in their grove and allies himself with the goddesses just before he curses his sons—a manifestation of his punitive side as a hero: now while still living against his sons, later when he is dead against the Thebans collectively, who march against the Athenians. For the curse of Oedipus, see further Hutchinson 1985, 170 *ad* 772–791.

19. Henrichs 1983, 96–97. Such propitiatory offerings were also given to a few non-chthonic deities such as the Tritopatores and heroes such as the Erechtheids and Leucaspis.

20. J. Jones (1962, 222–223) writes that when Oedipus arrives at Colonus, the action is "on the brink of fulfillment" but that such progression is interrupted by Theban politics.

21. Some of the suppliants that Athens accepts continue to pose a threat for the city politically, as does Medea and even the Danaids, whose father may subsequently have engineered a coup at Argos. Given this possibility, we can see that the play may have voiced concerns about preserving the democracy in the wake of the oligarchic coup of 411 BC that took place at Colonus.

22. On the imagery of wandering, see Segal 1981, 365–369.

23. Oedipus is impious in the eyes of the chorus on account of his trespass into the grove. On the sanctity of sacred groves, see Parker 1983, 146–148.

24. Mills (1997, 167) justifies the chorus' reaction by arguing that pollution is an added dimension to the danger of incurring war with Thebes, as it provokes divine displeasure.

25. Chaniotis (1996, 79–83) notes that petitions for asylum were often judged by the religious authorities of a particular sanctuary. The chorus appear to fulfill a similar role when they order Oedipus out of the city on account of his defilement.

26. When Antigone sees them arriving, she appears apprehensive, because they have come to spy out Oedipus' seat (σῆς ἕδρας ἐπίσκοποι, 112). On the chorus' role, see Travis 1999.

27. Contrast his own choice of seat (ἐπ᾽ ἀξέστου πέτρου, "on an unpolished stone," 19) in the idyllic setting of the grove; the rough and unpolished stone, a sign of purity, in the grove of the Eumenides, indicates that he too belongs in a realm that is sacred, pure, and chthonic.

28. The tripartite distinction between sacred, secular, and defiled replicates spatial boundaries that represent important hierarchical distinctions (Parker 1983, 11 n. 53).

29. Many critics have been concerned with the play's episodic structure. A large portion of the earlier scholarship is summarized in Burian 1974a, which counters earlier criticism of the play's structure. See also Winnington-Ingram 1980, 249–254. On the problems surrounding the Polyneices scene with respect to the play's structure, U. Wilamowitz-Moellendorff (1917, 329–337) defends the play's structure and interprets the Polyneices scene in light of the influence of earlier plays such as Euripides' *Phoenician Women*.

30. His pollution stems from incest and parricide and is hardly amenable to purification. Both here and in his defense speech, Oedipus avoids mentioning the specific nature of his deeds. On unspeakable words, see Clay 1982.

31. Parricide represents the worst kind of kin-killing—the father was considered inviolate—and it is doubtful whether it was expiable (Pl. *Lg.* 869c). Incest constitutes the very antithesis of normative social order and "lies in a sense beyond pollution, because it is beyond purification" (Parker 1983, 98). On sanctions pertaining to parricide and incest, see Parker 1983, 95–98, 122–130.

32. For the need to guard against the heavy pollution resulting from kin-killing, see S. *OT* 238–241; E. *HF* 1281–1286, *IT* 940–957. As Parker (1983, 123) notes, "Expulsion of homicidal relatives by the rest of the clan, and voluntary withdrawal 'in obedience to the law', are both found in mythology, but about the fate of actual kin-killers in Athens there seems to be no scrap of evidence."

33. There is a wide spectrum of responses to polluted outsiders in the suppliant plays. In Euripides' *Iphigenia in Tauris*, Orestes' pollution calls for his segregation and is part of the aetiological myth for the feast of the *Choes* at the festival of the *Anthesteria* (947–960). In Euripides' *Medea*, the chorus cannot envision the infanticide's reception in Athens, and they claim that the holy city of Athens will not be able to accept the impure Medea (850). Conversely, Theseus in Euripides' *Heracles* shows true compassion toward Heracles by disregarding his heavy defilement (1199–1201). Theseus in *OC* invites Oedipus to come to his palace, though Oedipus declines by saying that he must remain close to the grove (638–648).

34. For a narratological approach to the play, see Markantonatos 2002.

35. Parker 1983, 318–321. Mills 1997, 177–179, is more cautious in the evaluation of Oedipus' pollution; in particular, she views pollution as an obstacle for Oedipus' integra-

tion, which is overcome only through Theseus' ἐπιείκεια ("flexibility"). The issue in the play is not whether Oedipus can ever be freed of his pollution but how the issue of ritual defilement is handled to facilitate his reception in Athens. On ἐπιείκεια in the Athenian lawcourts, see Harris 2004.

36. On Oedipus' plea, see also Markantonatos 2007, 123–140. For the conception of the individual as dependent on communal roles, see Gill 1996, 1–93; Saïd 1978, 217–218; Mastrangelo 2000. For an inversion of his heroic identity, see Kuntz 1993, 143–148.

37. The view that he puts forth contrasts with Oedipus' conception of his responsibility in *Oedipus Tyrannus*. In the earlier play, acceptance of his criminal responsibility resulted not only in his blinding but also in self-imposed exile, since it was Oedipus himself who had pronounced this sentence on Laius' murderer (S. *OT* 1369–1385, 1436–1437). In comparing the two versions, Gellie 1972 argues that Oedipus' claim implies a change of moral attitude, according to which justice is judged, based on rational and intentional judgments rather than on actions alone. Winnington-Ingram 1980, 256, attributes to a certain degree Oedipus' change of attitude towards his crimes to the passage of time, "a staple Sophoclean theme." On Oedipus' guilt and innocence, see Linforth 1951; Knox 1957; Gellie 1972; Hester 1993; B. Williams 1993. On the connections between the *Oedipus at Colonus* and *Oedipus Tyrannus*, see Seidensticker, 1972.

38. Also in line 521 the manuscript reading is ἄκων, which Jebb adopts over Bothe's ἑκών, adopted by Lloyd-Jones (1994: 472). Edmunds 1996, 134–138, argues that Oedipus defends himself by arguing that the crime of parricide was unintentional. It is difficult to support the view that Oedipus' killing of Laius may be considered unintentional homicide, on the basis of ἔργων ἀκόντων ("unintentional deeds," 239–240) which refers to Oedipus' crimes and τό γ᾽ ἄκον πρᾶγμα ("unintentional act," 976), which refers to the murder of Laius (ἄκων/ἀέκων "unaware, ignorant" recurs in 521, 964, 987). While ἑκών as a technical term refers to unintentional homicide, Oedipus' crimes do not fit that category. Unintentional homicide was legally defined on the basis of the absence of premeditation. Oedipus argues that the murder of Laius was committed in self-defense in ignorance of his victim's identity (273, 548, 976). Note, however, that line 547 has been emended by Meckler on the basis of line 271. On the different types of homicide in Athenian law, see MacDowell 1963, 113–120; Gagarin 1981, 3–4.

39. On the theme of retaliation in the play, see Winnington-Ingram 1980, 260–264, 324–326. On self-defense, see MacDowell 1963, 75–76; Gagarin 1978. On the ethical code of "helping friends and harming enemies," see Blundell 1989, 226–259.

40. On homicide, see further Harris 2001.

41. Parker 1983, 251–256.

42. Burkert 1985b.

43. Slatkin 1986, 219, rightly notes that the city's values and reputation are at stake in determining Oedipus' reception or expulsion: "Theseus does not question; Creon does not listen. The essential dialogue takes place between Oedipus and the chorus. It is their conception of him that he must address and win over, and their collective entity that must make a place for him. By the time Theseus arrives, Oedipus and the chorus have achieved that end; when Theseus has declared him 'fellow-citizen' (637), their choral praise is not for the leader but for the state."

44. On the concept of ἱερός ("sacred"), see Burkert 1985a, 269.

45. On piety, see Burkert 1985a, 272–275, who notes that "outward *eusebeia* guided by *nomos* is civic duty" (p. 274).

46. Oedipus' benefit is expressed as ὄνησις in this passage (287–88). Slatkin 1986, 212,

notes that the political connotations of ὄνησις are evident at line 452, "where Oedipus accuses his sons of valuing power more than they value their own father, and predicts that they will gain no ὄνησις ("benefit") from ruling in Thebes." The benefit is also referred to as κέρδος ("profit," 72, 92, 578–579, 1421), ὠφέλησις ("benefit," 401), ἄρκεσις ("help," 73), δῶρον ("gift," 577) and ἀλκή ("protection," 1524). Oedipus is also cast as σωτήρ ("savior," 457–460, 463). See further, Edmunds 1996, 142–146.

47. Visser 1982.

48. For the law and requirements for naturalization, see Osborne 1981, 139–154, 186–192.

49. On the praise of Athens in Sophocles' *Oedipus at Colonus*, see Knox 1964, 154–156; Segal 1981, 362; Vidal-Naquet 1990; Zeitlin 1990, 155–167; Blundell 1993, 287–296.

50. The reference to δορυξενία ("spear-alliance") translates the diplomatic relationship between the two cities into the heroic tragic register and, moreover, links the two heroes, whose mythological careers did not otherwise overlap. On the aristocratic connotations of *xenia* in the context of the *Oresteia*, see also Griffith 1995, 68–81, 100.

51. For χάρις in fourth-century decrees of naturalization, see Osborne 1981, 146: "[ὅπως ἄ]ν εἰδῶσιν ἅπαντες ὅτι ὁ δῆμος [ὁ Ἀθ]ηναίων ἀποδίδωσι χάριτας μ[εγ]άλας τοῖς εὐεργετοῦσιν εἰαυτὸ[ν] καὶ διαμένουσιν ἐπὶ τῆς εὐνοία[ς το]ῦ δήμου» ("so that they all may know that the demos of the Athenians bestows great honors upon those who offer benefits and continue to act for the goodwill of the demos" (*IG* II² 222); see also p. 195 with Osborne's comments on [D.] 45.78.

52. Theseus later refers to Oedipus' religious heroization in these terms: χάρις ἡ χθονία ("favor bestowed by the nether world," 1752).

53. My interpretation differs substantially from Bakewell (1999), who argues that the Furies, Oedipus, and Eurystheus all become metics in Athens.

54. On the tension between the ideal and the reality, see further Grethlein 2003, 282–318.

55. Samons 2004, 87–93.

56. Th. 8.67–77; Sealey 1976, 359–362.

57. On the constitution of the four hundred, see Arist. *Ath.* 29–34.

58. See Krummen 1993, 216, and Edmunds 1996.

59. Sealey 1976, 355–358.

60. As A. Kelly 2009, 17, notes: "In a series of battles (Cynossema 411 BC, Abydus 410 BC, Cyzicus 410 BC, Arginusae 406 BC), however, the Athenians actually defeated Peloponnesian fleets, but the instabilities of domestic politics undermined their successes; after a loss at Notium in 406 BC, Alcibiades (reinstated in 411 BC) fell from favour once more and, when a storm prevented the retrieval of Athenian dead after Arginusae the responsible generals were executed or banished."

61. Demosthenes includes Oedipus' reception in Athens in his praise of the ancestors (18.186).

62. On Oedipus and Thebes, see Markantonatos 2002, 79–85; on the treatment of the Oedipus myth in this play, see, in general, A. Kelly 2009, 36–51.

63. κἀξεκηρύχθην φυγάς ("I was proclaimed an exile," 430) implies that Oedipus was officially expelled by the city, although he implicates his sons because they did not defend him. He then argues that it was Creon who banished him (770–771) and finally, holds Polyneices responsible for his exile (1362–1364).

64. Oedipus' exile is alluded to in Pi. *P.* 4.263. Oedipus' exile in S. *OT* is predicted by Teiresias (454–456), and Oedipus asks repeatedly that he be exiled (1340–1345, 1410–1415,

1436–1437, 1449–1454, 1518). The only other evidence regarding his banishment is Euripides' *Phoenician Women*, 1706–1707, even though the passage is considered to be an interpolation. See further Mills 1997, 161–162, n. 9 and 17.

65. While the chorus had already expressed feelings of pity, they had explicitly refrained from offering any kind of help (254–255).

66. On the purification ritual, described in lines 465–504, see Burkert 1985b.

67. Konstan 2005, 54–60, 62–64.

68. Tzanetou 2005, 99–104.

69. Jebb 1928, 97 *ad* 564; Mills 1997, 172.

70. See Mills 1997, 171–172; Lesky 1952, 100–105.

71. On Oedipus' secret tomb, see Androtion, *FGrH* 324F 62, who is probably combining the Boeotian version of Oedipus' burial at Eteonos (*FrGrH* 382F 2) with that of Sophocles. See further C. Robert 1915, 1–9; Mills 1997, 161 n. 5; Lardinois 1992. For the controversy surrounding the location of Oedipus' tomb, namely, whether it was situated at Colonus or under the Areopagus (Paus. 1.28.7 and Val. Max. 5.3.3), see Kearns 1989, 208–209. There is no evidence outside Sophocles' play to suggest that the cult existed.

72. On ritualized friendship, see Herman 1987.

73. Edmunds 1996, 95–100.

74. With the exception of Phrynichus' *Capture of Miletus* and Aeschylus' *Persians*, few plays reflect closely specific historical events. Among the suppliant plays, apart from Aeschylus' *Eumenides*, discussed in Chapter 1, Euripides' *Suppliant Women* is tied to the Athenian defeat at Delium in 424 BC. See further Bowie 1997, 39–62; Mills 1997, 91–97.

75. See further Mastrangelo 2000; Easterling 1967.

76. On moral values in the play, see especially Blundell 1993, 291–293.

77. Visser 1982.

78. Zeitlin 1990.

79. On Theseus as embodiment of Athenian values, see Mills 1997, 160–185. See also Segal 1981, 379–382; Walker 1995, 187–189.

80. See also S. *OC* 1003–1013, where Oedipus exposes Creon's dishonesty by underscoring the city's true sense of religious piety.

81. See Easterling 1984, 41: "The role of the king is plainly used here [i.e., in S. *OC*] not to discuss political theory but simply to characterise Athens. The implication seems to be that if the city was especially favoured in receiving Oedipus (who was to become her heroic protector) the favour was deserved: Athens was the best place Oedipus could find, and Theseus represents the Athenian self-image at its finest." For a detailed characterization of Theseus' democratic qualities in this play, see further Blundell 1993, 294–298; Mills 1997, 164–185.

82. Refugees and exiles often found asylum at the Theseum. Theseus is presented as the champion of democracy from 510 BC in literature and art. For the development of Theseus' figure in the fifth century, see Herter 1939; Connor 1970; Walker 1995, 35–81; Mills 1997, 1–42.

83. For Athens as represented by νόμος, see *OC* 913–914 and E. *Supp.* 430–431. For νόμος as an expression of Athenian democracy, especially in literary sources, see Ostwald 1986, 83, 250, 252, 258, 273.

84. Blundell 1993, 300–301, notes the difference between the pursuit of πολυπραγμοσύνη as characteristic of Pericles' democracy and Theseus' behavior whose policies are defensive rather than expansive: "Theseus' ideal is a far cry from Pericles' pride in an Athens whose adventurous spirit [τόλμα] has forced an entry into every sea and into every land.

---

His Athens is immune to the πολυπραγμοσύνη, which Thucydides portrays as the psychological foundation of Athenian imperialism" (p. 301).

85. On aspects of his religious heroization, see further Calame 1988; Markantonatos 2007, 157–166.

86. Knox 1964, 148.

87. Note that Oedipus insists that no one will have κράτος over him (408, 1207) and curses Polyneices never to acquire the κράτος that he desires (1386).

88. Contrast E. *HF* 1322–1323, where Heracles is told by Theseus to abandon Thebes for the sake of law. On the reception of Heracles by Theseus in *Heracles*, see Gregory 1991, 121–154.

89. Ellendt 1958; Paley 1872–1880.

90. Kamerbeek 1984; J. P. Wilson 1997, 63–90 and 67–68, with a detailed review of the bibliography.

91. Hesychius' lemma (e 2195) on ἔμπολις reads ὁ πατρίδα ἔχων ("one who has a homeland").

92. Vidal-Naquet 1990, 345.

93. Vidal-Naquet (1990) approximates Oedipus' status with that of a foreigner in Athens. He first argues that Oedipus cannot escape defilement nor be viewed as a repatriated exile such as Cimon or Alcibiades because he never returns to Thebes. Having rejected these two alternatives, he justifies his method as follows: "To say that he is a hero, that is to say more than a citizen, sharing that quality with other figures—such as Ajax—who have sometimes been annexed to Athens, is not enough. For it is both possible and necessary to integrate Oedipus more satisfactorily with the institutions and practices of the time of Sophocles" (pp. 350–351).

94. On exile and ἔγκτησις ("right to possession"), see Edmunds 1997, 113–114.

95. Vidal-Naquet 1990, 353–354. On metics, see Whitehead 1977.

96. Vidal-Naquet 1990, 345–346 and 489 with n. 55, with additional sources.

97. J. P. Wilson 1997, 69–70. Unlike Vidal-Naquet, Wilson argues that the word ἔμπολις does in fact mean citizen in the legal sense of the word.

98. Patterson 1981, 151–174. For women's designation as ἀσταί, see Patterson 1987, 54–57. On Pericles' citizenship law, see also Boegehold 1994.

99. Patterson 1981, 160–161 and 172 n. 28.

100. Patterson 1981, 54.

# BIBLIOGRAPHY

Aitken Bradshaw, E., and J. K. Berenson Maclean, eds. 2004. *Philostratus'* Heroikos*: Religion and Cultural Identity in the Third Century C.E.* Atlanta: Society for Biblical Literature and Leiden: Brill.

Allan, W. 2001. *Euripides: The Children of Heracles. Edition with Introduction, Translation and Commentary.* Warminster, England: Aris and Phillips.

Allison, R. H. 1984. "'This Is the Place': Why Is Oidipous at Kolonos?" *Prudentia* 10: 67-91.

Antonaccio, C. M. 1993. "Tomb and Hero Cult in Early Greece: The Archaeology of Ancestors." In Dougherty and Kurke 1993: 46-70.

———. 1994. *An Archaeology of Ancestors: Tomb Cult and Hero Cult in Early Greece.* Lanham, Md.: Rowman & Littlefield.

Auffarth, C. 1992. "Protecting Strangers: Establishing a Fundamental Value in the Religions of the Ancient Near East and Ancient Greece." *Numen* 39: 193-216.

Avery, H. C. 1971. "Euripides' *Heracleidai.*" *AJP* 92: 539-565.

Bacon, H. H. 2001. "The Furies' Homecoming." *CP* 96: 48-59.

Badian, E. 1993. *From Plataea to Potidaea: Studies in the History and Historiography of the Pentecontaetia.* Baltimore: Johns Hopkins University.

Bakewell, G, 1997. "*Metoikia* in the *Supplices* of Aeschylus." *CA* 16: 209-228.

———. 1999. "*Eunous kai polei sôtérios/metoikos*: Metics, Tragedy, and Civic Ideology." *Syllecta Classica* 10: 43-64.

———. 2007. "*Agamemnon* 437: *Chrysamoibos* Ares, Athens and Empire." *JHS* 127: 123-132.

Balot, R. K., ed. 2006. *Greek Political Thought.* Oxford: Blackwell.

Barron, J. P. 1964. "Religious Propaganda of the Delian League." *JHS* 84: 35-48.

Baslez, M-F. 1984. *L'étranger dans la Grèce antique.* Paris: Les Belles Lettres.

Belfiore, E. S. 1998. "Harming Friends: Problematic Reciprocity in Greek Tragedy." In Gill, Postlethwaite, and Seaford 1998: 139-158.

Bell, C. 1992. *Ritual Theory, Ritual Practice.* New York: Oxford University.

Bérard, C. 1982. "Récupérer la mort du prince: héroïsation et formation de la cité." In G. Gnoli and J. P. Vernant, eds. 1982. *La mort, les morts dans les sociétés anciennes*: 89-107. Cambridge: Cambridge University/Paris, Éditions de la MSH, 1982.

Betensky, A. 1978. "Aeschylus' *Oresteia*: The Power of Clytemnestra." *Ramus* 7: 11-25.

Bickerman, E. J. 1958. "*Autonomia*: Sur un passage de Thucydide." *RIDA* 5: 313-344.

Bierl, A. F. 1994. "Apollo in Greek Tragedy: Orestes and the God of Initiation." In Solomon 1994: 81-96.

Blickman, D. R. 1986. "The Myth of Ixion and Pollution for Homicide in Archaic Greece." *CJ* 3: 193–208.

Blomart, A. 2004. "Transferring the Cults of Heroes in Ancient Greece: A Political and Religious Act." In Aitken and Maclean 2004: 85–98.

Blundell, M. W. 1989. *Helping Friends and Harming Enemies: A Study in Sophocles and Greek Ethics.* Cambridge: Cambridge University.

———. 1993. "The Ideal of Athens in *Oedipus at Colonus.*" In Sommerstein, Halliwell, Henderson, and Zimmermann 1993: 287–306.

Boedeker, D. 1993. "Hero Cult and Politics in Herodotus: The Bones of Orestes." In Dougherty and Kurke 1993: 164–177.

Boedeker, D., and K. Raaflaub, eds. 1998. *Democracy, Empire and the Arts in Fifth-century Athens.* Cambridge, Mass.: Harvard University.

Boedeker, D., and D. Sider, eds. 2001. *The New Simonides: Contexts of Praise and Desire.* Oxford: Oxford University.

Boegehold, A. L. 1994. "Perikles' Citizenship Law of 451/0 B.C." In Boegehold and Scafuro 1994: 57–66.

Boegehold, A. L., and A. C. Scafuro, eds. 1994. *Athenian Identity and Civic Ideology.* Baltimore: Johns Hopkins University.

Bolmarcich, S. M. 2003. "Thucydidean Explanations: Diplomacy and Historiography in Archaic and Classical Greece." Ph.D. diss., University of Virginia.

Bonnechere, P. 1994. *Le sacrifice humain en Grèce ancienne. Kernos* Suppl. 3. Athènes-Liège.

Bosworth, A. B. 2000. "The Historical Context of Thucydides' Funeral Oration." *JHS* 120: 1–16.

Bothe, F. H. 1846. *Sophocles: Dramatum fragmenta.* Leipzig: Hahn.

Bowie, A. M. 1993. "Religion and Politics in Aeschylus' *Oresteia.*" *CQ* 43: 10–31.

———. 1997. "Tragic Filters for History: Euripides' *Supplices* and Sophocles' *Philoctetes.*" In Pelling 1997a: 39–62.

Bowra, C. M. 1961. *Greek Lyric Poetry from Alcman to Simonides.* 2d ed. Oxford: Clarendon.

Bradeen, D. W. 1960. "The Popularity of the Athenian Empire." *Historia* 9: 257–269.

———. 1969. "The Athenian Casualty Lists." *CQ* 19: 145–159.

Braun, M. 1998. *Die* "Eumeniden" *des Aischylos und der Areopag. Classica Monacensia* 19. Tübingen: Gunter Narr.

Braun, T. 1944. "ΧΡΗΣΤΟΥΣ ΠΟΙΕΙΝ" *CQ* 44: 40–45.

Bravo, B. 1980. "Sulān: Représailles et justice privée contre des étrangers dans les cités grecques." Études de vocabulaire et des institutions *ASNP* 10: 675–987.

Brelich, A. 1958. *Gli eroi greci: un problema storico—religioso.* Rome: Ateneo.

Bremmer, J. N., ed. 1987. *Interpretations of Greek Mythology.* London: Croom Helm.

———. 1997. "Myth as Propaganda: Athens and Sparta." *ZPE* 117: 9–17.

Brown, A. L. 1982. "Some Problems in the *Eumenides* of Aeschylus." *JHS* 102: 26–32.

———. 1983. "The Erinyes in the Oresteia. Real Life, the Supernatural and the Stage." *JHS* 103: 13–34.

———. 1984 "*Eumenides* in Greek Tragedy." *CQ* 34.2: 260–281.

Bruyn, O. de. 1995. *La compétence de l'Aréopage en matière de procès publics. Des origines de la polis athénienne à la conquête romaine de la Grèce (vers 700–146 avant J.-C.).* Stuttgart: Franz Steiner.

Burian, P. 1971. "Suppliant Drama." Diss. Princeton.

———. 1972. "Supplication and Hero Cult in Sophocles' *Ajax.*" *GRBS* 13: 151–156.

———. 1974a. "Pelasgus and Politics in Aeschylus' Danaid Trilogy." *WS* 8: 5–14.

———. 1974b. "Suppliant and Saviour: *Oedipus at Colonus*." *Phoenix* 28: 408–429.

———. 1977. "Euripides' *Heraclidae*: An Interpretation." *CP* 72: 1–21.

———. 1985. "*Logos* and *Pathos*: The Politics of the *Suppliant Women*." In Burian 1985: 129–155.

———. 1985. *Directions in Euripidean Criticism: A Collection of Essays*. Durham, N.C.: Duke University.

———. 1986. "Zeus *Soter Tritos* and Some Triads in Aeschylus' *Oresteia*." *AJP* 107: 332–342.

———. 2011. "Athenian Tragedy as democratic discourse." In Carter 2011: 95–117.

Burkert, W. 1979. *Structure and History in Greek Mythology and Ritual*. Berkeley: University of California.

———. 1985a. *Greek Religion*. Cambridge, Mass.: Harvard University.

———. 1985b. "Opferritual bei Sophokles: Pragmatik-Symbolik-Theater." *Der altsprachliche Unterricht* 27.2: 5–20.

———. 1996. *The Creation of the Sacred: Tracks of Biology in Early Religions*. Cambridge: Harvard University.

Burnett, A. P. 1976. "Tribe and City, Custom and Decree in *Children of Heracles*." *CP* 71: 4–26.

———. 1998. *Revenge in Attic and Later Tragedy*. Berkeley: University of California.

Butts, H. R. 1947. *The Glorification of Athens in Greek Drama*. Ann Arbor: University of Michigan.

Buxton, R. G. A., ed. 2000. *Oxford Readings in Greek Religion*. Oxford: Oxford University.

Calame, C. 1987. "Spartan Genealogies: The Mythological Representation of a Spatial Organisation," trans. A. Habib. In Bremmer 1987: 153–186.

———. 1998. "Mort héroïque et culte à mystères dans l' Oedipe à Colone de Sophocle: actes rituels au service de la recréation mythique." In Graf 1998: 326–356.

Calder, W. M., III 1981. "The Anti-Periklean Intent of Aeschylus' *Eumenides*." In Schmidt 1981: 217–223.

———. 1985. "The Political and Literary Sources of Sophocles' *Oedipus Coloneus*." In W. M. Calder III, U. K. Goldsmith, and P. B. Kenevan, eds. 1985. *Hypatia: Essays in Classics, Comparative Literature and Philosophy Presented to Hazel E. Barnes on Her Seventieth Birthday*: 1–14. Boulder: Colorado Associated University.

Cantarella, E. 2001. "Private Revenge and Public Justice: The Settlement of Disputes in Homer's *Iliad*." *Punishment & Society* 3: 473–483.

Cantarella, E., and G. Thür, eds. 2001. *Symposion 1997. Vorträge zur griechischen und hellenistischen Rechtsgeschichte*. Cologne: Böhlau.

Carter, D. M. 2004. "Was Attic Tragedy Democratic?" *Polis* 21: 1–25.

———. 2007. *The Politics of Greek Tragedy*. Exeter: Bristol Phoenix.

———. ed. 2011. *Why Athens? A Reappraisal of Tragic Politics*. Oxford: Oxford University.

Cartledge, P. 1979. *Sparta and Lakonia: A Regional History, 1300–362 BC*. London: Routledge.

———. 1987. *Agesilaos and the Crisis of Sparta*. Baltimore: Johns Hopkins University.

Cassella, P. 1999. *La supplica all'altare nella tragedia greca*. Naples: Bibliopolis.

Cawkwell, G. L. 1993. "Sparta and Her Allies in the Sixth Century." *CQ* 43.2: 364–376.

Chaniotis, A. 1996. "Conflicting Authorities: Asylia between Secular and Divine Law in the Classical and Hellenistic Poleis." *Kernos* 9: 65–86.

Clay, D. 1982. "Unspeakable Words in Greek Tragedy." *AJP* 103: 277–298.

Cohen, E. 2000. *The Athenian Nation*. Princeton: Princeton University.

Coldstream. J. N. 1976. "Hero-cults in the Age of Homer." *JHS* 96: 8–17.

Cole, J. R. 1977. "The *Oresteia* and Cimon." *HSCP* 81: 99–111.

Cole, S. G. 2004. *Landscapes, Gender, and Ritual Space: The Ancient Greek Experience.* Berkeley: University of California.

Collard, C. 1972. "The Funeral Oration in Euripides' *Supplices*." *BICS* 19: 39–53.

———. 1975. *Euripides' Supplices.* Groningen: Bouma's Boekhuis.

Collard, C., M. J. Cropp, and K. H. Lee, eds. 1995. *Euripides: Selected Fragmentary Plays,* vol. 1. Warminster, England: Aris and Phillips.

Conacher, D. J. 1967. *Euripidean Drama: Myth, Theme and Structure.* Toronto: University of Toronto.

———. 1987. *Aeschylus' Oresteia: A Literary Commentary.* Toronto: University of Toronto.

Connor, W. R. 1970. "The Theseus Myth in Classical Athens." In Ward, Connor, Edwards, and Tidworth 1970: 143–174.

———. 1990. "City Dionysia and Athenian Democracy." In Connor, Hansen, Raaflaub, and Strauss 1990: 7–32.

Connor, W. R., M. H. Hansen, K. A. Raaflaub, and B. S. Strauss, eds. 1990. "Aspects of Athenian Democracy." *Classica et Medievalia.* Copenhagen: Museum Tusculanum, University of Copenhagen.

Costa, C. D. N. 1962. "Plots and Politics in Aeschylus." *Greece & Rome* 9: 22–34.

Coy, J., and J. de Hoz, eds. 1984. *Estudios sobre los géneros literarios II.* Salamanca: University of Salamanca.

Craik, E. M., ed. 1990. *Owls to Athens. Essays on Classical Subjects in Honor of Sir Kenneth Dover.* Oxford: Oxford University.

Croally, N. 1994. *Euripidean Polemic: the Trojan Women and the Function of Tragedy.* Cambridge: Cambridge University.

———. 2005. "Tragedy's Teaching." In Gregory 2005: 55–70.

Cropp, M. 1980. "*Herakleidai* 603–604, 630 ff., and the Question of the Mutilation of the Text." *AJP* 101: 283–286.

Crotty, K. 1994. *The Poetics of Supplication: Homer's Iliad and Odyssey.* Ithaca, N.Y.: Cornell University.

Davidson, J., F. Muecke, and P. Wilson, eds. 2006. *Greek Drama III: Studies in Honour of Kevin Lee. Bulletin of the Institute of Classical Studies* Suppl. 87. London: Institute of Classical Studies.

Davies, J. K. 1977. "Athenian Citizenship: The Descent Group and the Alternatives." *CJ* 73: 105–121.

Delcourt, M. 1959. *Oreste et Alcméon. Étude sur la projection légendaire du matricide.* Paris: Les Belles Lettres.

Delebecque, E. 1951. *Euripide et la guerre du Péloponnèse.* Paris: C. Klincksieck.

Denniston, J. D., and D. Page, eds. 1957. *Agamemnon.* Oxford: Clarendon Press.

Dewald, C., and J. Marincola, eds. 2006. *The Cambridge Companion to Herodotus.* Cambridge: Cambridge University.

Dickins, G. 1912. "The Growth of Spartan Policy." *JHS* 32: 1–42.

Diggle, J., ed. 1984. *Euripidis Fabulae. Vol. 1.* Oxford: Clarendon.

Dillon, M. 2002. *Girls and Women in Classical Greek Religion.* London: Routledge.

Dodds, E. R. 1960. "Moral and Politics in the *Oresteia*." *PCPS* 6: 19–31.

———. 1973. "The Ancient Concept of Progress." In E. Dodds, ed. *The Ancient Concept of Progress, and other Essays on Greek Literature and Belief*: 1–25. Oxford: Clarendon Press, 1973.

Dougherty, C., and L. Kurke, eds. 1993. *Cultural Poetics in Archaic Greece. Cult, Performance, Politics*. Cambridge: Cambridge University.

Dover, K. J. 1957. "The Political Aspect of Aeschylus' *Eumenides*." *JHS* 77: 230–237.

Dreher, M. ed. 2003. *Das antike Asyl*. Kultische Grundlage, rechtliche Ausgestaltung und hellenistische Rechtsberichte 15. Köln: Böhlau.

Dubischar, M. 2001. *Der Agon Logon bei Euripides: Studien zu ausgewählten Dramen*. Stuttgart: Metzler.

Ducrey, P. 1968. *Le traitement des prisonniers de guerre dans la Grèce antique*. Paris: E. de Boccard.

Dué, C. 2006. *The Captive Woman's Lament in Greek Tragedy*. Austin: University of Texas.

Dunn, F. M. 1996. *Tragedy's End: Closure and Innovation in Euripidean Drama*. Oxford: Oxford University.

Dyer, R. R. 1969. "The Evidence for Apolline Purification Rituals at Delphi and Athens." *JHS* 89: 38–56.

Eagleton, T. 1991. *Ideology: An Introduction*. London: Verso.

Easterling, P. E. 1967. "Oedipus and Polyneices." *PCPS* 13: 1–13.

———. 1984. "Kings in Greek Tragedy." In Coy and de Hoz 1984: 33–45.

———. 1985. "Anachronism in Greek Tragedy." *JHS* 105: 1–10.

———. 1987. "Women in Tragic Space." *BICS* 34: 15–26.

———. 1997. "Constructing the Heroic." In Pelling 1997a: 21–37.

———, ed. 1997. *The Cambridge Companion to Greek Tragedy*. Cambridge: Cambridge University.

Ebbott, M. 2000. "The List of the War Dead in Aeschylus' *Persians*." *HSCP* 100: 83–96.

———. 2005. "Marginal Figures." In Gregory 2005: 366–376.

Edmunds, L. 1981. "The Cults and the Legends of Oedipus." *HSCP* 85: 221–238.

———. 1996. *Theatrical Space and Historical Place in Sophocles' Oedipus at Colonus*. Lanham, Md.: Rowman and Littlefield.

Ehrenberg, V. 1947. "Polypragmosyne: A Study in Greek Polistics." *JHS* 67: 46–67.

———. 1969. *The Greek State*. 2d ed. London: Methuen.

Ellendt, F. 1958. *Lexikon Sophocleum*. Hildesheim: Olms.

Euben, J. P., ed. 1986. *Greek Tragedy and Political Theory*. Berkeley: University of California.

Falkner, T. M. 1989. "The Wrath of Alcmene: Gender, Authority and Old Age in Euripides' *Children of Heracles*." In Falkner, T. M., and J. De Luce, eds. *Old Age in Greek and Latin Literature*: 114–131. Albany, N. Y.: State University of New York, 1989.

Falkner, T. M. N. Felson, and D. Konstan, eds. 1999. *Contextualizing Classics: Ideology, Performance, Dialogue: Essays in Honor of John J. Peradotto*. Lanham, Md.: Rowman and Littlefield.

Farnell, L. R. 1896–1909. *The Cults of the Greek States*. Oxford: Clarendon.

———. 1921. *Greek Hero-Cults and Ideas of Immortality*. Oxford: Oxford University.

Festugière, A. J. 1973. "Tragédie et tombes sacrées." *RHR* 184: 1–24.

Finley, M. I. 1978. "The Fifth-Century Athenian Empire: A Balance Sheet." In Garnsey and Whittaker 1978: 103–126.

———. 1985. *The Ancient Economy*. 2nd ed. Berkeley: University of California.

Fiske, J. 1992. "British Cultural Studies and Television." In Allen, R. C., ed. *Channels of Discourse, Reassembled*: 284–326. London: Routledge, 1992.

Fitton, J. W. 1961. "The *Suppliant Women* and the *Heraclidae* of Euripides." *Hermes* 89: 430–461.

Flower, M. A. 2000. "From Simonides to Isocrates: The Fifth-Century Origins of Fourth-Century Panhellenism." *CA* 19: 65–101.

Foley, H. P. 1982. "The 'Female Intruder' Reconsidered: Women in Aristophanes' *Lysistrata* and *Ecclesiazusae*." *CP* 77: 1–21.

———. 1985. *Ritual Irony: Poetry and Sacrifice in Euripides*. Ithaca, N.Y.: Cornell University.

———. 2001. *Female Acts in Greek Tragedy*. Princeton: Princeton University.

Fontana, B. 2000. "Logos and Kratos: Gramsci and the Ancients on Hegemony." *JHI* 61.2: 305–326.

Fornara, C. W. 1977. "*IG* i 2.39.52–57 and the 'Popularity' of the Athenian Empire." *CSCA* 10: 39–55.

Fornara, C. W., and L. J. Samons, II. 1991. *Athens from Cleisthenes to Pericles*. Berkeley: University of California.

Forrest, W. G. 1980. *A History of Sparta: 950–192 B.C.* 2nd ed. London: Duckworth.

Forsdyke, S. 2005. *Exile, Ostracism, and Democracy: The Politics of Expulsion in Ancient Greece*. Princeton: Princeton University.

Fraenkel, E. 1962. *Aeschylus* Agamemnon. Oxford: Oxford University.

Friis Johansen, H., and E. W. Whittle, eds. 1980. *Aeschylus: The Suppliants*. Copenhagen: Gyldendalske.

Furley, W. D. 1995. "Zur Aktualität der euripideischen *Herakleidai*." *Philologus* 139: 76–88.

Futo-Kennedy, R. 2006. "Justice, Geography and Empire in Aeschylus' *Eumenides*." *CA* 25: 35–72.

———. 2009. *Athena's Justice: Athena, Athens and the Concept of Justice in Greek Tragedy*. New York: Peter Lang.

Gagarin, M. 1978. "Self-defense in Athenian Homicide Law." *GRBS* 19: 111–120.

———. 1981. *Drakon and Early Athenian Homicide Law*. New Haven, Conn.: Yale University.

Galeotti Papi, D. 1995. "La scena di Macaria negli *Eraclidi* e l'oratoria funebre." *RFIC* 123: 140–154.

Garnsey, P. D. A., and C. R. Whittaker, eds. 1978. *Imperialism in the Ancient World*. Cambridge: Cambridge University.

Garvie, A. F. 2006. *Aeschylus' Supplices: Play and Trilogy*, 2nd ed. Bristol: Phoenix.

———. 1986. *Aeschylus*: Choephori. Oxford: Oxford University.

Gauthier, P. 1971. "Les *xenoi* dans les textes athéniens de la seconde moitié du Ve siècle av. J.-C." *REG* 84: 44–79.

———. 1988. "Métèques, périèques et paroikoi: bilan et points d'interrogation." In Lonis 1988: 23–46.

Gellie, G. H. 1972. *Sophocles: A Reading*. Melbourne: Melbourne University.

Gentili, B. and C. Prato. eds. 1979. *Poetae Elegiaci. Vol. 1. Fragmenta*. Leipzig: Teubner.

Georges, P. 1994. *Barbarian Asia and the Greek Experience*. Baltimore: Johns Hopkins University.

Gibert, J. 2011. "Hellenicity in Later Euripidean Tragedy." In Carter 2011: 383–401.

Gill, C. 1996. *Personality in Greek Epic, Tragedy and Philosophy: The Self in Dialogue*. Oxford: Oxford University.

Gill, C., Postlethwaite, N., and R. Seaford, eds. 1998. *Reciprocity in Ancient Greece*. Oxford: Oxford University.

Giordano, M. 1999. "La supplica: Rituale, istituzione sociale e tema epico." Diss. Naples.

Gödde, S. 2000. *Das Drama der Hikesie. Ritual und Rhetorik in Aischylos' Hiketiden*, (*Orbis Antiquus* 35). Münster: Aschendorff.

Goff, B., ed. 1995. *History, Tragedy, Theory: Dialogues on Athenian Drama*. Austin: University of Texas.

———. 1995a. "Aithra at Eleusis," *Helios* 22: 65–77.

———. 1999. "The Violence of Community: Ritual in the Iphigeneia in Tauris." In Padilla 1999: 109–125.

———. 2004. *Citizen Bacchae: Women's Ritual Practice in Ancient Greece*. Berkeley: University of California.

Goldhill, S. 1984. *Language, Sexuality, Narrative, the Oresteia*. Cambridge: Cambridge University.

———. 1987. "The Great Dionysia and Civic Ideology." *JHS* 107: 128–193.

———. 1992. *Aeschylus: The* Oresteia. Cambridge: Cambridge University.

———. 1997. "The Audience of Athenian Tragedy." In Easterling 1997: 54–68.

———. 2000. "Civic Ideology and the Problem of Difference: The Politics of Aeschylean Tragedy, Once Again." *JHS* 120: 34–56.

Goldhill, S., and R. Osborne, eds. 1999. *Performance Culture and Athenian Democracy*. Cambridge: Cambridge University.

Gomme, A. W., A. Andrewes, and K. Dover. 1945–1981. *A Historical Commentary on Thucydides*, 5 vols. Oxford: Oxford University.

Goossens, R. 1962. *Euripide et Athènes*. Brussels: Palais des Académies.

Gottesman, A. 2006. "A Branch at the Altar: Supplication and Symbolic Capital in Ancient Greece." Diss. University of Chicago.

Gould, J. 1996. "Tragedy and the Collective Experience." In Silk 1996: 217–256.

———. 1973. "*Hiketeia*." *JHS* 93: 74–103.

Graf, F., ed. 1998. *Ansichten griechischer Rituale: Geburtstags-Symposium für Walter Burkert*. Stuttgart: Teubner.

Gramsci, A. 1971. *Selections from Prison Notebooks*. Ed. and trans. Q. Hoare and G. Nowell Smith. London: Lawrence and Wishart.

Grasmück, E. L. 1978. *Exilium: Untersuchungen zur Verbannung in der Antike*. Rechts und Staatswissenschaftliche Veröffentlichungen der Görres-Gesellschaft N.F. 30. Paderborn: Schöningn.

Green, P. 1996. "The Metamorphosis of the Barbarian: Athenian Panhellenism in a Changing World." In Wallace and Harris 1996: 5–36.

Gregory, J. 1991. *Euripides and the Instruction of the Athenians*. Ann Arbor: University of Michigan.

———, ed. 2005. *A Companion to Greek Tragedy*. Oxford: Blackwell.

Grethlein, J. 2003. *Asyl und Athen. Die Konstruktion kollektiver Identitäten in der griechischen Tragödie*. (Drama, Beiträge zum antiken Drama und seiner Rezeption 21). Stuttgart: Metzler.

Griffin, J. 1998. "The Social Function of Attic Tragedy." *CQ* 48: 39–61.

———. 1999. "Sophocles and the Democratic City." In Griffin, J., ed. 1999. *Sophocles Revisited. Essays Presented to Sir Hugh Lloyd-Jones*: 73–94. Oxford: Clarendon, 1999.

Griffith, M. 1995. "Brilliant Dynasts: Power and Politics in the *Oresteia*." *CA* 14: 62–129.

———. 1998. "The King and the Eye: The Rule of the Father in Greek Tragedy." *PCPS* 44: 20–86.

———. 2005. "Authority Figures." In Gregory 2005: 333–351.

Grube, G. M. A. 1941. *The Drama of Euripides*. London: Methuen.

Guerrini, R. 1972. "La morte di Euristeo e le implicazioni eticopolitiche negli *Eraclidi* di Euripide." *Athenaeum* 50: 45–67.

Hägg, R., ed. 1996. *The Role of Religion in the Early Greek Polis*. Stockholm: Swedish Institute.

———, ed. 1999. *Ancient Greek Hero Cult*. Stockholm: Swedish Institute.

Hahneman, C. 1999. "Mount Oita Revisited: Sophocles' *Trachiniai* in Light of the Evidence of Aischylos' *Herakleidai*." *ZPE* 126: 67–73.

Hall, E. 1989. *Inventing the Barbarian: Greek Self-Definition through Tragedy*. Oxford: Clarendon.

———. 1997. "The Sociology of Athenian Tragedy." In Easterling 1997: 93–126.

Hall, J. M. 1997. *Ethnic Identity in Greek Antiquity*. Cambridge: Cambridge University.

———. 1999. "Beyond the Polis? The Multilocality of Heroes." In Hägg 1999: 49–56.

———. 2002. *Hellenicity: Between Ethnicity and Culture*. Chicago: University of Chicago.

Hammond, N. G. L. 1967. "The Origins and the Nature of the Athenian Alliance of 478/7 B.C." *JHS* 87: 41–61.

———. 1969. "Strategia and Hegemonia in Fifth-Century Athens." *CQ* 19.1: 111–144.

Hansen, M. H. 1976. *Apagoge, Endeixis and Ephegesis against Kakourgoi, Atimoi, and Pheugontes: A Study in the Athenian Administration of Justice in the Fourth Century B.C.* (Odense University Classical Studies 8). Odense: Odense University.

Harris, E. M. 2001. "How to Kill in Attic Greek. The Semantics of the Verb apokteinein and their Implications for Athenian Homicide Law." In Cantarella and Thür 2001: 75–87.

———. 2004. "Le rôle de l'*epieikeia* dans les tribunaux athéniens." *Revue historique de droit français et étranger* 82: 1–13.

Harrison, J. E. 1903. *Prolegomena to the Study of Greek Religion*. Cambridge: Cambridge University.

———. 1927. *Themis*. 2nd ed. Cambridge: Cambridge University.

Harrison, T., ed. 2002. *Greeks and Barbarians*. New York: Routledge.

Headlam, W. G. 1906. "The Last Scene of the *Eumenides*." *JHS* 26: 268–277.

———. 1906. "The Last Scene of the *Eumenides*." *JHS* 26: 268–277.

Hellström, P., and B. Alroth, eds. 1996. *Religion and Power in the Ancient Greek World*. Uppsala: University of Uppsala.

Henderson, J. 2003. "Demos, Demagogue, Tyrant in Attic Old Comedy." In Morgan 2003: 155–180.

Henrichs, A. 1981. "Human Sacrifice in Greek Religion." *Entretiens Hardt* 27: 195–235.

———. 1983. "The 'Sobriety' of Oedipus: Sophocles *OC* 100 Misunderstood." *HSCP* 87: 87–100.

———. 1984. "The *Eumenides* and Wineless Libations in the Derveni Papyrus." *Atti del XVII congresso internazionale di papirologia II*: 255–268.

———. 1991. "Namenlosigkeit und Euphemismus: Zur Ambivalenz der chthonischen Mächte im attischen Drama." In Hofmann and Harder 1991: 161–201.

———. 1993. "The Tomb of Aias and the Prospect of Hero Cult in Sophokles." *CA* 12: 165–180.

———. 1994. "Anonymity and Polarity: Unknown Gods and Nameless Altars at the Areopagus." *ICS* 19: 27–58.

Herington, C. J. 1986. *Aeschylus*. New Haven, Conn.: Yale University.

Herman, G. 1987. *Ritualized Friendship and the Greek City*. Cambridge: Cambridge University.

———. 2006. *Morality and Behaviour in Democratic Athens: A Social History*. Cambridge: Cambridge University.

Hermann, G. 1824. *Euripidis Tragoediae*. Leipzig: Weidmann.

Herter, H. 1939. "Theseus der Athener." *RhM* 88: 177–239.

Hester, D. A. 1977. "To Help One's Friends and Harm One's Enemies: A Study in the *Oedipus at Colonus*." *Antichthon* 11: 22–41.

———. 1993. "The Ignorance of Oedipus." *Prudentia* 25.1: 1–23.

Hofmann, H., and A. Harder, eds. 1991. *Fragmenta Dramatica: Beiträge zur Interpretation der griechischen Tragikerfragmente und ihrer Wirkungsgeschichte*. Göttingen: Vandenhoeck and Ruprecht.

Hölscher, T. 1998. "Images and Political Identity: The Case of Athens." In Boedeker and Raaflaub 1998: 153–183.

Honig, B. 2003. *Democracy and the Foreigner*. Princeton: Princeton University.

Hornblower, S. 1991. *A Commentary on Thucydides*, vol. 1. Oxford: Clarendon.

———. 1991a. *The Greek World 479–323 BC*. 3rd ed. London: Routledge. (1st ed., 1983, Methuen.)

———. 1996. *A Commentary on Thucydides*, vol. 2. Oxford: Clarendon.

Hubbard, T. K. 1992. "Remaking Myth and Rewriting History: Cult Tradition in Pindar's Ninth Nemean." *HSCP* 94: 77–111.

Hutchinson, G. O. 1985. *Aeschylus: Septem contra Thebas*. Oxford: Oxford University.

Huxley, G. 1979. "Bones for Orestes." *GRBS* 20: 145–148.

Jacoby, F. 1944. "Patrios Nomos: State Burial in Athens and the Public Ceremony in the Kerameikos." *JHS* 64: 37–66.

———. 1954. "Some Athenian Epigrams from the Persian Wars." *Hesperia* 14: 157–211.

Jebb, R. C. 1885. *The Oedipus Tyrannus*. Cambridge: Cambridge University.

———. 1928. *Sophocles: The Plays and Fragments. Part II. The Oedipus Coloneus*. Cambridge: Cambridge University.

Johnson, J. F., and D. C. Clapp. 2005. "Athenian Tragedy: An Education in Pity." In Sternberg 2005: 123–164.

Johnston, S. I. 1999. *Restless Dead: Encounters between the Living and the Dead in Ancient Greece*. Berkeley: University of California.

Jones, C. P. 1999. *Kinship Diplomacy in the Ancient World*. Cambridge, Mass.: Harvard University.

Jones, J. 1962. *Aristotle and Greek Tragedy*. London: Chatto and Windus.

Jones, L. A. 1987. "The Role of Ephialtes in the Rise of Athenian Democracy." *CA* 6: 53–76.

Just, R. 1989. *Women in Athenian Law and Life*. London: Routledge.

Kagan, D. 1969. *The Outbreak of the Peloponnesian War*. Ithaca, N.Y.: Cornell University.

Kallet, L. 1993. "*Demos Tyrannos*: Wealth, Power and Economic Patronage." In Morgan 1993: 117–154.

———. 1998. "Accounting for Culture in Fifth-Century Athens." In Boedeker and Raaflaub 1998: 43–58.

Kamerbeek, J. 1984. *The Plays of Sophocles, Part VII: The* Oedipus Coloneus. Leiden: Brill.

Kavoulaki, A. 1999. "Processional Performance and the Democratic Polis." In Goldhill and Osborne 1999: 293–320.

Kearns, E. 1989. *The Heroes of Attica. Bulletin of the Institute of Classical Studies* Suppl. 57. London: Institute of Classical Studies.

————. 1990. "Saving the City." In Murray and Price 1990: 323–344.

Kelly, A. 2009. *Sophocles: Oedipus at Colonus*. Duckworth Companions to Greek and Roman Tragedy. Duckworth: London.

Kelly, T. 2009. *A History of Argos to 500 B.C.* Minneapolis: University of Minnesota.

Kierdorf, W. 1966. *Erlebnis und Darstellung der Perserkriege: Studien zu Simonides, Pindar, Aischylos und den Attischen Rednern* (*Hypomnemata* 16). Göttingen: Vandenhoeck and Ruprecht.

Kirchoff, A. 1867. *Euripidis Fabulae*. Berlin: Weidmann.

Kirkwood, G. M. 1986. "From Melos to Colonus: τίνας χώρους ἀφίγμεθ'." *TAPA* 116: 99–117.

Knox, B. M. W. 1957. *Oedipus at Thebes*. New Haven, Conn.: Yale University.

————. 1964. *The Heroic Temper: Studies in Sophoclean Tragedy*. Berkeley: University of California.

Koch, C. 1991. *Volksbeschlüsse in Seebundangelegenheiten. Das Verfahrensrecht Athens im Ersten attischen Seebund*. Frankfurt am Main: P. Lang.

Konstan, D. 1998. "Reciprocity and Friendship." In Gill, Postlethwaite, and Seaford 1998: 279–301.

————. 2001. *Pity Transformed*. London. Duckworth.

————. 2005. "Pity and Politics." In Sternberg 2005: 48–66.

Kopperschmidt, J. 1967. "Die Hikesie als dramatische Form." Ph.D. diss., Tübingen.

Kovacs, D. 1995. *Euripides: Children of Heracles, Hippolytus, Andromache, Hecuba*, vol. 2. Loeb Classical Library. Cambridge, Mass.: Harvard University.

Kowalzig, B. 2006. "The Aetiology of Empire? Hero-Cult and Athenian Tragedy." In Davidson, Muecke, and Wilson 2006: 79–98.

Kron, U. 1999. "Patriotic Heroes." In Hägg 1999: 61–83.

Krummen, E. 1993. "Athens and Attica: Polis and Countryside in Greek Tragedy." In Sommerstein, Halliwell, Henderson, and Zimmermann 1993: 191–217.

Kuntz, M. 1993. *Narrative Setting and Dramatic Poetry* (*Mnemosyne* Suppl. 124). Leiden: Brill.

Lape, S. 2010. *Race and Citizen Identity in the Classical Athenian Democracy*. Cambridge: Cambridge University.

Lardinois, A. 1992. "Greek Myths for Athenian Rituals." *GRBS* 33: 313–327.

Larsen, A. O. 1940. "The Constitution and Original Purpose of the Delian League." *HSCP* 51: 175–213.

Larson, J. 1995. *Greek Heroine Cults*. Madison: University of Wisconsin.

Leahy, D. M. 1955. "The Bones of Teisamenos." *Historia* 4: 26–38.

————. 1958. "The Spartan Defeat at Orchomenos." *Phoenix* 12: 141–165.

Lebeck, A. 1971. *The* Oresteia. *A Study in Language and Structure*. Cambridge, Mass.: Harvard University.

Lesky, A. 1952. "Zwei Sophokles-Interpretationen." *Hermes* 80: 91–105.

————. 1977. "On the *Heraclidae* of Euripides." *YCS* 25: 227–238.

Linforth, I. M. 1951. "Religion and Drama in *Oedipus at Colonus*." *University of California Publications in Classical Philology* 14: 75–191.

Lissarrague, F. 2006. "Comment peindre les Érinyes?" *Métis* N.S. 4: 51–70.

Lloyd, M. 1992. *The Agon in Euripides*. Oxford: Clarendon.

Lloyd-Jones, H. 1983. *The Justice of Zeus*. 2nd ed. Berkeley: University of California.

————. 1990. "Erinyes, Semnai Theai, Eumenides." In Craik 1990: 203–211.

————. 1994. *Sophocles: Antigone, Women of Trachis, Philoctetes, Oedipus at Colonus*, vol. 2. Loeb Classical Library. Cambridge, Mass.: Harvard University.

Lloyd-Jones, H., and Wilson, N. G. H. 1990. *Sophoclis: Fabulae.* Oxford: Oxford University.

Lonis, R. 1987. "Extradition et prise de corps de réfugiés politiques en Grèce." In Lonis 1987: 69–88.

Lonis, R., ed. 1987. *L'étranger dans le monde grec.* Nancy: Presses Universitaires de Nancy.

Loraux, N. 1986. *The Invention of Athens: The Funeral Oration in the Classical City.* Trans. A. Sheridan. Cambridge, Mass.: Harvard University.

———. 2000. *Born of the Earth. Myth and Politics in Athens.* Trans. S. Stewart. Ithaca, N.Y.: Cornell University.

———. 1993. *The Children of Athena. Athenian Ideas about Citizenship and the Division between the Sexes.* Trans. C. Levine. Princeton: Princeton University.

———. 2002. *The Divided City: On Memory and Forgetting in Ancient Athens.* Trans. C. Pache and J. Fort. New York: Zone.

Low, P. 2007. *Interstate Relations in Classical Greece: Morality and Power.* Cambridge: Cambridge University.

———, ed. 2008. *The Athenian Empire.* Edinburgh: Edinburgh University.

Lynn George, M. 1988. *Epos: Word, Narrative and the* Iliad. London: Macmillan.

Ma, J., N. Papazarkadas, and R. Parker. 2009. *Interpreting the Athenian Empire.* London: Duckworth.

MacDowell, D. M. 1963. *Athenian Homicide Law in the Age of the Orators.* Manchester: Manchester University.

———. 1978. *The Law in Classical Athens.* Ithaca, N.Y.: Cornell University.

Macleod, C. W. 1982. "Politics and the *Oresteia.*" *JHS* 102: 124–144.

Malkin, I. 1987. *Religion and Colonization in Ancient Greece.* Leiden: Brill.

———. 1994. *Myth and Territory in the Spartan Mediterranean.* Cambridge: Cambridge University.

Manville, P. B. 1990. *The Origins of Citizenship in Ancient Athens.* Princeton: Princeton University.

———. 1994. "Toward a New Paradigm of Athenian Citizenship." In Boegehold and Scafuro 1994: 21–33.

Marinatos, N., and R. Hägg, eds. 1993. *Greek Sanctuaries: New Approaches.* London: Routledge.

Markantonatos, A. 2002. *Tragic Narrative: A Narratological Study of Sophocles'* Oedipus at Colonus. Berlin: de Gruyter.

———. 2007. *Oedipus at Colonus: Sophocles, Athens and the World.* Berlin: de Gruyter.

Mastrangelo, M. 2000. "Oedipus and Polyneices: Characterization and the Self in Sophocles' *Oedipus at Colonus.*" *MD* 44: 35–81.

Mastronarde, D. J. 2010. *The Art of Euripides: Dramatic Technique and Social Context.* Cambridge: Cambridge University.

Mattingly, H. B. 1996. *The Athenian Empire Restored: Epigraphic and Historical Studies.* Ann Arbor: University of Michigan.

———. 2008. "Periclean Imperialism." In Low 2008: 81–112.

McCauley, B. 1999. "Heroes and Power: The Politics of Bone Transferral." In Hägg 1999: 85–98.

McClure, L. 1999. *Spoken Like a Woman: Speech and Gender in Athenian Drama.* Princeton: Princeton University.

McGregor, M. F. 1987. *The Athenians and Their Empire.* Vancouver, B.C.: University of British Columbia.

McLean, J. 1934. "The *Heraclidae* of Euripides." *AJP* 55: 197–224.

———

Méautis, G. 1942. *Sophocle: Essai sur le héros tragique.* Paris: A. Michel.

Meier, C. 1990. *The Greek Discovery of Politics.* Trans. D. McClintock. Cambridge, Mass.: Harvard University.

———. 1993. *The Political Art of Greek Tragedy.* Trans. A. Webber. Baltimore: Johns Hopkins University.

Meiggs, R. 1972. *The Athenian Empire.* Oxford: Clarendon.

Mendelsohn, D. 2002. *Gender and the City in Euripides' Political Plays.* Cambridge: Cambridge University.

Mercier, C. E. 1990. "Suppliant Ritual in Euripidean Tragedy." Diss. Columbia University.

Mikalson, J. 1991. *Honor Thy Gods: Popular Religion in Greek Tragedy.* Chapel Hill: University of North Carolina.

Mills, S. 1997. *Theseus, Tragedy, and the Athenian Empire.* Oxford: Clarendon.

Missiou, A. 1998. "Reciprocal Generosity in the Foreign Affairs of Fifth-Century Athens and Sparta." In Gill, Postlethwaite, and Seaford 1998: 181–197.

Mitchell, L. G. 2007. *Panhellenism and the Barbarian in Archaic and Classical Greece.* Swansea: Classical Press of Wales.

Mitchel-Boyask, R. 2009. *Aeschylus. Eumenides.* Duckworth Companions to Greek and Roman Tragedy. Duckworth: London.

Morgan, K. A., ed. 2003. *Popular Tyranny: Sovereignty and Its Discontents in Ancient Greece.* Austin: University of Texas.

Morris, I. 1988. "Tomb Cult and the 'Greek Renaissance': The Past in the Present in the 8th Century BC." *Antiquity* 62: 750–761.

———. 2000. *Archaeology as Cultural History: Words and Things in Iron age Greece.* Oxford: Blackwell.

Moulinier, L. 1975. *Le pur et l'impur dans la pensée des Grecs d'Homère à Aristote.* New York: Arno.

Murray, O., and S. Price, eds. 1990. *The Greek City from Homer to Alexander.* Oxford: Clarendon.

Musgrave, S. 1800. *Sophocles,* 2 vols. Oxford.

Nagy, G. 1999. *The Best of the Achaeans: Concepts of the Hero in Archaic Greek Poetry.* Baltimore: Johns Hopkins University. (Revised ed., 1st ed., 1979.)

Naiden, F. S. 2000. "Greek Supplication prior to 300 BCE." Ph.D. diss., Harvard University.

———. 2006. *Ancient Supplication.* Oxford: Oxford University.

Nancy, C. 1983. "Φάρμακον σωτηρίας: Le mécanisme du sacrifice humain chez Euripide." In H. Zehnacker, ed., *Théâtre et spectacle dans l'antiquité: Actes du Colloque de Strasbourg. 5–7 novembre 1981:* 17–30 (Travaux du centre de recherche sur le Proche-Orient et la Grèce antiques 7). Leiden: Brill.

Neitzel, H. 1991. "Zur Reinigung des Orest in Aischylos' 'Eumeniden.'" *WJfA* 17: 68–89.

Nemeth, G. 1983. "On Dating Sophocles' Death." *Homonoia* 5: 115–128.

Nilsson, M. P. 1951. *Cults, Myths, Oracles, and Politics in ancient Greece.* Acts of the Swedish Institute in Athens, vol. 1. C. W. K. Gleerup: Lund.

Ober, J. 1989. *Mass and Elite in Democratic Athens: Rhetoric, Ideology and the Power of the People.* Princeton: Princeton University.

———. 1996. *The Athenian Revolution: Essays on Ancient Greek Democracy and Political Theory.* Princeton: Princeton University.

Ober, J., and T. Hedrick, eds. 1996. *Democratia. A Conversation on Democracies, Ancient and Modern.* Princeton: Princeton University.

O'Connor-Visser, E. A. M. E. 1987. *Aspects of Human Sacrifice in the Tragedies of Euripides*. Amsterdam: Grüner.

O'Higgins, L. 2003. *Women and Humor in Classical Greece*. Cambridge: Cambridge University.

Osborne, M. J. 1981. *Naturalization in Athens*, vols. 3–4 (*Verhandelingen van de Koninklijke Academie voor Wetenschappen, Letteren en Schone Kunsten van België. Klasse der Letteren 98*). Brussels: Paleis der Academien.

Ostwald, M. 1982. *Autonomia: Its Genesis and Early History*, Atlanta, Ga.: Scholars.

———. 1986. *From Popular Sovereignty to the Sovereignty of Law: Law, Society, and Politics in Fifth-Century Athens*. Berkeley: University of California.

Padel, R. 1992. *In and Out of the Mind: Greek Images of the Tragic Self*. Princeton: Princeton University.

———. 1995. *Whom Gods Destroy: Elements of Greek and Tragic Madness*. Princeton: Princeton University.

Padilla, M. W., ed. 1999. *Rites of Passage in Ancient Greece*. Lewisburg, Penn.: Bucknell University.

Page, D. 1973. *Aeschyli Septem quae supersunt tragoediae*. Oxford. Oxford University.

Paley, F. A. 1872–1880. *Euripides: With an English Commentary*. 2nd ed. London: Whittaker and Bell.

Palmer, M. 1992. *Love of Glory and the Common Good: Aspects of the Political Thought of Thucydides*. Lanham, Md.: Rowman and Littlefield.

Parker, R. B. 1983. *Miasma: Pollution and Purification in Early Greek Religion*. Oxford: Oxford University.

———. 1996. *Athenian Religion: A History*. Oxford: Clarendon.

———. 2008. "Religion and the Athenian Empire." In Low 2008: 146–158.

Patterson, C. 1981. *Pericles' Citizenship Law of 451–450 B.C.* Salem, N.H.: Ayer.

———. 1987. "*Hai Attikai*: The Other Athenians." *Helios* 13: 49–67.

———. 2009. "Citizenship and Gender in the Ancient World: The Experience of Athens and Rome." In S. Benhabib and J. Resnik, eds. *Migrations and Mobilities: Citizenship, Borders, and Gender*: 47–75. New York: New York University.

Pearson, A. C., ed. 1907. *Euripides: The Heraclidae*. Cambridge: Cambridge University.

Pelling, C. B. R., ed. 1997a. *Greek Tragedy and the Historian*. Oxford: Oxford University.

———. 1997b. "Aeschylus' *Persae* and History." In Pelling 1997a: 1–15.

———. 1997c. "Conclusion." In Pelling 1997a: 213–235.

———. 2000. *Literary Texts and the Greek Historian*. London: Routledge.

Petzold, K. E. 1994. "Die Gründung des Delisch-Attischen Seebundes: Element einer 'imperialistischen' Politik Athens?: II. Zielsetzung des Seebundes und die Politik der Zeit." *Historia* 43: 1–31.

Pfeiffer, R. ed. 1949. *Callimachus. Volumen 1. Fragmenta*. Oxford: Clarendon.

Podlecki, A. J. 1966. *The Political Background of Aeschylean Tragedy*. Ann Arbor: University of Michigan. (2nd ed., 1999.)

———. 1989. *Aeschylus: Eumenides*. Warminster, England: Aris and Phillips.

Pohlenz, M. 1930. *Die griechische Tragödie*. Leipzig: Teubner.

Polignac, F., de. 1984. *La naissance de la cité grecque. Cultes, espace et société, VIIIe–VIIe siècles avant J.-C.* Paris: Découverte.

Popp, H. 1968. "Zum Verhältnis Athens zu seinen Bündnern im attisch-delischen Seebund." *Historia* 17: 425–443.

Powell, A., ed. 1990. *Euripides, Women, and Sexuality*. London: Routledge.

Pozzi, D. C. 1991. "The Polis in Crisis." In Pozzi and Wickersham 1991: 126–163.

Pozzi, D. C., and J. M. Wickersham, eds. 1991. *Myth and the Polis*. Ithaca, N.Y.: Cornell University.

Prag, A. J. N. W. 1985. *The Oresteia: Iconographic and Narrative Tradition*. Chicago: Bolchazy Carducci.

Price, J. J. 2001. *Thucydides and Internal War*. Cambridge: Cambridge University.

Pritchett, K. W. 1969. "The Transfer of the Delian Treasury." *Historia* 18: 17–21.

Quincey, J. H. 1964. "Orestes and the Argive Alliance." *CQ* 14: 190–206.

Quinn, T. J. 1964. "Thucydides and the Unpopularity of the Athenian Empire." *Historia* 13: 257–266.

Raaflaub, K. 2003. "Stick and Glue: The Function of Tyranny in Fifth-Century Athenian Democracy." In Morgan 2003: 59–93.

———. 2004. *The Discovery of Freedom in Ancient Greece*. Trans. R. Franciscono. Chicago: University of Chicago.

Rabinowitz, N. S. 1981. "From Force to Persuasion: Aeschylus' *Oresteia* as Cosmogonic Myth." *Ramus* 10: 159–191.

Rawlings, H. R. 1977. "Thucydides on the Purpose of the Delian League." *Phoenix* 31: 1–8.

Reckford, K. J. 1968. "Medea's First Exit." *TAPA* 99: 329–359.

Rehm, R. 1988. "The Staging of Suppliant Plays." *GRBS* 29: 263–307.

———. 1994. *Marriage to Death: The Conflation of Wedding and Funeral Rituals in Greek Tragedy*. Princeton: Princeton University.

Reinhardt, K. 1949. *Aischylos als Regisseur und Theologe*. Bern: Francke.

Rhodes, P. J. 1981. *A Commentary on the Aristotelian Athenaion Politeia*. Oxford: Clarendon.

———. 1985. *The Athenian Empire* (*Greece and Rome*: New Surveys in the Classics 17). Oxford: Oxford University.

———. 2003. "Nothing to Do with Democracy: Athenian Drama and the *Polis*." *JHS* 123: 104–119.

———. 2007. "Democracy and Empire." In Samons 2007: 24–45.

Rivier, A. 1944. *Essai sur le tragique d'Euripide*. Lausanne: Rouge.

Robert, C. 1915. *Oidipus*. Berlin: Weidemann.

Roberts, D. H. 1984. *Apollo and His Oracle in the Oresteia. Hypomnemata 78*. Göttingen: Vandenhoeck and Ruprecht.

Robertson, N. D. 1980. "The True Nature of the Delian League." *AJAH* 5: 64–96.

Rohde, E. 1925. *Psyche: The Cult of Souls and Belief in Immortality among the Greeks*. Trans. by W. B. Hillis. London: Kegan Paul, Trench, Trübner.

Romilly, J. de. 1963. *Thucydides and Athenian Imperialism*. Oxford: Blackwell.

Rose, P. W. 1999. "Theorizing Athenian Imperialism and the Athenian State." In Peradotto, Falkner, Felson, and Konstan 1999: 19–40.

Roselli, D. K. 2007. "Gender, Class and Ideology: The Social Function of Virgin Sacrifice in Euripides' *Children of Herakles*." *CA* 26: 81–169.

Rosenbloom, D. 1995. "Myth, History and Hegemony in Aeschylus." In Goff 1995: 91–130.

———. 2006a. *Aeschylus: Persians*. London: Duckworth.

———. 2006b. "Empire and Its Discontents: *Trojan Women, Birds*, and the Symbolic Economy of Athenian Imperialism." In Davidson, Muecke, and Wilson 2006: 245–271.

———. 2011. "Panhellenism of Athenian Tragedy." In Carter 2011: 353–381.

Rosenmeyer, T. G. 1952. "The Wrath of Oedipus." *Phoenix* 6: 92–112.

Rosivach, V. J. 1978. "The Altar of Zeus Agoraios in the *Heracleidae*." *PP* 33: 32–47.

Saïd, S. 1978. *La faute tragique.* Paris: Maspero.

———. 1993. "Tragic Argos." In Sommerstein, Halliwell, Henderson and Zimmermann 1993: 167–189.

———. 2002. "Greeks and Barbarians in Euripides' Tragedies: The End of Differences?" Trans. A. Nevill. In Harrison 2002: 62–100.

Samons, L. J., II, ed. 1998. *Athenian Democracy and Imperialism.* Boston: Houghton Mifflin.

———. 1998–1999. "Aeschylus, the Alkmeonids and the Reform of the Areopagos." *CJ* 94: 221–233.

———. 2000. *Empire of the Owl: Athenian Imperial Finance (Historia Einzelschriften 142).* Stuttgart: Steiner.

———. 2004. *What's Wrong with Democracy? From Athenian Practice to American Worship.* Berkeley: University of California.

———, ed. 2007. *The Cambridge Companion to the Age of Pericles.* Cambridge: Cambridge University.

Sansone, D. 1988. "The Survival of the Bronze-Age Demon." *ICS* 13: 1–17.

Saxonhouse, A. W. 1992. *Fear of Diversity. The Birth of Political Science in Ancient Greek Thought.* Chicago: University of Chicago.

Schaps, D. 1979. *The Economic Rights of Women in Ancient Greece.* Edinburgh: Edinburgh University.

Schauer, M. 2002. *Tragisches Klagen. Form und Funktion der Klagedarstellung bei Aischylos, Sophokles und Euripides* (Classica Monacensia 26). Tübingen: Gunter Narr.

Schlesinger, E. 1933. "Die griechische Asylie." Diss. Grießen.

Schlunk, R. R. 1976. "The Theme of the Suppliant Exile in the *Iliad.*" *AJP* 97: 199–209.

Schmidt, E. G., ed. 1981. *Aischylos und Pindar.* Berlin: Akademie-Verlag.

Schröder, O. 1914. "De laudibus Athenarum a poetis tragicis et ab oratoribus epidicticis excultis." Ph.D. diss., Göttingen.

Schuller, W. 1974. *Die Herrschaft der Athener im Ersten Attischen Seebund.* Berlin: de Gruyter.

Scullion, S. 2002. "Tragic Dates." *CQ* 52: 81–101.

Seaford, R. 1994. *Reciprocity and Ritual: Homer and Tragedy in the Developing City-State.* Oxford: Clarendon.

———. 1995. "Historicizing Tragic Ambivalence: The Vote of Athena." In Goff: 203–221.

Sealey, R. 1966. "The Origins of the Delian League." In V. Ehrenberg and E. Badian, eds., *Ancient Society and Its Institutions: Studies Present to Victor Ehrenberg on His 75th Birthday,* 233–255. Oxford. Blackwell.

———. 1976. *A History of the Greek City-States, 700–338 B.C.* Berkeley: University of California.

———. 1990. *Women and Law in Classical Greece.* Chapel Hill: University of North Carolina.

Segal, C. P. 1981. *Tragedy and Civilization: An Interpretation of Sophocles.* Cambridge, Mass.: Harvard University.

Seidensticker, B. 1972. "Beziehungen zwischen den beiden Oidipusdramen des Sophokles." *Hermes* 100: 255–274.

———. 1995. "Women on the Tragic Stage." In Goff 1995: 151–173.

Sfyroeras, P. 1994. "The Ironies of Salvation: The Aigeus Scene in Euripedes' *Medea.*" *CJ* 90: 125–142.

Shapiro, H. A. 1996. "Athena, Apollo and the Religious Propaganda of the Athenian Empire." In Hellström and Alroth 1996: 101–113.

Shaw, M. H. 1975. "The Female Intruder in Fifth-Century Drama." *CP* 70: 255–266.

Sickinger, J. P. 2007. "The Bureaucracy of Democracy and Empire." In Samons 2007: 196–214.

Sidwell, K. 1996. "Purification and Pollution in Aeschylus' *Eumenides*." *CQ* 46: 44–57.

Silk, M. S., ed., 1996. *Tragedy and the Tragic: Greek Theatre and Beyond*. Oxford: Oxford University.

Sinn, U. 1993. "Greek Sanctuaries as Places of Refuge." In Marinatos and Hägg 1993: 70–87.

Skinner, M., ed. 1987. *Rescuing Creusa: New Methodological Approaches to Women in Antiquity. Helios* Special Issue 13.2.

Slatkin, L. 1986. "*Oedipus at Colonus*: Exile and Integration." In Euben 1986: 210–221.

Smarczyk, B. 1986. *Bündnerautonomie und athenische Seebundspolitik im Dekeleischen Krieg.* (Beiträge zur klassischen Philologie 177). Frankfurt am Main: Hain.

———. 1990. *Untersuchungen zur Religionspolitik und politischen Propaganda Athens im Delisch-Attischen Seebund.* Munich: Tuduv.

———. 2007. "Religion und Herrschaft: Der Delisch–Attische Seebund." *Saeculum: Jahrbuch für Universalgeschichte* 58: 205–228.

Snodgrass, A. M. 1971. *The Dark Age of Greece.* Edinburgh: Edinburgh University.

———. 1987. *An Archaeology of Greece: The Present State and Future Scope of a Discipline* (Sather Classical Lectures 50). Berkeley: University of California.

———. 2000. "The Archaeology of the Hero." In Buxton 2000: 180–190.

Solmsen, F. 1949. *Hesiod and Aeschylus.* Ithaca, N.Y.: Cornell University.

Solomon, J., ed. 1994. *Apollo: Origins and Influence.* Tucson: University of Arizona.

Sommerstein, A. H. 1989. *Aeschylus' Eumenides.* Cambridge: Cambridge University.

———. 1997. "The Theatre Audience, the Demos, and the *Suppliants* of Aeschylus." In Pelling 1997a: 63–79.

———, ed. 2009. *Aeschylus*: Oresteia. Trans. A. H. Sommerstein, vol. 2. Loeb Classical Library. Cambridge, Mass.: Harvard University.

———. 2010. *Aeschylean Tragedy.* 2d ed. London: Duckworth.

Sommerstein, A. H, S. Halliwell, J. Henderson, B. Zimmermann, eds. 1993. *Tragedy, Comedy and the Polis: Papers from the Greek Drama Conference: Nottingham, 18–20 July 1990.* Bari: Levante Editori.

Sourvinou-Inwood, C. 2003. *Tragedy and Athenian Religion.* Lanham, Md.: Lexington Books.

Spranger, J. A. 1925. "The Political Element in the *Heracleidae* of Euripides." *CQ* 19: 117–128.

Stadter, P. 2006. "Herodotus and the Cities of Mainland Greece." In Dewald and Marincola 2006: 242–256.

Ste. Croix, G. E. M. de. 1954. "The Character of the Athenian Empire." *Historia* 3: 1–41.

———. 1972. *The Origins of the Peloponnesian War.* London: Duckworth.

Sternberg, R., ed. 2005. *Pity and Power in Ancient Athens.* Cambridge: Cambridge University.

Stevens, P. T. 1971. *Euripides: Andromache.* Oxford: Clarendon.

Stoessl, F. 1956. "Die Herakliden des Euripides." *Philologus* 100: 207–234.

Strassburger, H. 1958. "Thucydides und die politische Selbstdarstellng der Athener." *Hermes* 86: 17–40.

Strohm, H. 1957. *Euripides: Interpretationen zur dramatischen Form* (Zetemata 15). Munich: Beck.

Suter, A. 2008. "Male Lament in Greek Tragedy." In A. Suter, ed., *Lament: Studies in the Ancient Mediterranean and Beyond*: 156–180. Oxford: Oxford University.

Tanner, R. G. 1966. "The Composition of the *Oedipus Coloneus.*" In Kelly, M., ed. *For Service to Classical Studies in Honor of Francis Letters*: 153–192. Melbourne: F. W. Cheshire.

Taplin, O. 1977. *The Stagecraft of Aeschylus: The Dramatic Use of Exits and Entrances in Greek Tragedy.* Oxford: Clarendon.

Tarkow, T. 1977. "The Glorification of Athens in Euripides' *Heracles.*" *Helios* 5: 27–33.

Thomson, G. 1941. *Aeschylus and Athens.* 2nd ed. London: Lawrence and Wishart.

———. 1966. *The Oresteia of Aeschylus: A Study in the Social Origins of Drama.* 2nd ed. Prague: Academia.

Travis, R. 1999. *Allegory and the Tragic Chorus in Sophocles' Oedipus at Colonus.* Lanham, Md.: Rowman and Littlefield.

Turner, C. 2001. "Perverted Supplication and Other Inversions in Aeschylus' Danaid Trilogy." *CJ* 97: 27–50.

Tzanetou, A. 2005. "A Generous City: Pity in Athenian Oratory and Tragedy." In Sternberg 2005: 98–122.

Van Hook, L. 1934. "The Praise of Athens in Greek Tragedy." *CW* 27: 185–188.

Vellacott, P. 1975. *Ironic Drama: A Study of Euripides' Method and Meaning.* Cambridge: Cambridge University.

Vernant, J-P., and P. Vidal Naquet, eds. 1990. *Myth and Tragedy in Ancient Greece*, vol. 2. Trans. J. Lloyd. New York: Zone Books.

Vidal-Naquet, P. 1990. "Oedipus between Two Cities." *An Essay on Oedipus at Colonus.* In Vernant and Vidal-Naquet 1990: 329–359.

———. 1997. "The Place and Status of Foreigners in Tragedy." In Pelling 1997a: 109–119.

Vinh, G. 2011. "Athens in Euripides' *Suppliants*: Ritual, Politics and Theater." In Carter 2011: 325–344.

Visser, M. 1982. "Worship Your Enemy: Aspects of the Cult of Heroes in Ancient Greece." *HTR* 75: 403–428.

———. 1984. "Vengeance and Pollution in Classical Athens." *JHI* 45: 193–206.

Visvardi, E. 2011. "Pity and Panhellenic Politics: Choral Emotion in Euripides' *Hecuba* and *Trojan Women.*" In Carter 2011: 269–291.

Walker, H. J. 1995. *Theseus and Athens.* Oxford: Oxford University.

Wallace, R. W. 1989. *The Areopagus Council to 307 B.C.* Baltimore: Johns Hopkins University.

Wallace, R. W., and E. M. Harris, eds. 1996. *Transitions to Empire: Essays in Greco-Roman History, 360–146 B.C., in Honor of E. Badian.* Norman: University of Oklahoma.

Ward, A. G., W. R. Connor, R. B. Edwards, and S. Tidworth, eds. 1970. *The Quest for Theseus.* New York: Praeger.

Watson, L. 1991. *Arae: The Curse Poetry of Antiquity.* Leeds: Cairns.

Westbrook, R. 1992. "The Trial Scene in the *Iliad.*" *HSCP* 94: 53–76.

Whitehead, D. 1977. *The Ideology of the Athenian Metic.* *PCPS* Suppl. 4. Cambridge: Cambridge University.

———. 1986. "The Ideology of the Athenian Metic: Some Pendants and a Reappraisal." *PCPS* 32: 145–158.

Whitley, J. 1988. "Early States and Hero Cults: A Reappraisal." *JHS* 108: 173–182.

Wilamowitz-Moellendorff, U. von. 1882. *De Euripidis Heraclidis Commentatiuncula.* (= *Kleine Schriften*, vol. 1, 62–81).

———

———. 1882. "Exkurse zu Euripides Herakliden." *Hermes* 17: 337–64 (*Kleine Schriften*, vol. 1, 82–109).

———. 1917. "Oedipus auf Kolonus." In von Wilamowitz–Moellendorff. T. *Die dramatische Technik des Sophokles* (Philologische Untersuchungen 22: 313–376. Berlin: Weidmann, 1917.

Wiles, D. 1997. *Tragedy in Athens: Performance Space and Theatrical Meaning*. Cambridge: Cambridge University.

Wilkins, J. 1990. "The State and the Individual." In Powell 1990: 177–194.

———. 1990a. "The Young of Athens: Religion and Society in the *Herakleidai* of Euripides." *CQ* 40: 329–339.

———. 1993. *Euripides*, Heraclidae. Oxford: Clarendon.

Williams, B. 1993. *Shame and Necessity*. (Sather Classic Lecture Series). Berkeley: University of California.

Williams, R. 1977. *Marxism and Literature*. Oxford: Oxford University.

Wilson, J. P. 1997. *The Hero and the City: An Interpretation of Sophocles'* Oedipus at Colonus. Ann Arbor: University of Michigan.

Wilson, P. J. 2000. *The Athenian Institution of the Khoregia: the Chorus, the City and the Stage*. Cambridge: Cambridge University.

———. 2009. "Tragic Honours and Democracy: Neglected Evidence for the Politics of the Athenian Dionysia." *CQ* 59: 8–29.

———. 2011. "The Glue of Democracy? Tragedy, Democracy, Structure and Finance." In Carter 2011: 19–43.

Winkler, J. J., and F. Zeitlin, eds. 1990. *Nothing to do with Dionysos? Athenian Drama in its Social Context*. Princeton: Princeton University.

Winnington-Ingram, R. P. 1954. "A Religious Function of Greek Tragedy: A Study in the Oedipus Coloneus and the Oresteia." *JHS* 74: 16–24.

———. 1980. *Sophocles: An Interpretation*. Cambridge: Cambridge University.

———. 1983. *Studies in Aeschylus*. Cambridge: Cambridge University.

Yates, D. C. 2005. "The Archaic Treaties between the Spartans and their Allies." *CQ* 55:65–76.

Zacharia, K. 2003. *Converging Truths: Euripides'* "Ion" *and the Athenian Quest for Self-Definition* (*Mnemosyne* Suppl. 242). Leiden: Brill.

Zeitlin, F. 1965. "The Motif of Corrupted Sacrifice in Aeschylus' *Oresteia*." *TAPA* 97: 463–508.

———. 1966. "Postscript to Sacrificial Imagery in the *Oresteia* (*Ag.* 1235–37)." *TAPA* 97: 645–653.

———. 1978. "The Dynamics of Misogyny: Myth and Mythmaking in the *Oresteia* of Aeschylus." *Arethusa* 11: 149–184.

———. 1990. "Theater of Self and Society in Athenian Drama." In Winkler and Zeitlin 1990: 130–167.

Zelnick-Abramovitz, R. 1988. "Request and Supplication by Foreigners to the Athenian Polis." *Mnemosyne* 51: 554–573.

Ziolkowski, J. E. 1981. *Thucydides and the Tradition of Funeral Speeches at Athens*. New York: Arno.

Zuntz, G. 1947. "Is the *Heraclidae* Mutilated?" *CQ* 41: 45–52.

———. 1955. *The Political Plays of Euripides*. Manchester: Manchester University.

# INDEX LOCORUM

24.22: 141n14
45.78: 170n51
59.16: 128
59.79–81: 112
59.89: 114
60.4: 96
60.8–9: 155nn2, 3
60.27–31: 164n135
60.29: 162n100

Diodorus Siculus
11.33.3: 138n92
11.46.6–47: 137n85
11.56.1–3: 159n60
11.63: 140n4
11.77.6: 140n5
12.9.4: 159n60
13.72: 122
17.108.7: 159n60

Dionysius of Halicarnassus
5.17.4: 138n92

Dinarchus
1.46–47: 153n148
1.47: 62, 152n134

Euripides
*Andromache*
877–879: 163n123
*Children of Heracles*
12–17: 82
15–22: 76
15–25: 78
32: 158n46
40–44: 92
55–56: 89
55–62: 76
61–62: 77
62: 76
64: 159n61
67–68: 159n64
68: 159nn61,64
70: 80, 158n46
101–104: 134n41
111–113: 81
112–113: 76
118–164: 28

130–133: 11
134–143, 134–179: 82
135, 139–140: 159n61
139–142, 140, 140–141, 141–143: 82
147–152: 87
150–155: 78
152, 153–168, 154: 87
155–157: 161n94
155–249: 103
158, 162–168: 87
181–183: 159n67
181–190: 83
181–231: 81
182, 185, 186, 187–188, 190–191: 83
191–196: 77, 78
197–198: 77
198: 76
219–237: 164n145
229–230: 78
243–246: 14, 77
244–245: 76
284–287: 14
310–311: 101
329–330: 85
329–331: 99
329–332: 14
339–349: 102
410, 410–414, 415–417, 415–424, 419,
    420, 420–422: 85
422, 425: 161n88
435–438: 161n91
437–439: 85
439–450, 442: 86
451–457: 85
461: 161n91
461–463: 86
474–483: 92
475, 476–477, 479–480: 93
494–497, 498, 499: 88
500: 94
501: 88
501–502: 95
502: 91, 95
503–506, 503–510: 99
509–510, 511–517: 96
522–524: 97
537, 539–541, 549–551: 96
550–551: 91

559: 91, 97
563: 96
612: 159n64
621–622: 97
625–627: 96
625–637: 97
626–627: 96
629: 162n101
660–670: 88
786–787, 800–818, 815–817, 843–863:
   100
873–878: 159n63
873–888: 101
918, 924: 159n64
936–937: 100
961–974: 164n144
962–982: 165n148
1000–1008: 82
1015: 102
1027–1037: 101
1032–1037: 40, 145n42
1033: 102
1036: 101
*Electra*
15–18: 159n63
1238–1275: 26
1270–1272: 153n141
*Hecuba*
378: 164n137
382–400: 161n91
798–801: 134n41
975: 163n123
*Heracles*
1–169: 135n55
155–161: 79
243–245, 286–287: 79
922–940: 48
1199–1201: 168n33
1281–1286: 168n32
1322–1323: 172n89
*Iphigenia in Aulis*
821–834: 163n123
1028–1032: 163n123
1385: 164n137
1398–1399: 94
*Iphigenia in Tauris*
30–41: 160n86
940–957: 168n32

943–960: 140n8
944: 152n134
947–960: 141n18, 168n33
968–969: 153n141
1216: 148n78
1435–1474: 26, 140n8
*Medea*
214–218: 163n122
223–224: 167n15
749–751: 159n70
846–850: 142n22
850: 168n33
*Orestes*
38: 152n134
46: 147n67
321, 836: 152n134
1276: 163n123
1644–1652: 26
1650: 152n134
1650–1652: 141n18
*Phoenician Women*
88–95: 163n123
588–589: 160n84
962–969: 161n91
1276–1283: 163n123
1706–1707: 171n65
*Trojan Women*
210–213: 155n6
*Suppliant Women*
155–249: 103
187–189: 155n6
220–249: 104
226–236: 134n36
246–249: 161n96
247–249: 11
253–256: 155n17
258–262: 134n41
297–300: 163nn122, 123
301–313: 103, 165n150
306–325: 163n122
315–333: 14
337–341: 103, 165n150
339–342: 14
341: 155n17
346–348: 155n17
347: 157n35
350–353: 11
352–353: 104

Isocrates
  4.41: 136n78
  4.54–60: 155nn2, 3
  4.57: 22
  4.63: 161n89
  4.80: 138n97
  4.103–109: 136n71
  4.120: 154n7
  5.33–34: 155nn2, 3
  8.80–90: 138n97
  8.82: 25
  10.31: 155nn2, 3
  12.194: 155n3
  14.1–2: 161n87
  14.1–2, 6, 14.53–54, 14.57: 137n82

Lysias
  2.3: 96
  2.11–16: 155nn2, 3
  2.14: 156n20
  2.15: 161n98
  2.23: 164n140
  2.23–24: 98
  2.24–26: 164n135
  26.11–12: 141n14

Pausanias
  1.17.6: 144n39
  1.28.6: 62, 153n143
  1.28.7: 171n72
  1.30.4: 167n14
  1.32.6: 155n2, 162n99
  2.11.4: 153n138
  3.3.6–7: 42
  3.3.7: 42, 144n39
  3.11.10: 146n58
  3.19.9: 147n65
  7.1.8: 42
  7.25.1: 153n142
  7.25.2: 153nn141

Pindar
  *Nemean Odes*
  11.34: 147n68
  *Olympian Odes*
  7.89–90: 128
  *Pythian Odes*

  4.263: 171n65
  9.78–83: 165n146
  11.31–37: 147n68

Plato
  *Apology*
  25c–26a: 112
  *Crito*
  44c–45b: 159n71
  *Laws*
  716e–717a: 112
  849a–d: 128
  869c: 168n31
  *Menexenus*
  237a: 96
  244e1–3: 161n95
  246d1–248d6: 164n135
  *Protagoras*
  342a–d: 136n79

Plutarch
  *Aristides*
  23–25: 137n85
  *Cimon*
  6.2–3: 137n85
  8.6: 42
  8.7–9: 25
  14.3–5: 140n5
  16.8: 140n4
  17.3: 32
  *Demosthenes*
  25: 159n6
  *Moralia*
  292b: 146n60
  *Pelopidas*
  27: 145n49
  *Pericles*
  10.7–8: 140n5
  12–17: 136n71, 160n76
  17: 153n150
  *Phocion*
  21.2: 159n60
  *Publicola*
  2.35.1: 138n92
  *Solon*
  9.1: 146n56
  12.1: 153n141

637: 121, 127, 169n43
638–641: 115
638–648: 168n33
643–644: 115
714–715: 108
737–738: 123
761–799: 123
765–775: 124
770–771: 171n63
772–775: 125
781–790: 115
782: 124
785, 785–786: 125
787–790: 167n18
818–819: 123
913–914: 171n84
913–918: 124
922–923: 123
927–928: 128
939–959: 124
944–949: 126
964, 976: 169n38
977: 112
987: 169n38
1003–1013: 171n80
1207: 172n87
1299: 167n18
1309: 149n90
1362–1364: 171n63
1370–1396: 123
1386: 172n87
1390–1392: 167n18
1421: 170n46
1156: 127
1156–1157: 127
1524: 170n46
1524–1537: 122
1657–1666: 145n42
1752: 170n52
*Oedipus Tyrannus*
1–77: 135n55
238–241: 168n32
454–456: 171n65
1228: 148n78
1340–1345: 171n65
1369–1385: 169n37
1410–1415: 171n65
1436–1437: 169n37, 171n65

1449–1454, 1518: 171n65
*Philoctetes*
930: 149n90
*Trachiniae*
358: 127

Strabo
8.4.6: 162n99
8.6.19: 165n146

Thucydides
1.2.5–6: 19, 136n76
1.23.6: 70
1.75: 157n31
1.75.2–4: 23
1.75–78: 136n71, 160n76
1.76: 133n3
1.76.2–3: 137n83
1.77.1–4: 160n78
1.77–78: 133n3
1.88: 23, 70
1.96: 67, 162n107
1.96–97.1: 77
1.96.1: 67, 137n86
1.97: 90, 160n78
1.97–101: 67
1.97.1: 69
1.98.1: 138n90, 143n27
1.98.2: 143n27
1.98.4: 21
1.99: 21, 137n89
1.99.2: 160n78
1.99.3: 162n107
1.100, 1.100.2: 21
1.100.2–3: 143n27
1.102: 140nn2, 4
1.102.4: 32, 140n10
1.104: 37
1.104–105: 21
1.105–106: 141n10
1.107.4: 140n5
1.118.2: 23, 70
1.122.3, 1.124.3: 78
1.126.10–11: 153n142
1.126.11: 152n134, 153n139
1.136: 159n60
1.139.3: 70
1.140: 157n39

# GENERAL INDEX

Eumenides of Colonus, 107–108
Euphemus, 24
Euripides. See *Children of Heracles*; *Electra*; *Erechtheus*; *Heracles*; *Medea*; *Suppliant Women*; *Trojan Women*
Eurystheus, 39–40, 54, 70, 73–74, 76, 79, 83, 88–91, 100–102, 156n11, 157nn16, 35; as *metoikos*, 165n149, 170n170
exile: as alternative to death, 83; purificatory, 51–52

Foley, H. P., 94
foreigners/outsiders: annexation as heroes, 39–42; in audience, 4, 25–26; secondary status in Athens, 116–118; shift in Athens' reception towards, 106–107; treatment by Athens vs. Sparta, 19–21, 123
freedom: and democracy, 84, 103–104; and empire, 7, 68–69, 75–80, 84; of speech, 4, 83
funeral oration: differences from tragedy, 22–26, 29, 73; and sacrifice of Heracles' daughter, 94–98
Furies/Erinyes, 54–59, 64–65; association with weddings, childbirth, 61; avengers of kin-killers, 56–57; and madness, disease, 46, 57; as chthonic, polluted, 55, 57; in Homer, 56, 151n117; incorporation into Athenian cult, 53–54, 60–61, 64–65; and Orestes, 33–35, 46–49; and purification, 49–50
Furley, William, 89
Futo-Kennedy, Rebecca, 5–6

Gagarin, M., 112
Gender, 91–94; and sacrifice, 94–98
Giordano, Manuela, 11
Gödde, Suzanne, 7
Goldhill, Simon, 3
Gould, John, 12
Gramsci, Antonio, 28
Grethlein, Jonas, 7, 74
Griffith, Mark, 3

hegemony, defined, 18–19, 22–24, 28–29, 129–132. *See also* Athenian hegemonic ideology

Helen, 56, 153n138
Hellenic shared identity, 41–42, 44
Henrichs, Albert, 60, 108
Heracles, 2, 26–27, 131, 149–150n96, 168n33
*Heracles* (Euripides), 2, 11, 26, 48
Heracles' children, 8, 22, 40, 81–84; daughter's self-sacrifice, 88–90
hero-cults. *See* cult-heroes
Herodotus, 22, 43, 143n26; on Sparta and Athens, 63, 137n86; Sparta and Orestes' bones, 42–43
Hesiod, 41, 55, 58
historical context of plays, 4–5, 129–132; Argive alliance, 31–32; Argive/Spartan relations, 31–32, 42–44; and Athenian hegemonic ideology, 2–3, 6–7, 17–18, 22–24, 27, 67; Athens' rule, 15, 67–69; Athens' tribute requirements, 3, 89–91; battle at Arginusae, 122; end of Peloponnesian War, 74, 106, 117, 122–126; Sparta's influence in Peloponnesian war, 42–43, 75, 78
Hölscher, Tonio, 5
Homer, 8–9, 41
homicide, 45, 51–53, 56, 62, 110–112; Areopagus, 32–34, 51, 61–63; exile alternative to death, 83; purification for, 49–51
hoplites, 94–96
Hyllus, 73, 88, 100

ideology, and hegemony, 28–29. *See also* Athenian hegemonic ideology
Iolaus, 75–78, 80–83, 85–86, 92
Iphigeneia, 8, 26, 94, 151n120
*isegoria*, 83
Ismene, 113, 119–120, 125

Jason, 49, 149n97
Jebb, R. C., 127
Jocasta, 105

Kamerbeek, J., 127
kin murder, 33, 45–47, 57, 110–113, 148n83
kinship, 56, 78, 147n77, ritual, 62, 107–108, 116
Knox, Bernard, 125, 127

Konstan, David, 87, 103, 120
Kore, 73, 84

Laius, 105, 112, 169nn37–38
Larson, Jennifer, 88
Lattimore, Richmond, 11
law, in Athenian democracy, 70–71, 80–81, 124
Lloyd, Michael, 80
Lloyd-Jones, H., 127
Loraux, Nicole, 7, 24, 98
Lycurgus, 63, 164n132

MacDowell, D. M., 112
Marathon, 22, 24, 67, 73, 76, 81, 97
marriage, and virgin sacrifice, 94, 97
Medea, 2, 11, 26–27, 49, 163n122, 168n33
*Medea* (Euripides), 2, 26–27, 48
Melanippus, 145n39
Melian debate, 23
Mendelsohn, Daniel, 74, 91
Menelaus, 10, 43–44, 146n54
metics ("resident aliens"), 13, 16, 19, 24–25, 81, 98, 128, 165n149
Mills, Sophie, 5–6, 23–24
Musgrave, S., 127–128
Mytilenaean debate, 23, 76, 84, 102–103

Naiden, Fred, 12–13, 81
naturalization, requirements for, 113–114
Nausicaa, 8–9
Naxos, 21, 68, 90

oaths, 38, 39–41, 62, 69
Oedipus: heroization of, 27, 107, 114–115, 120–123; naturalization of, 28, 113–116; and pollution, 107–108, 110–113, 115; and prophecy, 121–122, 125. See also *Oedipus at Colonus* (Sophocles)
*Oedipus at Colonus* (Sophocles), 7, 30, 54, 105–109, 124; coup of 411 BCE, 122, 166–167n21; stage setting, 108, 109. See also Oedipus
*Oedipus Tyrannus*, 105, 169n37
*oikos* (household): Furies associated with, 53, 54, 61–62; guest-friendship and, 9, 54; Homeric supplication, 9; justice, 45, 56, 94

*Oresteia* (Aeschylus), 21, 44
*Oresteia* (Stesichorus), 43, 45
Orestes: and Argive Alliance, 31–33, 37–40; Argive identity, 41; bones of, 33, 42–43; burial, 33, 41–43; as cult-hero, 38–42; matricide, 45–46; purification, 46–48, 52; supplication of Athena, 33–41. See also *Eumenides* (Aeschylus)
outsiders. See foreigners/outsiders

Paley, F. A., 127
panegyric, Athenian. See Athenian hegemonic ideology
Panhellenic laws, 4, 17, 75, 81, 103–104, 160n74
Panhellenic myth, 41–42, 44
Paris, 56, 137n87, 147n69, 153n138
Parker, R. B., 51–52, 57, 112
Patterson, C., 128
Peace of Callias, 68, 137n87, 154n7
Peisistratus, 63
Pelasgus, 10–11, 13–15, 34, 81, 142n22
Pelling, Christopher, 7
Peloponnesian War, 3, 42–43, 78, 89–91, 105–107, 116–118
Pericles, 19–20, 38, 78, 84, 89, 96, 100–102; on Athens' democracy, 70; Athens versus Sparta, 24, 26, 38, 64, 98, 122–123; citizenship law, 19, 128
*Persians* (Aeschylus), 6
Persian Wars, 2, 21–24, 43, 64
piety, Athenian, 4–5, 7, 105–106, 117, 119, 123–124, 129
Pindar, 43
pity, 8, 20, 23, 30, 85–87, 103, 120–123, 131
Plataea, 22
Plato, 112
plays: civic ceremonies preceding, 3–4; staging of, 47–50, 108–109; theater at Dionysus, 4, 25, 49. See also audience for plays
pollution, 18, 28, 45–47, 51–52, 57, 115, 125–126; and Oedipus, 107–108, 110–113, 115; and Orestes, 44–45, 49–53
Pollux, 116, 127–128
Polyneices, 54, 120, 123, 127, 134n36, 167n18, 168n29

Poseidon, 95, 108
Praxithea, 95–98
Priam, 8, 9
Proclus, 52
*prohairesis*, 96
prophecy: of Eurystheus, 74, 101; of
    Oedipus, 121, 122–123, 125
purification ritual, 35, 44–53, 57, 113
Pythia, 46–48, 58–59, 149n94, 150n97

Quincey, J. H., 31

Raaflaub, Kurt, 76, 79
reciprocity, 26–27, 64–65, 70, 99–100,
    121
refugee, 54, 77, 83, 158n60, 161n89,
    171n83
repatriation, 31, 125, 159n63
Roselli, David, 92
Rosenbloom, David, 6, 70, 103

sacrifice: and gender, 94–97; and hege-
    mony, 97–100; Heracles' daughter, 84,
    87–97; as imperial tribute, 88–91
Saïd, Suzanne, 15
Saxonhouse, Arlene, 94
Seaford, Richard, 3
self-defense, 112
self-sacrifice, 84, 88–90, 94–97
*Semnai Theai*: Athenian cult of, 61–62;
    identification of Furies with, 54,
    59–61; role in homicide trials, 62–63
Sophocles. See *Oedipus at Colonus*
Sparta, 32, 63, 78, 101; use of genealogy,
    44; identified with Heraclids, 101–102;
    relations with Argos, 41–44; return of
    Orestes bones to, 42–43; treatment of
    foreigners, 19–20
staging of plays: Aeschylus' *Eumenides*,
    47–50; Sophocles' *Oedipus at Colonus*,
    108–109
Stesichorus. See *Oresteia*
suppliant(s), 9–11, 16–19, 20–23; asymme-
    try in suppliant relationship, 16–17, 29,
    38, 78; children of Heracles as, 80–84;
    Furies as, 54; Oedipus as, 108–113;
    Orestes as, 33–34, 38. *See also* asylum
suppliant plays: characteristics of, 9–11,

14–16; and empire, 16–19; and hege-
    monic ideology, 16–18, 20–21, 26–28;
    and hegemony, 14–16; settings for,
    1–2, 13–14
*Suppliant Women* (Aeschylus), 2, 10–11,
    13–16, 34, 79, 81
*Suppliant Women* (Euripides), 2, 80, 120;
    Athens and Thebes, 157n37; Athens
    as haven for foreigners, 22, 26–27,
    69–70; development of Athenian
    hegemonic ideology, 102–104; im-
    perial democracy, 67, 69–70, 102–
    104, 164n145; Theseus in, 11, 120, 124
*Supplicandus/a*: Argos as, 15–16; Athena/
    Athens as, 10, 13–19; and inequality to
    suppliant, 16–17, 29, 38, 78
supplication: at the altar, 8–9, 13, 46–48,
    78, 80–81; and aristocratic society,
    8–9, 145n49; in Athenian Assembly,
    80–84; in Athenian law, 12–13; of
    Oedipus, 109–113; of Orestes, 36–38;
    in Homer, 8–9; in tragedy, 9–11,
    26–28; participation of community,
    8–11, 13; origins of Athenian panegyric
    of, 19–21, 54, 85–87; and ritual, 12, 36

Taplin, Oliver, 47–48
Tartarus, 55
Telemachus, 9
Thasos, 21
Thebes, 102, 119–120, 122–126
Theoclymenus, 9
Theseus, 10–11, 27–28, 102–104, 105–107,
    114–116, 119, 123–125, 127–128, 158n57,
    164n145–146; as archetypal Athenian
    hero/king, 5, 103, 118, 122–124, 171n82;
    hero-cult of, 42; and pity and gener-
    osity, 120–122, 125, 165n150
Thucydides: on Athens and Sparta, 19–20,
    78; Athens as haven for foreigners, 19;
    and Athenian imperialism, 21, 23–24,
    67–68, 76–78; Pericles' funeral ora-
    tion, 20–21, 38, 139n103, 162n109,
    172n85; on tribute, 90, 137n89
Thyestes, 56, 148n83
Tisamenus, 42, 146n54
tomb cult, 33, 145n39
tragedies, political interpretations of, 3–4

tribute, 3, 19, 21, 23, 69, 90–91; human
 sacrifice as, 88–91, 96
*Trojan Women* (Euripides), 5

vengeance. *See* blood vengeance
Vidal-Naquet, P., 127–128
virgin sacrifice, 88, 94–96

Wilkins, John, 96
Wilson, Joseph, 127
women: sacrifice of compared to and

death in battle, 93–97; social norms
 and standing, 92–94

*xenia* (guest-friendship), 8–9
*Xenios*, 80
Xerxes, 6

Zeitlin, Froma, 15, 123
Zeus: Agoraios, 11, 73, 80–81, 93, 144n33;
 *Hikesios*, 80; Purifier, 49–50; *Soter*, 80
Zuntz Günther, 74

www.ingramcontent.com/pod-product-compliance
Ingram Content Group UK Ltd.
Pitfield, Milton Keynes, MK11 3LW, UK
UKHW042152060225
454777UK00004B/469